Investigating
Vatican II

Investigating Vatican II

Its Theologians, Ecumenical Turn,
and Biblical Commitment

Jared Wicks, SJ

The Catholic University of America Press
Washington, D.C.

Copyright © 2018
The Catholic University of America Press
All rights reserved
The paper used in this publication meets the minimum requirements of American National Standards for Information Science—Permanence of Paper for Printed Library Materials, ANSI z39.48-1984.
∞

Cataloging-in-Publication Data available from the Library of Congress
ISBN 978-0-8132-3047-4

Contents

Acknowledgments

The articles in this book were originally published in other sources. Those sources are acknowledged on the opening pages of each chapter. I am grateful to the chief editors of *Concordia Journal*, *Ecumenical Trends*, and *Josephinum Journal of Theology*, along with SAGE Journals (*Theological Studies*) and Paulist Press (*Doing Theology*).

Investigating
Vatican II

Introduction

This book presents the Second Vatican Council as an event to which theologians contributed in major ways and from which Catholic theology even today can gain enormously. The following chapters aim to inform readers, especially theology students and their teachers, about Vatican II as an event of theological discussion, argument, and exposition. This event began with Pope John XXIII's first announcement of the council on January 25, 1959, and went on to the end of the council's work on December 8, 1965. The council's episcopal members, headed by the pope, issued the sixteen Vatican II documents, by putting their stamp of approval on the theological work of the many council experts, who included mid-twentieth-century theologians of the highest caliber. Chapter 2 presents their dedicated theological work before and during the council.

Gathering these texts into a single volume aims to promote re-reception of Vatican II's theologically rich documents by a renewed appropriation more than fifty years after the council concluded. This book proposes a re-visitation of Vatican II's articulation of God's revelation of himself in Christ, which chapters 3, 9, and 10, below, present from different perspectives. The incarnate and saving word of God to humankind is the centerpiece of faith and theological work inspired by Vatican II. Re-reception will also be a fresh turning to the ecumenical engagement for which Vatican II laid theological foundations, as chapters 4 and 5 set forth. Four narrative parts, chapters 6 through 9, take the reader through the sessions of Vatican II, highlighting several dramas as the council took on, with increasing clarity, major tasks of theological reformulation, ecclesial updating, ecumenical grounding, and turning to the modern world with a new "face" of respect and new commitment to serving the whole human family. Underlying and animating the whole process were Pope John XXIII's "Tridentine motivations" of reform and rejuvenation in the church, as chapter 1 relates.

Taking up Vatican II has a special importance in the present era, as Pope Francis is putting Vatican II into practice in new ways in the Catholic church. The pope's promotion of synodality, as a constitutive element at all levels in a listening church, rests on the council's affirmation of the "sense of faith" given to believers and the council's urging that collegial consultation, for example, in pastoral councils, mark Catholic practice throughout the church and its ministries.[1] Pope Francis's Apostolic Exhortation, *The Joy of the Gospel*, instructing on how God's saving love and mercy come near to us in the person of Jesus Christ, is a magnetic actualizing of Vatican II's account of divine revelation and faith.[2] Even the pope's practice of spiritual reading during the day from his "pocket gospel," which he urges people, often at the Sunday "Angelus," also to do, is a loud echo today of an exhortation made insistently

1. Pope Francis spoke at length on synodality in his address on the fiftieth anniversary of the Synod of Bishops, October 17, 2015. See the text in *Origins* 45, no. 22 (October 29, 2015): 381–84, or online at www.vatican.va. The Vatican II bases are in the Dogmatic Constitution on the Church, *Lumen Gentium*, November 21, 1964, nos. 12 and 22–23; the Decree on the Pastoral Office of Bishops, *Christus Dominus*, October 28, 1965, nos. 24 and 27; the Decree on the Apostolate of Lay People, *Apostolicam Actuositatem*, November 18, 1965, no. 26; and the Decree on the Church's Missionary Activity, *Ad Gentes*, December 7, 1965, nos. 30–31 and 35–41.

2. *The Joy of the Gospel*, Apostolic Exhortation, November 24, 2013, pars. 3, 11, 35–36, 128, 164, and 264–67, which rest on Vatican Council II, *Dei Verbum*, November 18, 1965, especially nos. 1–4.

by the Second Vatican Council.[3] For understanding Pope Francis and his program, one needs to know Vatican II well, especially its overriding concern to make pastoral concerns prevail.

Another motivation for this book is the urgency of receiving Vatican II in a contemporary manner in the Catholic church. Sadly, many Catholics have not received and embraced Vatican II's attractive and rejuvenating vision of faith, worship, and life. A first reception of the council took place, but in many places this was done poorly. Nearly twenty years after the council ended, Cardinal Joseph Ratzinger gave lectures and interviews on the poor communication of the sublime contents of the Vatican II documents.[4] In May 1985, Pope John Paul II told the Belgian bishops that while the council gave the church basic principles and means for a spiritual renewal, "some have badly studied, interpreted, and applied [the council], causing confusion and divisions.... We must supply a remedy for the causes of the spiritual weakness of Christians."[5]

Today, many readers will know from their extended families and circle of acquaintances the low level or even absence of religious engagement in the lives of many "emerging adult" Catholics. The Notre Dame sociologists, Christian Smith and his associates, make this current crisis clear in *Young Catholic America: Emerging Adults In, Out of, and Gone from the Church*.[6] Further investigation of those "out of and gone" reveals that often their parents did not receive the uplifting and motivating influence of the council, which left them bereft of ability and commitment for passing on a heritage of renewed Catholic life to their children, who are

3. See *Dei Verbum*, no. 25, treated in the final section of chapter 10, below.

4. Joseph Cardinal Ratzinger, "Sources and Transmission of the Faith," *Communio* 10 (1983): 17–34, and *The Ratzinger Report: An Exclusive Interview on the State of the Church*, ed. Vittorio Messori (San Francisco: Ignatius Press, 1985).

5. *Osservatore Romano*, English Edition (June 24, 1985), 9. Gerard O'Connell reported the pope's judgment in the first part of his informative chronicle of the 1985 Extraordinary Synod of Bishops on the Reception of Vatican II, in *The Month* 19 (1986): 44.

6. Christian Smith, Kyle Longest, Jonathan Hill, and Kari Christoffersen, *Young Catholic America: Emerging Adults In, Out of, and Gone from the Church* (New York: Oxford University Press, 2014).

now young adults. In many families, the transmission of Catholic convictions and values broke down during the years 1965 to 1985, so that many parents of today's emerging adults (i.e., those aged eighteen to twenty-three) could not effectively form their children as Catholics. Certainly, in scattered pockets, impressive emerging young adult Catholics are living out an informed and committed Catholic engagement, but they are dwarfed by the large numbers of their contemporaries who are "out and gone" and sadly lack Vatican II's inspirations and depth in their spiritual lives.

The present book aims to make known from the perspective of theology the "golden bits" of teaching and inspired guidance for faith-formation still at hand for us in the doctrinal and spiritual riches of the principal Vatican II documents.[7] The following chapters arose from the conviction that Catholic teaching and formation urgently need to recapture the magnetic appeal of what Vatican II can give us, for example, in *Dei Verbum*, no. 4, on the revelation of God-with-us-to-save expressed in concentrated form in the Christ-event. Catholic theology would do well to refurbish its self-understanding from *Dei Verbum*, no. 24, which portrays theological work as "investigating, by the light of faith, all the truth stored up in the mystery of Christ." These can be fundamental Vatican II contributions to Catholic renewal, along with a whole series of further profound theological proposals set forth in the chapters to come.

Preview of the Chapters

The five chapters of the first part of the book selectively introduce major figures of the Vatican II theological renewal and reforms.

---

7. On finding "golden bits" embedded in Vatican II documents, see Gerald O'Collins, *The Second Vatican Council: Message and Meaning* (Collegeville, Minn.: Liturgical Press, 2014), ix.

Chapter 1 introduces Angelo Giuseppe Roncalli (Pope John XXIII), featuring his conviction of the church's potential to become ever again *rejuvenated*. His fifty-year work of editing for publication the records of St. Charles Borromeo's visitation of the Diocese of Bergamo in 1575 showed him how implementing reforms mandated by the Council of Trent gave the church of Bergamo new vitality and higher standards of Catholic life and pastoral dedication. John XXIII convoked Vatican II to promote such a renewal in the whole church in a mid-twentieth-century manner. Gradually the council's bishops adopted this aim, turning *to* renewal and *against* many of the lackluster prepared draft-texts on doctrine and service in the church.

Chapter 2 relates moments of Vatican II when theological experts made crucial contributions. This began with theologically acute responses to the initial announcement of the council in January 1959 and continued during the council's preparation and its autumn sessions of 1962 to 1965. The whole process was marked by engagement and input of theological experts, who first served the preparatory and conciliar commissions on topics of their competence and then helped the council members evaluate draft-texts and formulate critical and constructive interventions. This account leads to a valuable generalization about the relation between theological expertise and the church's Magisterium.

Chapter 3 focuses on interventions in 1962 by theological experts who circulated critical assessments of the prepared draft, "The Sources of Revelation," leading to alternative texts offered by theologians such as Joseph Ratzinger, Pieter Smulders, Karl Rahner, and Jean Daniélou. Leading Vatican II bishops gave public expression to the theologians' behind-the-scenes criticism and suggested alternatives, so that today we find traits of those theologians' proposals in the foundational first chapter of *Dei Verbum* on God's salvific revelation in Christ.

Chapters 4 and 5 focus on the Secretariat for Promoting the

Unity of Christians, instituted by John XXIII in 1960, where theologians crafted elegant, biblically based proposals on ecclesial office under Christ the exalted Lord of the late Pauline letters, on the priestly people of God, and on the effective, life-giving word of God. The Secretariat shepherded major texts through the council process, not only on Catholic ecumenical aims and method, but also on non-Christian religions, especially Judaism, and on religious liberty. Chapter 5 introduces the Catholic ecumenical commitment and shows the foundations laid by Vatican II, especially in its careful account of degrees of church membership and the significance of the separated Christian communities. These led to key revisions on the way to the Dogmatic Constitution on the Church, directed by Gérard Philips (Louvain), while the expert service of Jan Witte (Gregorian University) helped frame a basic Catholic principle of ecumenical theology and activity, namely, the saving significance of word, sacrament, and formation given in the presently separated Christian communities.

The second part of this book, on the outcomes and global traits of Vatican II, moves through the council's four periods of work from 1962 to 1965. Chapter 6 returns to Pope John XXIII's goals for the council, which arose during his long service, first in his own diocese and in Rome (1904 to 1924), then from 1925 to 1953 in Bulgaria, Turkey, and France, and from 1953 to 1958 as patriarch-archbishop of Venice. As pope, John XXIII was initially alone in his vision of Catholic transformation through a council, but three cardinals (Suenens, Frings, and Bea) grasped his aims, as did a majority of council members during the first period of deliberations in 1962. Pope John declared these goals afresh in early December 1962, which led to their broad impact as guidelines of the early 1963 second preparation of Vatican II.

Chapter 7 describes a typical day's work during a General Congregation of the council's second period in 1963, before dwelling on the newly elected Pope Paul VI's profound opening discourse of that period. On ecclesiology, bishops, and ecumenism, Vatican II made solid progress in 1963 and completed the first of its sixteen documents, the constitution on liturgical renewal. But a culminating vote on it occurred November 22, 1963, a date portending that the council's reception would unfold amid social and cultural turmoil during the later 1960s.

Chapter 8 examines the Vatican II centerpiece that is the Dogmatic Constitution on the Church, completed during the third period in 1964. *Lumen Gentium*'s teaching was applied in the nine council decrees on roles and practice in the church, for example, on ecumenism which is grounded in the constitution's account of the groups making up the people of God. As the third period ended, the council went through rough waters churned up by Paul VI's interventions regarding the pope's role in the collegial hierarchy, postponing a vote on religious liberty, and late revisions inserted into the ecumenism decree. But more serious long-term problems for Catholic theology appeared in the rift appearing in 1964 among the theologians of renewal, when Henri de Lubac found secularizing currents in Eduard Schillebeeckx's lectures on the relation between the church and the world.

Chapter 9 treats Vatican II's fourth period in 1965, when it completed eleven documents. The Constitution on the Church in the Modern World gained theological depth by having a profound Christological perspective permeate its opening chapters. The Dogmatic Constitution on God's saving revelation offers theological rejuvenation to Catholics by its evangelical central focus. But in 1964 another theology, from early twentieth-century antimodernism, had come on the scene in minority attacks mounted vigorously against the Pastoral Constitution and the declarations on non-Christian religions and on religious freedom. Penetratingly, Joseph Ratzinger saw these Vatican II documents as the council's "counter-syllabus" to the "Syllabus of Errors" of Pius IX issued in 1864. Since the minority was harkening back to an outdated vision, Pope Paul VI in time wrote a profound theological letter to Archbishop Marcel Lefebvre on the vital adaptability of tradition, as Vatican II set this forth (pp. 232–35).

While the chapters just sketched make clear many global traits of Vatican II, chapter 10 uncovers basic traits from the final chapter of *Dei Verbum*. Few council interpreters have noted how this text gives guidelines sharply contrasting with what had been set down in 1962 in scripture in the church. The contrasts attest to a major change in priorities, as Vatican II highlights the pastoral contributions desired from exegetes and recommends theological work immersed in scripture, for "scrutinizing all the truth stored up in the mystery of Christ." Climactically *Dei Verbum* insists wholeheartedly that all the faithful engage in prayerful Scripture reading, *lectio divina*, to deepen their lives in Christ.

Practical Notes

Some readers may find it helpful to begin their reading with chapters 6–9, to gain basic familiarity with Vatican II's dramatic history from 1962 to 1965. However, chapter 2 includes aspects of Vatican II's preparation, before the formal inauguration in October 1962, especially as the preparation engaged theologians. The other chapters take up selected theological issues as these developed before and during the council.

Because the chapters of this work originated in different times and places between 2009 and 2015, I have edited the texts to reduce some, but not all, repetitions, to give internal cross-references, and to update the notes by indicating other works which promote theological enrichment from the Second Vatican Council.

Part I

Major Figures and Aims of the Vatican II Renewal and Reform

1

Tridentine Motivations of Pope John XXIII before and during Vatican II

Commonly, people see opposition between the style and content of the Council of Trent and the event and documents of the Second Vatican Council. The latter is often taken as ending the Counter Reformation era that Trent embodied in notable ways.[1] However, a careful review of the debates and documents of Vatican II shows that while this quite different council abstained from anathematizing any doctrines and reversed several practices mandated by Trent, it did not depart from any of Trent's doctrinal definitions. Trent's teachings even played some positive roles at Vatican II.[2] In fact, in inaugurating Vatican II, Pope John XXIII spoke of ad-

This chapter was originally published as "Tridentine Motivations of Pope John XXIII Before and During Vatican II," *Theological Studies* 75 (2014): 847–62. Published by SAGE Publishing, all rights reserved. https://doi.org/10.1177/0040563914548656. It expands a lecture given at the Georgetown University conference held on November 8, 2013, to commemorate the 450th anniversary of the completion of the Council of Trent.

1. See, e.g., John W. O'Malley, *Trent: What Happened at the Council* (Cambridge, Mass.: Belknap Press of Harvard University Press, 2012), 11.

2. Joseph A. Komonchak, "The Council of Trent at the Second Vatican Council," in *From Trent to Vatican II: Historical and Theological Investigations*, ed. Raymond F. Bulman and Frederick J. Parrella (New York: Oxford University Press, 2006), 61–80.

herence to the church's teaching at Trent and Vatican I as basic in the new council's effort to penetrate "in a fuller and deeper way" (*amplius et altius*) the Catholic heritage and then to reformulate in a contemporary manner the same meaning in ways to enlarge its influence on souls.[3]

Beyond a comparison of the content of documents, the slippery topic remains of Vatican II's spirit, especially the grand impulses given it by its convener, Pope John XXIII. Some light on the latter domain comes from the recent publication of excerpts from the diary of Fr. Roberto Tucci, SJ, who at the time of Vatican II headed the Jesuit editorial team of *La Civiltà cattolica* in Rome. Tucci's texts include notes on nine personal audiences with Pope John XXIII during the council years. The volume's editor begins his introduction by stating that John did not convene Vatican II to be like previous councils which defined dogmas. Instead, it "should give new impulses and new dynamism to the church spiritually, pastorally, and in its missionary action, as did occur after the Council of Trent, which he [John XXIII] knew well and admired."[4] John wanted Vatican II to have certain characteristics of the post-Tridentine era, about which he was well-informed.

To develop this topic, the following pages present several marks that the Council of Trent made on Angelo Giuseppe Roncalli (John XXIII). These came both from Trent's decrees on church reform and from individuals who, after Trent closed in December 1563, carried out the implementation of Trent's reform decrees in different locales.[5] This trio of Trent's decrees, implementers, and

3. John XXIII, "Gaudet Mater Ecclesia," October 11, 1962, in *Acta Apostolicae Sedis* 54 (1962): 786–96, at 792.

4. Giovanni Sale (ed.), *Giovanni XXIII e la preparazione del concilio Vaticano II nei diari del direttore della "Civiltà cattolica"* (Milan: Jaca Book, 2012), 13. The volume gives Tucci's notes after private audiences with Pope John beginning in September 1959 and extending to February 1963.

5. Trent issued reform decrees during its three periods. In the first period (1545–47), the council promulgated three reform decrees; see *Decrees of the Ecumenical Councils*, ed. Norman Tanner (Washington, D.C.: Georgetown University Press, 1990), 2:667–70, 681–83,

local impacts is, I believe, a useful lens through which to perceive the motivations and objectives that John XXIII gave to the Second Vatican Council as he convened and led it until his death on June 3, 1963. Before speaking of Vatican II, it is essential to visit some stations in the life of Angelo Roncalli, in order to grasp the impact on him of the Tridentine reform.

Roncalli as Patriarch/Archbishop of Venice

On March 14, 1953, Cardinal Roncalli entered Venice as the newly named archbishop and patriarch. Less than a year later, he announced visitations of parishes and other diocesan institutions, to continue and complete the unfinished visitation-program of his predecessor. Shortly after, Roncalli wrote this in his diary: "Pastoral visitation *in the spirit of the Council of Trent*, as shepherd and father *(pastor et pater)*."[6] Two months into the visitation, he drafted a letter for Pope Pius XII, expressing gratitude for appointing him at the sunset of his life to pastoral care around the charming *laguna* of Venice, where he is meeting "beautiful souls, who are more precious than the marble, paintings, and mosaics" of the city's artistic heritage. In the parishes, he is noting defects and urgent needs, while evaluating persons and situations, and so coming to know the realities. He tries to improve them, while not imagining he can attain everything or even something immediately by the touch of a magic wand or by applying a whip.[7] This was his acting "in the spirit of Trent," as he understood it.

---

and 686–89. Two more reform decrees followed during the second period (1551–52): see *Decrees* (ed. Tanner), 2:698–701 and 714–18. The third period (1562–63) saw five reform decrees issued: see *Decrees* (ed. Tanner), 2:728–32, 737–41, 744–53, 759–83, and 784–96.

6. Entry of February 28, 1954, in *Pace e Vangelo: Agende del patriarca 1953–1958*, ed. Enrico Galavotti (Bologna: Istituto per le scienze religiose, 2008), 6.1:229–30 (emphasis added). During the parish visits, Roncalli had help in reviewing conditions in the parishes from his secretary, Don Loris Capovilla, and from the Master of Ceremonies of St. Mark's Basilica.

7. Letter drafted April 18, 1954, but not sent, addressed to Monsignor Giovanni Battista Montini, the *sostituto* in the Secretariat of State of the Roman Curia who had daily

Over three years later, in early November 1957, Roncalli made the final parish visit, to San Lorenzo di Mestre. But he had already announced that the "conclusion and crown of the pastoral visitation," would be a three-day diocesan synod scheduled for late November 1957. Roncalli's official letter announcing the synod described its preparation with another Tridentine echo: "The priests are making themselves ready for this celebration, which reminds us of the era after the Council of Trent and of the fervor shown then by churchmen and laypeople animated to undertake a reestablishment [un'instaurazione] of Catholic life, which thanks be to God succeeded well, and so such an action still corresponds to the needs of modern times."

Roncalli's pre-synod statement of 1957 concretizes the purpose of the synod with a term that became well known. "Haven't you heard the word *aggiornamento* repeated many times? Here is our church, always young and ready to follow different changes in the circumstances of life, with the intention of adapting, correcting, improving, and arousing enthusiasm. In summary, this is the nature of the synod, this is its purpose."[8] Thus, during Roncalli's five-year ministry in Venice, 1953 to 1958, he carried out a pastoral action which for him imitated Trent's mandated episcopal visitations of dioceses, and he followed the synodal practice on the local level that many post-Tridentine dioceses adopted as means of promulgating new norms to guide and enliven Catholic life.[9]

---

appointments with Pope Pius XII. Angelo G. Roncalli and Giovanni Battista Montini, *Lettere di fede e amicizia: Corrispondenza inedita (1925–1963)*, ed. Loris F. Capovilla and Marco Roncalli (Rome: Edizioni Studium, 2013), 135–37. On his pastoral governance, he wrote earlier about following the rule that he as a young priest had heard from the bishop of Bergamo, Giacomo M. Radini-Tedeschi, "Omnia videre, multa dissimulare, pauca corregere" (see everything, pass over many things, correct a few of them). Diary entry of December 7, 1953, in *Pace e Vangelo* (ed. Galavotti), 1:178.

8. *Pace e Vangelo* (ed. Galavotti), 2:503n826.

9. Council of Trent, Session 24, Reform Decree, November 11, 1563, c. 3, on episcopal visitation of dioceses, in *Decrees* (ed. Tanner), 2:761–62. Giuseppe Alberigo surveyed research on the visitations and synods of Italian church provinces and dioceses in application

Among the sources of Roncalli's mid-1950s references to the Tridentine reforms were two intensive exposures to outcomes of the Council of Trent that he had earlier in his life. One of these was documentary and of long duration, while the other was spiritual in nature through his favorite models of exemplary service in the church during the Tridentine era.

Roncalli as Editor of the Records of Charles Borromeo

After Roncalli's ordination to the priesthood for the Diocese of Bergamo in 1904, he became personal secretary to the new bishop, Giacomo M. Radini-Tedeschi, whom he served for a decade until the bishop died in 1914. Roncalli also taught church history in the seminary beginning in 1906. Early in these years, he visited in Milan the archive of the archdiocese in the Ambrosian Library, where he came upon thirty-nine bound volumes of manuscripts concerning his own diocese in the post-Tridentine era. He came back several times to peruse them, enthused about "so many and such interesting documents regarding the church of Bergamo from the era marked by the renewal of its religious life after the Council of Trent. Here was evidence of the warm fervor of the Catholic counter-reformation." In volumes VI and VII of this collection, he found the records of the visitation of the Diocese of Bergamo in 1575 by Metropolitan St. Charles Borromeo, who came to Bergamo under a mandate given by Pope Gregory XIII, bringing with him ten assistant visitators or inspectors. After Roncalli's discovery, Bishop Radini made it a diocesan project of Bergamo to publish the records of this apostolic visitation in homage to Borromeo on the third centenary in 1910 of his canonization.[10]

---

of Trent's reforms. See "Studi e problemi relativi all'applicazione del concilio di Trento in Italia (1945–1958)," *Rivista storica italiana* 70 (1958): 239–98, at 256–83.

10. This information and cited text is from Roncalli's Introduction, composed in

The publication project gained the approval of the Prefect of the Ambrosiana, Monsignor Achille Ratti (the future Pope Pius XI), who had the documents unbound and photographed. Soon, however, what was projected as a work by a commission of Bergamo's seminary professors devolved on Roncalli alone. He trained seminarians to transcribe the Latin texts of relevant correspondence, reports (*verbali*) on churches, parish life, clergy, and other institutions, and ordinances (*decreti*) of reform issued by St. Charles. The work advanced from its beginning in 1910, with some parts being printed but not published, but in 1914 it came to a halt due to the death of Bishop Radini and the outbreak of World War I, in which Roncalli served in the Italian army as a military hospital chaplain.

The publication project remained suspended for sixteen years, during which Roncalli had several assignments: first, three years as seminary spiritual director and animator of a Catholic women's association in Bergamo (1918–20), then over four years operating from Rome as national organizer of the Italian office to coordinate support for the missions (1921–25), and then nine years outside Italy after his consecration as bishop and sending as apostolic visitor and then apostolic delegate to the scattered Catholic minority in Bulgaria (1925–34). He returned to the editorial work after his transfer to Turkey, in late 1934, with residence in Istanbul, as apostolic delegate to the Catholics of both Turkey and Greece. By then he had a helper in work on the visitation edition, the Bergamo priest Don Pietro Forno. Three parts of the edition, *The Acts of the Apostolic Visitation by St. Charles Borromeo in Bergamo in 1575*, came out in 1936, 1937, and 1938, but Don

---

Istanbul in April 1936, to the first published volume: *Gli atti della visita apostolica di S. Carlo Borromeo a Bergamo (1575)*, ed. Angelo Giuseppe, Roncalli (Florence: Olschki, 1936–57), 1.1:xix–xlvi, at xix–xxiii. The work has been studied comprehensively by Max Vodola in "John XXIII, Vatican II, and the Genesis of *aggiornamento*: A Contextual Analysis of Angelo Roncalli's Works on San Carlo Borromeo in Relation to Late Twentieth Century Church Reform" (PhD diss., Monash University, 2010). See Vodola's article, "I met Charles Borromeo ... and he brought me to Vatican II," *Pacifica* 26 (2013): 171–83.

Forno died and World War II intervened. The last two parts came out in 1946 and in 1959.[11]

The documents of the publication seem at first glance to immerse the readers in external matters. From inspection of each of the 250 parishes of the diocese, the reports covered topics such as the physical condition of the buildings and windows of churches and outlying chapels, the solidity of the tabernacles, whether there is a monstrance for eucharistic exposition, the positioning of side altars, whether there is a confessional, whether the baptismal and marriage registers are kept up, whether the pastor lives nearby, whether he preaches and gives classes in Christian doctrine, and whether the parish cemetery is maintained and protected against wandering animals. In many of the subsequent mandates, Borromeo ordered parishes to have a proper confessional installed within thirty days and to establish within two months a school of Christian doctrine governed by statutes modeled on those of the schools of the Archdiocese of Milan.

The 1936 introduction to the first published part gave the historical context of the records Roncalli was publishing. But he found the practical aspects of the visitation to be imbued with a profound spiritual dimension in its activation and direction of zeal for pastoral care. It was a world in which one central event stood out.

The Council of Trent offered the spectacle of a vigorous renewal of Catholic life ... [in] a period of mysterious and fruitful rejuvenation and, what seemed still more marvelous, of efforts by the most remarkable individuals of the church to implement the new legislation. The pastoral ardor burning in them drove them to realize as perfectly as possible the conciliar mandates aimed at the perfection and spiritual elevation of the clergy and people.... [It was] a time of potent reawakening of energies which has no equal in any other period of church history.

---

11. Although the final published volume is dated 1957, it came out in 1959, when its editor was pope. He regularly spoke of *Gli atti* as his fifty-year project and task.

This reawakening became manifest in the provincial councils and synods ... among which those of the Province of Milan remained classic examples of applying and implementing the Tridentine legislation in an entire region. But it was above all evident in the pastoral visitations by bishops of their own dioceses and in the apostolic visitations carried out with higher authority under a direct mandate of the pope.[12]

This account of the post-Tridentine era in Roncalli's native Lombardy stresses the church's potential to become ever again rejuvenated, which was a centerpiece of Roncalli's theology of the church's nature and life. This he held dear and loved to articulate on occasions throughout his lifetime, for example, in preaching on Christmas, Easter, and Pentecost; in interpreting major figures and events of church history; and in October 1958, just before he and the other cardinals entered the conclave to elect the successor of Pope Pius XII. At that moment, Roncalli expressed his hopes of what the new pope, whoever he may be, would bring to the Catholic church. This should be, "not a solution of continuity, but instead of progress in pursuing the youthfulness of holy Church, whose mission is always to lead souls to the divine heights of realizing the Gospel and sanctifying human life in view of eternal life."[13] After his election as Pope John XXIII, he undertook to promote such a rejuvenation, similar to what followed Trent, by making it a central objective of the Second Vatican Council.

Of interest on the western side of the Atlantic is the earliest known occasion on which Roncalli wrote about ecclesial youthfulness. This is a notebook entry in which he copied parts of an

12. *Gli atti della visita* (ed. Roncalli), 1.1:xxiv. An "apostolic" visitation by papal mandate would include examining and, in cases, laying down corrections of the ministry of the diocesan bishop, whereas this was not foreseen in a bishop's visitation of his own diocese.

13. Cited here is Roncalli's letter about his prayer before the conclave, sent from Rome, October 16, 1958, the second day of pre-conclave congregations, to the rector of the seminary of Venice. *Pace e Vangelo* (ed. Galavotti), 2:754n756. Roncalli's diaries published in the Italian national edition contain at least twenty-one passages from 1903 to 1960 on the church's perennial youthfulness.

address given in Rome in March 1900 by Bishop John Lancaster
Spalding of Peoria, Illinois. Roncalli wrote out extracts exuding
Spalding's optimism about the "better things ... before us, not
behind us," about the new times that require new persons, and
about the ancient faith which requires, "if it is to be held vitally,
[that] we celebrate it with an energy that is wholly youthful."[14] In
the last days of Leo XIII, a circle of thinkers in Rome was fasci-
nated by "the Americanists," including Cardinal James Gibbons
and Bishops John Ireland and John Lancaster Spalding. Roncalli,
then in his early twenties, shared, at least for a moment, that fas-
cination with the young church across the Atlantic.[15]

The Spiritual Impact on Roncalli by Model Figures of Church Service in Tridentine Era

The writings of Angelo Roncalli attest to the spiritual impact
on him of the ideals and labors of three individuals of the post-
Tridentine era—a historian (Cesare Baronio) and two episcopal
implementers of Trent's reforms (Charles Borromeo and Gregorio Barbarigo).

(1) A year after beginning to teach church history in the seminary of Bergamo, Roncalli gave the inaugural lecture of the academic year 1907–8 on Cardinal Cesare Baronio, a disciple of
St. Philip Neri in the Oratory of Rome. The lecture came out the
next year in a journal and was republished in 1961.[16] Baronio was

14. *Giornale dell'Anima. Soliloqui, note e diari spirituali*, critical and annotated edition
by Alberto Melloni. *Edizione nazionale dei diari di Angelo Giuseppe Roncalli Giovanni XXIII*
(Bologna: Istituto per le scienze religiose, 2003), 1:213–14n25, cites the Spalding excerpt to
further illustrate Roncalli's notes during his retreat of December 1903, before his diaconate
ordination.

15. Spalding had lectured at the Church of the Gesù in Rome from a text translated and
published in Italian later that year in the journal *Rassegna nazionale*. The original came out
as "Education and the Future of Religion" in Spalding's collection of essays, *Religion, Agnosticism, and Education* (Chicago: McClurg, 1902), 147–92.

16. Angelo Roncalli, "Il cardinale Cesare Baronio," *La scuola cattolica* 36 (1908): 3–29,

the author-compiler of twelve volumes of the *Annales Ecclesiastici* (1588–1607), an account of the first twelve centuries of the church's history.

In his lecture, Roncalli presented Baronio, in his resoluteness and self-effacing dedication, as emblematic of the era of Catholic renewal. He gave to that church an essential element, namely, documented and cogently argued church-historical exposition. A generation earlier, the Lutherans of Magdeburg had produced their history of the church down to 1400, featuring the suppression of the pure New Testament Christianity by floods of papally sanctioned abuses, with only scattered witnesses to the truth (*testes veritatis*) in the pre-Reformation centuries. Many Catholics felt disarmed and humiliated, but here Baronio stepped into the breach to show that in the field of history the Catholic cause was not lost. He did this by going beyond just chronicling to offer vast documentation and incisive argumentation. In a characteristic image, Roncalli had Baronio recomposing the dry bones of texts and facts, clothing them, and making them sing the harmonies of a glorious past, "through which the church was continuing its perennial song of youth and life."[17]

Baronio was relevant in the first decade of the twentieth century, which for Roncalli was a troubled time because of historicist and modernist currents of deconstructive higher criticism. Catholics must meet this challenge, much as Baronio did in his time, with the well-grounded historical scholarship already promoted by Pope Leo XIII, and they must show no fear of the results of historical studies. Baronio remained present to Roncalli, and in 1925 his episcopal motto, *Obedientia et pax*, came from Baronio's motto as cardinal.

(2) In admiring and striving to imitate St. Charles Borromeo, Angelo Roncalli joined vast numbers of Italian priests and es-

---

republished separately with an introduction by Giuseppe de Luca (Rome: Edizioni di storia e letteratura, 1961).

17. Roncalli, *Il cardinale Cesare Baronio* (1961), 42.

pecially bishops who revered St. Charles during his lifetime and long after his death in 1584.[18] But as church historian and editor of the records of Borromeo's visitation of Bergamo in 1575, Roncalli had his own perspective on the man he once called a "colossus of *pastoral* sanctity."[19]

In introducing the first part of the records of the visitation, Roncalli wrote in 1936 of St. Charles as "the teacher of bishops," who both instructed on and exemplified episcopal life and service at a high level in the decades after Trent. The records then coming out to document Borromeo's activity in Bergamo will, Roncalli claims, show Trent's reform mandates being applied in detail and will reveal St. Charles as a zealous pastor devoting his intelligence and practical sense to grasp situations and give admonitions and directives full of pastoral wisdom. Borromeo acted in Bergamo, with dignity and resolve, to restore Christian life across the variegated span of its forms of expression. The visitation records permitted Roncalli to contemplate "apostolic and pastoral wisdom" in action, which he clearly aspired to have as marks of his own pastoral service.

In the records of the visitation, he [Borromeo] himself appears, alive and operative. He is here ... as one whom his contemporaries encountered and venerated for his high level of intelligence as a man of government who sees everything and gets to the point, along with his noble,

18. See Giuseppe Alberigo, "Carlo Borromeo come modello di vescovo nella chiesa post-tridentina," *Rivista storica italiana* 79 (1967): 1031–52, and Alberto Melloni, "History, Pastorate, and Theology: The Impact of Carlo Borromeo upon A. G. Roncalli / Pope John XXIII," in *San Carlo Borromeo: Catholic Reform and Ecclesiastical Politics in the Second Half of the Sixteenth Century*, ed. John M. Headley and John B. Tomaro (Washington, D.C.: Folger Shakespeare Library, 1988), 277–99. It is indicative that Hubert Jedin's classic essay on the ideal bishop of the Catholic Reform concludes with Borromeo and even inserts the shrewd remarks of a contemporary on what *not* to imitate in St. Charles's life and ministry. "Das Bischofsideal der katholischen Reformation," originally published in 1942, reprinted in Jedin's *Kirche des Glaubens Kirche der Geschichte. Ausgewälte Aufsätze und Vorträge* (Freiburg: Herder, 1966), 2:75–117.

19. From an article on St. Charles in Bergamo's *La vita diocesana*, November 4, 1909, cited by Melloni, "History, Pastorate, and Theology," 279. Roncalli instinctively stressed the pastoral side of St. Charles, while omitting his rigorous ascetical practices.

elevated heart of a bishop and a saint. He emerges from these pages in his full stature, and with him a whole world comes alive around him. The documents make known his collaborators. We hear the voices of the clergy and the people, of men and women of every social class who receive him, who present themselves to him, to whom he gives admonitions and directives. . . . This is the Christian people that remains the same, always quite sensitive to holiness when it passes in their midst. More than the directives laid down by councils and synods, the records of the visitation give the correct and authentic tone of this act of apostolic and pastoral wisdom, which Borromeo knew how to combine with his inner religious fervor. He had the exquisite art of providing for everything with the proper means, to bring ordered results, perfect organization, doing this calmly, in spite of certain oppositions he had to deal with, but which he met with great dignity and goodness.[20]

Over two decades later, Angelo Roncalli was elected pope on October 28, 1958, and was pleased to schedule his coronation liturgy on November 4, the day of the liturgical memorial of St. Charles. His homily first expanded on the image of Christ the Good Shepherd, his ideal as pope. He then devoted three paragraphs to Borromeo, whom he had long venerated. St. Charles lived in a time when the church suffered a weakening of its vigor and had to gain new energy. In such an era, St. Charles worked for restoration, especially by promoting observance of the decrees of the Council of Trent. He is rightly called *Magister Episcoporum* and he manifested admirably "episcopal sanctity."[21] Such was John XXIII's emphatic attachment to the great pastoral figure of Charles Borromeo.

(3) A third Tridentine figure dear to Roncalli was the seventeenth-century Venetian patrician Gregorio Barbarigo, who was bishop for seven years in Bergamo and then for thirty-three years

20. *Gli atti della visita*, 1.1:xxxvi–xxxvii.

21. Pope John XXIII, "Homily at the Solemn Pontifical Mass of His Coronation," in his *Discorsi, Messaggi, Colloqui del Santo Padre Giovanni XXIII*, vol. 1, *Primo anno del Pontificato* (Vatican City: Vatican Polyglot Press, 1960), 10–14, at 13–14.

in Padua until his death in 1697. Barbarigo had been beatified in 1761 and John XXIII canonized him two centuries later in 1960, after having held him for many years among his personal patrons and protectors.[22] A particular attraction lay in Barbarigo's having made a six-year visitation of the Diocese of Bergamo. In a letter of October 1960, Pope John even suggested to the bishop of Bergamo that a publication of the records of Barbarigo's episcopal visitation could make possible a fascinating comparison with the apostolic visitation by Borromeo nearly a century earlier—but nothing came of this.[23]

At Barbarigo's canonization Mass in May 1960, Pope John said that the new saint would now radiate into the universal church a divine ray of light, from his "pastoral holiness" (*santità pastorale*), which aids people toward salvation and extends the Lord's kingdom. Barbarigo, John pointed out, imitated Borromeo by ongoing application of the Tridentine norms in governing his dioceses. He was also modern, in having gained knowledge at a good seventeenth-century level of physics, mathematics, and even Oriental languages. But under these externals was Barbarigo's holiness of priestly virtues and energetic charity toward his people as their father and shepherd (*pater et pastor*).[24]

To conclude this section on Trent's formative influence on Roncalli, we can turn to the introduction he composed for the fifth and final part of the published records of the reforming visitation of Bergamo under Archbishop Charles Borromeo. Roncalli wrote the short preface eighty days before he would be elected pope, and in the text he alluded once more to his characteristic

22. *Giornale dell'Anima* (ed. Melloni), 298, in a note on the occasion of Roncalli's episcopal ordination in 1925, and 465n33, recalling Barbarigo among the saints and blessed to whom his godfather Xaverio taught him as a young boy to turn for help and protection.

23. Letter of October 24, 1960, to Bishop Giuseppe Piazzi of Bergamo. Cited by Alberto Melloni, in *Papa Giovanni. Un cristiano e il suo concilio* (Turin: Einaudi, 2009), 112n113.

24. Pope John XXIII, "Homily during the Canonization of St. Gregorio Barbarigo," May 26, 1960, in his *Scritti, messaggi, colloqui del Santo Padre Giovanni XXIII* (Vatican City: Tipografia poliglotta Vaticana, 1961), 2:335–65, at 360–62.

ecclesiology of the church-in-history with its potential for rejuvenating developments. Referring to the five volumes with their
documentary record from 1575, he wrote:

From the complex whole and from the particular points of these papers, a final impression springs forth, namely, a fact about the Catholic Church throughout all the variations of persons and eras of history.
It did have times of defective adherence to its principles, when it gave
in to compromises in accord with our weakened human nature and was
in danger of decline and weakened resistance. But it has as well always
looked toward its own renewal and toward recapturing its youthfulness,
enlivened by a holy passion for authentic spiritual advancement. This
positive reality of the church, as enlightened by evangelical truth and
seeking superior values, gives to souls and to whole peoples guidance
and encouragement for living and acting well.[25]

Thus Roncalli wrote in August 1958. Six months later, as Pope
John XXIII, he will announce that he intends to convene a synod
of the Diocese of Rome and an ecumenical council of the whole
church. The objectives of both were present for Roncalli already
in the Borromean records: recapturing ecclesial youthfulness,
correcting sub-standard practice, giving the impetus of evangelical truth toward superior values, and helping souls with guidance and encouragement for living well. All these sprang from an
idealized vision of Trent's reforms and their impact when applied
by bishops like Charles Borromeo and Gregorio Barbarigo.

Pope John XXIII Giving Vatican II
Its Objectives

In 1960, it was ten days before Pentecost when Pope John canonized Gregorio Barbarigo and underscored his pastoral holiness. Pentecost 1960 then became a major date for Vatican II, for

---

25. *Gli atti della visita*, ed. Roncalli, 2.3:v, completed at Sotto il Monte, August 5, 1958.

on that day John established ten preparatory commissions, two secretariats, and a Central Preparatory Commission to work on drafting texts which would come before Vatican II for deliberation, revision, further amendment, approval, and promulgation.

It is a commonplace of Vatican II history that as these preparatory bodies took shape, with their cardinal presidents, secretaries, members, and consultors, only a few of them were ready to pursue the objective of launching a renewing impact upon the Catholic church and the world beyond. Still, there were pockets of orientation toward renewal, for example, in the Preparatory Commissions on Liturgical Worship and on the Lay Apostolate. A particular ferment enlivened the newly created Secretariat for Promoting the Unity of Christians. But the other eight commissions, especially the Preparatory Theological Commission, were marked by narrow horizons, by desires to confirm recent papal encyclicals and current canon law, and by suspicion regarding the renewal currents of Catholic thought which had been flowing during the middle decades of the twentieth century in the biblical, liturgical, patristic, pastoral, and ecumenical fields.

From 1960 to 1962, Pope John spoke on several occasions in ways contrasting with much of the document preparation in the pre-conciliar commissions. He spoke of a church-wide rejuvenation which he hoped would result from the coming council—recalling what followed the Council of Trent. In this he was setting the stage for a major early drama at Vatican II. On three occasions, Pope John gave ordered accounts of his aims for the council, while hoping that these would "take hold" among future leaders and members of Vatican II.

(1) At Christmas 1961, John formally convened Vatican II to meet in 1962. He noted the existence of crises in society, in which "distrustful souls see only darkness burdening the face of the earth," but he reaffirmed his trust in Christ "who has not left

the world that he redeemed."[26] Where there is spiritual poverty in the world, this contrasts with the vibrant vitality of the church of Christ. (John wants the future participants in the council to think well of themselves and of their potential for good.) The coming council will promote the sanctification of church members and articulate revealed truth. It will turn to the problems and worries of the world, concerned to heighten in people a proper sense of their human dignity, to reaffirm the moral order and Catholic social doctrine, and so to benefit family life, education, and civil society. John wanted his own optimistic ideals, based in his view of history, to inspire the council. But, as 1962 began, he knew of hardly any church leaders around the world who were embracing such high expectations for the coming council.

(2) A month before Vatican II opened Pope John spoke on the radio about the council.[27] Seven draft documents from the preparatory commissions were by then in the hands of the council's members and John had studied the texts. He stated the common expectation that the council will concern itself with the church's vitality within, by presenting the light of its doctrine and the sanctifying power of grace.

But John then spoke expansively on issues outside the church, about human aspirations which will find their echo in the council: issues of the family, work, peace within and between nations, education, culture, social duties, and the freedom that corresponds to human dignity. This longer portion of the address featured topics not present in the draft-texts already sent to the council's members. The contrast was striking and had to raise the question whether John XXIII did not have serious reservations about the

---

26. Constitution *Humanae Salutis*, convening the council to meet during 1962, cited from *Council Daybook: Sessions 1 & 2*, ed. Floyd Anderson (Washington, D.C.: National Catholic Welfare Conference, 1965), 6–9. The Latin original is in *Acta Apostolicae Sedis* 54 (1962): 5–13.

27. Address of September 11, 1962, given in *Council Daybook* (ed. Anderson), 18–21, and in the Italian original in *Acta Apostolicae Sedis* 54 (1962): 678–85.

first draft-texts. His heart seemed directed to reaching out in solidarity to embrace the wider world of the human family.

(3) Then, as Vatican II opened, Pope John gave his famous inaugural address of October 11, 1962.[28] One objective of the assembly, he said, is to enhance Catholic teaching, with a view to the penetration of souls. Truth can be reformulated. The council should undertake this, and in doing so, it should act as a Magisterium which is especially pastoral in nature (*cuius indoles praesertim pastoralis est*). During the council's first working period in 1962, this little definition came to have notable influence on the assembly of council members. Many of them began to think and act as a preeminently pastoral Magisterium, leading them to demand revised draft documents corresponding to pastoral objectives—in doctrine formulated in a manner capable of deepening personal adherence and in decrees orienting church members to dedicated service as a leaven for good in the world.

One month into the council's work, on November 14, 1962, 98 percent of the members voted the basic acceptance of a draft calling for a wide-ranging liturgical renewal. This text would be the basis of their work, in spite of objections voiced by prominent individuals in the previous three weeks of debate. Next on the agenda was the Preparatory Theological Commission's draft-text. In four days of debate on this text, Pope John's pastoral aim of renewal began to function forcefully as the criterion of critical judgments on the work of the Preparatory Theological Commission.[29]

For example, Cardinal Joseph Frings (Cologne, Germany) said that the tone of the prepared text was that of a professor de-

28. The original Latin text is in *Acta Apostolicae Sedis* 54 (1962): 786–95; an English translation, with useful section headings, is given in *Council Daybook* (ed. Anderson), 25–29. A revised and corrected the translation is included in my *Doing Theology* (Mahwah, N.J.: Paulist Press, 2009), 141–51.

29. Chapter 6, below, recounts the interventions of November 14–19, 1962, in greater detail, on 157–60.

fending theses. It lacks that "pastoral note with which the Holy
Father ardently wants the council statements to be imbued."
Cardinal Paul-Émile Léger (Montréal, Canada) said that fear of
errors underlay the text, making it dissonant with "the spirit of
positive renewal desired by the pope in this council." Cardinal
Augustin Bea (Unity Secretariat) charged that with this text the
council would be failing in its work to give Catholic teaching a
fresh expression to affect souls, for as the pope said, our Magisterium is "especially pastoral."[30] Similar appeals to Pope John's
statement of the council's aims were heard in the following days.
Of eighty-eight speakers, thirty-two declared the text unsatis-
factory—a little over one-third (36 percent). But the critics had
a weighty argument, as eighteen of them appealed to Pope John's
pastoral objective as a main reason for setting aside the draft.
When a motion was made to remove the text from the agenda, 62
percent agreed, showing that the appeals to the pope's objectives
were taking hold in the minds of many council members.

Pope John removed from the immediate agenda the prepared
text on tradition and scripture as sources of revelation. For its
revision, he ordered the Doctrinal Commission to cooperate with
the Unity Secretariat of Cardinal Bea in preparing a revision better serving the pastoral aims then taking hold in the council.[31]
One reason for including the Bea Secretariat was the existence of
its own attractive text on the renewing power of the word of God
in the life of the church, which the Central Preparatory Commission had approved on June 20, 1962, but in November was not in
the hands of the council members.[32]

30. *Acta Synodalia Sacrosancti Concilii Vaticani II* (Vatican City: Tipografia Poliglotta
Vaticana, 1970–99), 1.3:34 (Frings), 41 (Léger), and 49 (Bea). But at the end, Archbishop
Morcillo Gonzalez spoke for forty-seven Spanish bishops who judged *De Fontibus* acceptable
as a foundation for the council's work (59–62), as had Cardinals Ruffini (Palermo, Italy), Siri
(Genoa, Italy), and Quiroga y Palacios (Compostella, Spain) earlier (37–38, 38–39, 39–41).

31. *Acta Synodalia*, 1.3:259.

32. Chapter 4, below, describes the Secretariat's draft-text on the word of God in the
framework of that body's prepared contributions of Vatican II. I treated it more at length in
"Scripture Reading Urged *vehementer* (DV No. 25): Background and Development," *Theological*

As Vatican II's first period ended, John laid down guidelines that the council's commissions were to follow in recasting their texts, an activity now seen as Vatican II's "second preparation." To give the commissions their criteria of revision, John's mandate cited a portion of his opening discourse, centered on the council's preeminently pastoral teaching office.[33] The second preparation in the first half of 1963 turned out fourteen revised texts, and with them Vatican II was on the way toward realizing to a considerable extent the aims John XXIII had set before it. By June 1963 the council members had in hand draft-texts on seminaries, Catholic schools, priestly ministry, the lay apostolate, bishops and diocesan governance, the pastoral care of souls, religious life, the Eastern Catholic churches, divine revelation, the church (two chapters on its mystery and hierarchy), ecumenism, and the Virgin Mary. Two further schemas went out in August on the sacrament of marriage, followed by chapters on the church concerning laity and religious.[34] Struggles and drama remained, but by appropriating John's pastoral objective Vatican II overcame its faulty first preparation and made a decisive turn toward being a pastoral council of rejuvenation and *aggiornamento*.

Conclusion: Two Remarks

Because Trent's reform decrees had a broad impact on the local churches that he knew well, Angelo Roncalli saw Trent as a model for the Catholic church even in the mid-twentieth century. To

---

Studies 74 (2013): 555–80, at 560–64 and 573–77 (English translation), reprinted in *50 Years on: Probing the Riches of Vatican II*, ed. David G. Schultenhover (Collegeville, Minn.: Liturgical Press, 2015), 365–90.

33. *Acta Synodalia*, 1.1:96–98, with a partial English translation in *Council Daybook* (ed. Anderson), 114.

34. Jan Grootaers gives an ample narrative in "The Drama Continues between the Acts: the 'Second Preparation' and Its Opponents," in *History of Vatican II*, ed. Guiseppe Alberigo and Joseph A. Komonchak (Maryknoll, N.Y.: Orbis, 1995–2006), 2:359–514. Grootaers's reference to "opponents" indicates resistance to the new directions, especially in council commissions where some influential members held doggedly to the drafts already prepared.

realize this, he had to contest a notion of church teaching focused wholly on doctrinal correctness and the exclusion of error. The pastoral dimension of the teaching's formative influence had to be present all through its formulation. Moreover, to make Vatican II a comprehensive council, it imitated Trent by complementing the doctrinal reformulations of its four constitutions with a broad program of renewed practice in worship, ministerial service, and the apostolate. This program finds expression in Vatican II's nine decrees, which give ideals and mandates for implementation in roles of service and action within the ecclesial body of God's people.

Finally, Vatican II was much too large an undertaking to be adequately explained under one rubric or by a single goal. Besides being a council of pastoral *aggiornamento*, as Pope John oriented it, the council also became a doctrinal council of ecclesiology, giving the church's self-definition. Furthermore, it became, in its Pastoral Constitution on the Church in the Modern World and its Declarations on Non-Christian Religions and on Religious Liberty, the organ issuing what Joseph Ratzinger astutely called a "counter-syllabus" to the tradition introduced by Pope Pius IX's "Syllabus" of the errors of the modern age (1864).[35] These further achievements belong to the essence of Vatican II, but along with these it still pursued the purpose that is stated first in the first paragraph of its first document, on the Catholic liturgy, namely, "to impart an ever increasing vigor to the Christian lives of the faithful." Angelo Roncalli called this a "rejuvenation" of the church in its members, a reality he found foreshadowed in the post-Tridentine era.

35. The "counter-syllabus" reversed the negativity about modern culture and political life expressed incisively by Pope Pius IX and then concisely in the preface added to Vatican I's Constitution on the Catholic Faith (1870; see *Decrees*, ed. Tanner, 804–5), and by many popular accounts of modern cultural and intellectual history from a Catholic perspective. In this view, decline proceeded downward through rejections of the church (Protestants), of Christ (critical Enlightenment), and of God (nineteenth century, e.g., Marx, Nietzsche), to leave, outside the Catholic church, confused chaos about answers to life's major questions. Vatican II selectively received developments of the modern age and indicated ways of integrating them into the Catholic vision of faith and human life. See J. Ratzinger, *Principles of Catholic Theology* (San Francisco: Ignatius Press, 1987), 381. Chapter 9, below, develops this notion in greater detail.

Theologians at Vatican II

The Ways and Means of Their Contribution
to the Council

Popular accounts of the Second Vatican Council at times emphasize
the critical, and even combative, activity of the theologian-experts,
especially during the first period (October–December 1962). Individual council theologians such as Karl Rahner, Yves Congar,
and Eduard Schillebeeckx appear as significant protagonists in
the conciliar drama. In fact, the papers of these theologians document their considerable involvement both just before the council opened and then during its first weeks, when they circulated
among the council members and other experts critiques of the initial official drafts and even offered alternative texts on the sources
of revelation, the deposit of faith, and the nature of the church.

But the conciliar activity of theologians began more than three
years before Vatican II opened on October 11, 1962. Their lectures
and writings had aimed to sketch the context of the coming council, to identify its priorities, and to propose topics that it should

This chapter was originally published as "Theologians at Vatican Council II," in Jared
Wicks, *Doing Theology* (Mahwah, N.J.: Paulist Press, 2009), 187–223.

treat. Numerous theologians had worked for the council's preparatory commissions from mid-1960 into summer 1962.

During the four autumn periods of council sessions (1962–65), and for some during the three intersessions, Vatican II demanded much of numerous theologians, called *periti* in the council's Latin terminology. They provided a variety of services, including consultations offered to the council members and even composition of their Latin interventions in the council hall and of the comments they handed in on draft-texts under discussion. Well-known experts were invited to give lectures to groups of bishops on the council topics. As the council moved ahead, more experts were called into service of the conciliar commissions, including several mixed commissions and numerous sub-commissions. As draft documents were being revised, the commissions asked their theologian-associates to examine in detail the oral and written interventions of the council fathers on earlier texts and to draw up proposed revisions reflecting the interventions.

But in all this, the ultimate outcome of the theologians' work was decided by others, that is, by those who were members of the council and of commissions, who voted to approve or not approve the texts. The ideas, preferences, and texts drawn up by the theologians were consultative proposals of experts, about which the council members in different moments decided whether, and in what form, these theological contributions might appear in the draft "schemas" placed before the council and then in the documents approved by the council. [1]

The aim of this chapter is to indicate the principal moments in which theologian-experts contributed to the huge ecclesial event that was the Second Vatican Council. To keep within reasonable limits, practically nothing will appear here about the decisive in-

---

1. I gave an annotated list of the theologians' contributions in the article, *"De revelatione* Under Revision (March–April 1964). Contributions of C. Moeller and Other Belgian Theologians," in *The Belgian Contribution to the Second Vatican Council*, ed. Doris Donnelly et al. (Leuven: Peeters, 2008), 461–94, at 461–64.

fluence exercised on the council by Popes John XXIII and Paul VI, and I will make only passing references to the major players of Vatican II such as Cardinals Augustin Bea, Léon Joseph Suenens, and Julius Döpfner. Other accounts of the council treat them amply. Here the emphasis is on the "ways and means" by which theologians influenced the council, with examples of the topics they presented both in preparation for and during Vatican II. I hope to verify the actual degree, beyond mythic narratives, of the influence on the experts on the work of the council and on its results.[2]

The Pre-Preparatory Phase (1959–60)

Pope John XXIII announced his intention of convoking an ecumenical council of the Catholic church on January 25, 1959, to a small gathering of cardinals at the Basilica of St. Paul Outside the Walls. Around the world, people were still getting used to the new pope, Angelo Giuseppe Roncalli, who had been papal nuncio in Bulgaria, Turkey, and France, but most recently was patriarch of Venice when he was elected to succeed Pius XII (1939–58) on October 28, 1958, just eighty-eight days before he announced the coming council.[3] But some theologians quickly went into action and many followed during the next three-and-a-half years with contributions to help prepare the council.

In France, Yves Congar, OP, brought out in mid-February 1959 a survey on councils in the life of the church, to which he added his hopes that the coming council would refrain from any new definition of privileges given to the Virgin Mary, that it would create a better balance in church governance between the wide scope

2. Étienne Fouilloux spoke of a tendency to legendary amplification of the influence of the theologians in the first lines of his paper, "Comment devient-on expert à Vatican II? Le cas du Père Yves Congar," in *Le duxième Concile du Vatican 1959–1965* (Rome: École Français, 1989), 307–31.

3. On the factors surrounding Pope John's decision and announcement, see chapter 1, above, and Joseph A. Komonchak, "Pope John XXIII and the Idea of an Ecumenical Council," available at https://jakomonchak.wordpress.com/category/Vatican-II.

of papal action and the restricted roles of bishops, that it would manifest a genuine solicitude for the good of human life in this world, and that it would give a positive impulse to better relations with non-Catholic Christians, for whom at the moment there was no designated office for contact and dialogue in the Vatican.[4]

In autumn 1959, Congar was at an ecumenical congress at the Benedictine Abbey of Chevetogne, Belgium, where the topic was general councils, and Congar stressed the importance of the first four such councils, because of the overriding significance (for both Eastern Orthodox and Catholics) of their dogmatic teachings. For the new council for which the Catholic church was preparing, Congar named two doctrinal topics calling for further clarification because of their ecumenical import: the "collegiality" of all the bishops in governing the whole church, and a clarification of the relations between scripture and the tradition coming from the apostles and preserved in the church.[5]

Another theologian who went to work shortly after Pope John's announcement was the historian of the Council of Trent, Hubert Jedin, professor of modern church history in the faculty of Catholic theology of the University of Bonn, Germany. Jedin assembled a concise history of the church's general councils in a book frequently reprinted in the original German and translated into seven other languages. Jedin also recommended to his Italian scholar-friends that they prepare a handy one-volume edition of all the decrees of the general councils from Nicaea (325) to Vatican I (1869–70).[6]

---

4. "Les conciles dans la vie de l'Église," *Informations catholiques internationales* 90 (February 15, 1959): 17–26. The article was unsigned, but É. Fouilloux, in the article mentioned in note 2 (above), related that it was written by Congar.

5. *Le Concile et les conciles* (Chevetogne: Abbaye de Chevetogne, 1960), 75–109 and 285–334.

6. Jedin's history came out as *Kleine Konziliengeschichte* (Freiburg: Herder, 1959), followed by its translation, *Ecumenical Councils of the Catholic Church: An Historical Outline* (New York: Herder and Herder, 1960). The volume of council decrees is *Conciliorum oecumenicorum Decreta*, ed. Giuseppe Alberigo et al. (Basel: Herder, 1962), from which came

Hans Küng spent his summer vacation of 1959 composing his widely-read book on the just-announced council, featuring its potential for initiating reforms in the Catholic church which would pave the way for reunion with the presently divided Christian churches.[7] By a happy accident, Küng had been invited to Basel in January 1959 by the Reformed theologian Karl Barth and lectured there about ongoing reform of the church (*ecclesia semper reformanda*) just a week before Pope John announced the coming council. His book on reform and reunion was also influenced by a meeting around July 1, 1959, with two Dutch priests, Jan Willebrands and Frans Thijssen, the coordinators of the Catholic Conference on Ecumenical Questions, which had been quietly promoting ecumenism among European Catholic theologians during the 1950s. Küng stressed in his book that the very holding of a council signaled a change of climate in the Catholic church, in which there was now good reason to hope for concrete changes, in a new receptivity to the justified proposals of the Protestant Reformation, which would then lead toward recomposing the fractured unity of Western Christianity.

Joseph Ratzinger, a young professor of fundamental theology in the faculty of Catholic theology of the University of Bonn, Germany, anticipated a major theme of Vatican II in an early lecture on the council as expressing the collegial nature of the church's pastoral leadership on the model of the twelve apostles. Many had forgotten this after Vatican I in 1870 had treated only the successor of Peter and his infallibility in certain moments of

---

the bilingual edition with English translations, including the documents of Vatican II, in *Decrees*, ed. Tanner.

7. *Konzil und Wiedervereinigung. Erneuerung als Ruf in die Einheit* (Freiburg: Herder, 1960), translated as *The Council, Reform, and Reunion* (New York: Sheed and Ward, 1961). Just before Vatican II opened, Küng's *Strukturen der Kirche* appeared, translated as *Structures of the Church* (London: Burns and Oates, 1965), in the series *Quaestiones disputatae*, then under the supervision of Karl Rahner. Küng narrates the circumstances surrounding the preparation of both works in the first volume of his memoirs, *My Struggle for Freedom* (Grand Rapids, Mich.: Eerdmans, 2004).

his teaching. Still, the council is not a parliament of the peoples' representatives, as the bishops gathered in council are the body bearing a primary responsibility in this later age for giving witness to the word of Christ from which believers live.[8]

In the Vatican, a Pre-Preparatory Commission was formed and made known on Pentecost Sunday, May 16, 1959. It included the coordinating secretary of each of the ten offices or congregations of the church's central government, with Cardinal Secretary of State Domenico Tardini directing the group and reporting on its work to Pope John. A then-unknown official of the Vatican marriage tribunal, Monsignor Pericle Felici, became secretary of this pre-preparatory group.

Cardinal Tardini got the council machinery moving with a letter of June 18, 1959, to 2,594 bishops and major superiors of clerical orders, who by canon law would be called to be participating members of the council. The letter expressed Pope John's desire to hear views, advice, and suggestions about the questions and topics the council should take up.

The survey had a response rate of 77 percent, with answers differing greatly, from short indications about points of church doctrine, law, and administration to lengthy proposals with arguments to back them up. Tardini's letter of June had asked for a response by the end of September, but the answers kept arriving well into spring 1960, which gave the Pre-Preparatory Commission the needed time to organize the vast material, which came to about nine thousand different proposals, with many items coming from several or more respondents, under a chosen set of headings. The cardinal's letter initiating the canvas said explicitly that in preparing the answer, each bishop or religious superior could, if he wished, formulate his suggestions in consultation with persons who were experts in the various ecclesiastical fields.

---

8. Joseph Ratzinger, "Zur Theologie des Konzils," *Catholica* 15 (1961): 292–304, originally a lecture of February 25, 1961.

Scattered Signs of Theological Input

The suggestions made in 1959–60 by bishops and religious superiors for the council agenda were printed in the Vatican II *Acta et Documenta* (Series I, vol. II, in eight parts). These were originally published for use in the second phase of preparation, in composing draft-texts of decrees to put before the council members. But recently these texts have attracted the attention of those interested in Catholic history, especially of Vatican II, because they present a portrait of the church's leadership in its transition from the pontificate of Pope Pius XII to that of John XXIII and Vatican II.

Recent studies of the proposals, often treating those from one nation, indicate that the future fathers of the council were not widely interested in gathering ideas by consulting experts in theology. This, at least, is implied in reviews of the proposals that came from France, England, Spain, Canada, and Italy.

But there were exceptions. In the Netherlands, four bishops proposed that the council sanction a positive Catholic engagement in the ecumenical movement. The bishops used for this a memorandum drawn up by Frs. Willebrands and Thijssen of the Catholic Conference on Ecumenical Questions.[9]

In Strasbourg, France, Archbishop Jean Julien Weber inserted into his proposal several suggestions of Congar, then living in Strasbourg. The council should center its teaching on the Gospel, proclaiming before the world the lordship of Jesus Christ, and stressing the great truths of God as Trinity and his redemptive work, which are held in common with Christians of other confessions. In this recentering, the church would present itself as

---

9. J. Jacobs, "Les *vota* des évêques néerlandais pour le concile," in *À la veille du Concile Vatican II*, ed. Mathijs Lamberigts and Claude Soetens (Leuven: Leuven University Press, 1992), 99–110. Peter De Mey sketched the work of the Catholic Conference in "Johannes Willebrands and the Catholic Conference for Ecumenical Questions (1952–1963)," in *The Ecumenical Legacy of Johannes Cardinal Willebrands*, ed. Adelbert Denaux and Peter De Mey (Leuven: Peeters, 2012), 49–77.

the "gathered congregation of those joined to Christ by faith and baptism," with such an ample vision allowing Catholics to acknowledge the saving action of the Holy Spirit not just in their own life and sacraments but in other Christian bodies as well. Such thinking puts into practice, even before the council urged it, the principle of "the hierarchy of truths," intending thereby to offer a corrective to overemphasis in Catholic piety on special devotions, especially to the Virgin Mary.[10]

In his study of the responses from the United States, Joseph Komonchak discovered some documentation of American bishops' consultations of theologians.[11] Cardinal Richard Cushing of Boston formed a committee of ten, including four theologians of St. John's Seminary, to draw up possible proposals for the council. The cardinal selected twenty items, including a request for a new systematic account of the church as the mystical body of Christ, which should lead to social conclusions, for example, toward overcoming exaggerated nationalism in one part of the body.

Cardinal Francis Spellman of New York asked his seminary professors for a list of possible suggestions. However, among the topics submitted, the cardinal declined to pass on to Rome proposals to restore the diaconate as a permanent ministry in the church and to let the vernacular take the place of Latin in the celebration of the Catholic liturgy. One of the professors proposed that the council bring clarity in an area then under discussion, namely whether ideally a government is obliged to favor the true faith, while only tolerating heretical and schismatic sects. Cardinal Spellman, who later brought Fr. John Courtney Murray, SJ,

---

10. Vatican II, *Decree on Ecumenism*, no. 11. A reference to his drafting for Bishop Weber can be found in Congar's council diary, *My Journal of the Council* (Collegeville, Minn.: Liturgical Press, 2012), 10. Based on the two-volume French original of 2002, I presented this work in "Yves Congar's Doctrinal Service of the People of God," *Gregorianum* 84 (2003): 499–550.

11. J. Komonchak, "U.S. Bishops' Suggestions for Vatican II," *Cristianesimo nella storia* 15 (1994): 313–71.

to Vatican II as his adviser, crossed out with a big "X" the topic of state favor of one religious confession.

At the Catholic University of America, the moral theologian Fr. Francis Connell, CSSR, drafted twenty points of doctrine for the council, from which Archbishop Patrick Aloysius O'Boyle of Washington selected nine for inclusion in his proposal, including a request that the council solemnly condemn racism and all discrimination against persons of other races. But these cases were very few among the 138 responses sent in by bishops of the United States.

Among the suggestions of the future council members, two can be mentioned because of the roles that they will have at Vatican II. In Münster, Germany, Bishop Michael Keller incorporated into his proposal a series of topics worked out by professors of the Catholic theology faculty of the University of Münster. In teaching on what the church is, the council should draw more fully on scripture, so that the topic of the body of Christ, from St. Paul, would be accompanied by insistence on the Holy Spirit who unites and gives life to the community and on the notion of "the people of God" who are on pilgrimage toward the fullness of God's kingdom and reign. Bishop Keller took over a paragraph composed by Professor Hermann Volk, who was then dean of the University of Münster's faculty of Catholic theology, stating that the council should declare solemnly that scripture is the principal source of Catholic truth, while tradition, which is not creative of divine revelation, is for us a source from which God's revealed truths become manifested. The council should show the invalidity of the popular idea that the Catholic church lives from the sacraments, while Protestants live from the word they hear read and preached. Taking its cue from the letter to the Hebrews, "The word of God is living and active, sharper than any two-edged sword" (Heb 4:12), the council should acknowledge the saving efficacy of the word, as it is read during the liturgy, applied in the homily, and explained in catechesis, always according to the meaning that the church holds to be true.

Together with this topic, well known from writings of Professor Volk, Bishop Keller took over another idea of the faculty, namely, that Catholic seriousness about the value of scripture should lead to a revision of the liturgical lectionary, so that people would not hear the same Sunday readings every year, but should be exposed to many more biblical passages by selections arranged in a three-year cycle of readings.[12] After contributing these preparatory proposals for Vatican II, Professor Volk was appointed bishop of Mainz in spring 1962 and so became a member of the Second Vatican Council, where he promoted his theology of God's word as a member of the Secretariat for Promoting Christian Unity and the council's Doctrinal Commission.

In October 1965, when the Commission was working on the final revisions of its Constitution on Divine Revelation, Volk voiced his dissatisfaction over the way the beginning of text then stood, that is, by naming the council as the subject or speaker of the teaching (*Sacrosancta Synodus*). For Volk, the opening words should indicate briefly the topic and should not call attention to the council. In a short consultation between Volk and the Louvain theologian Gérard Philips, a new opening phrase was formulated, which the Commission members immediately voted to accept: "Hearing the word of God reverently and proclaiming it confidently, this holy synod ..." (*Dei verbum religiose audiens et fidenter proclamans ...*). Thus, the theologian Hermann Volk affected Vatican II both early in its preparation and later near the end of its work.[13]

---

12. Bishop Keller's proposal: *Acta et Documenta Concilio Oecumenico Vaticano Secondo Apparando*, Series I (Antepraeparatoria), 2.2:629–33. The faculty's suggestions: ibid., 4.2:799–803. H. Volk published "Wort Gottes: Gabe und Aufgabe" in *Catholica* 16 (1962): 241–51, and *Zur Theologie des Wortes Gottes* (Münster: Regensburg, 1962). The two texts are in Volk's *Gesammelte Schriften* (Mainz: Grünewald, 1966–78), 2:89–100, and 3:19–35.

13. The incident at the October 25, 1965, meeting of the Doctrinal Commission was

At Milan, the deadline for suggestions by September 1959, fixed by Cardinal Tardini, was not observed, as it left little time for the maturation of ideas. The theological faculty of Milan held meetings on proposals for Vatican II from October 1959 into April 1960, with reports being presented to the Archbishop Cardinal Giovanni Battista Montini (the future Pope Paul VI). This interaction resulted in two documents sent to the Pre-Preparatory Commission in early May 1960, which showed complementarity between the faculty's doctrinal proposals and the cardinal's comprehensive pastoral suggestions. Cardinal Montini said it was time to adopt a new way of dealing with men who left the priesthood to marry, namely, to offer them reconciliation and dispensations from celibacy. To ensure real progress toward the ecumenical hopes that John XXIII had been mentioning in talks on the council, Montini urged the holding of pre-conciliar hearings with representatives of the Eastern Orthodox and Protestant churches, so that in the coming council Catholic bishops would have accurate ideas of their faith and life and not think of these groups in ways derived from outdated textbooks.[14]

Studies Submitted by Theological Faculties

A second part of the pre-preparatory Vatican II survey was the formulation of proposals by professors teaching in Catholic theology faculties. In July 1959, Cardinal Tardini wrote to sixty-two such bodies around the world, asking for "brief studies, clear and precise, looking to practical conclusions that the council might de-

---

recorded in the diary of Fr. Umberto Betti, OFM, *Diario del Concilio* (Bologna: Edizioni Dehoniane, 2003), 71.

14. Cardinal Montini's proposal is given in *Acta et Documenta* I, 2.3:374–81. The faculty wanted the council to clarify the supernatural destiny of humans in relation to life in this world and to work out doctrine on the role of bishops in the church (*Acta et Documenta* I, 4.2:667–96). On Montini's preparation, see A. Rimoldi, "La preparazione del Concilio," in *Giovanni Battista Montini Arcivescovo di Milano e il Concilio Ecumenico Vaticano II: Preparazione e primo periodo* (Brescia: Istituto Paolo VI, 1985), 202–41, esp. 212–22.

cide to adopt." The deadline was set for April 1960 and fifty-three faculty groups submitted responses, now published in the *Acta et Documenta* (Series I, vol. IV, in three parts). Most of these studies were collegial products, coming out of discussions of proposals by individuals and amendments accepted by vote in faculty meetings, as was done in Milan and Münster.

A notable exception was the collection of sixteen individually signed studies by professors of theology at the Pontifical Lateran University in Rome, where Pope John had studied as a young priest of the Diocese of Bergamo. One of these studies, by a Spanish Capuchin professor of the Old Testament, Fr. Teofilo Garcia, urged the council to give an example for all Catholic theologians to follow by adopting biblical themes in its documents of teaching and renewal of pastoral practice.[15] But Fr. Garcia died in 1960 and so had no chance for a personal influence on the work of the council.

The case of the rector of the Lateran University, Monsignor Antonio Piolanti, was different, for he became in 1960 a member of the Preparatory Theological Commission and from 1962 to 1965 he was an officially named expert of Vatican II. In his study, submitted in early 1960, Piolanti decried tendencies which he found in present-day Catholic theology toward an autonomy subversive of the faith. The council should intervene to reaffirm the clear principles laid down by the popes, beginning with Gregory XVI and Pius IX in the nineteenth century and continuing in the twentieth century in teachings by Pius X and most recently by Pius XII, especially in his encyclical *Humani Generis* (1950). The tendencies needing correction are especially of French origin, in the work of theologians whom Piolanti named, such as Henri Bouillard, SJ, and Marie-Dominique Chenu, OP, who relativize the value of doctrinal terms by holding that they are tied to thinking of past ages. Another tendency is the work of Jesuits who had

---

15. *Acta et Documenta* I, 4.1:189–94.

been based at Lyon, such as Henri de Lubac, Jean Daniélou, and Hans Urs von Balthasar, who promote a return to the theology of the early Church Fathers as an alternative to the disciplined thought of scholastic theology. This group, in Piolanti's reading, advances the idea that theological statements derive their validity not from objective grounds of fact and reason but from their correspondence with the religious experience that gives rise to positions and which theological discourse intends to explain.

Monsignor Piolanti called for the council to censure these tendencies by affirming the immutability of the truths of faith, which sound theology receives from the authoritative teaching office of the successor of Peter. This gives theology its positive basis, for as Pius XII said in *Humani Generis*, theology's task is to show how the truths now being taught were already present in some real way in the Bible and the works of the Church Fathers. Then, in a second methodological step, theology should investigate the deposit of doctrine to discover by rational reflection further truths that are there by implication.[16]

Monsignor Piolanti was a typical member of one stream of the theology then in vogue in Rome, and he had the satisfaction of seeing his proposal against the "new theology" of French origin taken over in the council proposal of the Vatican Congregation for Seminaries and Studies, for which Piolanti was a consultant. The Congregation omitted names of the theologians whom Piolanti singled out, but it submitted the main parts of his study as one of its own proposals for the Vatican II conciliar agenda.[17]

16. *Acta et Documenta* I, 4.1:248–63. The passage of Pius XII's *Humani Generis* to which Piolanti referred is given in *The Papal Encyclicals 1939–1958*, ed. Claudia Carlen (Ann Arbor, Mich.: Pierian Press, 1990), 178 (no. 21).

17. The proposal of the Congregation for Seminaries, incorporating Piolanti's critical essay, is in *Acta et Documenta* I, 3:321–28. Fouilloux studied the Lateran University proposals, along with publications of its professors in the journal *Divinitas*, in "Théologiens romains et Vatican II (1959–1962)," *Cristianesimo nella storia* 15 (1994): 373–90, concluding that this group took as its starting point the authoritative documents of the current Magisterium and frequently called attention to contemporary deviations from such authoritative

Among the other proposals made by theological faculties in early 1960, three are of interest because of their subsequent influence during the council, which occurred by their members serving as experts for the council's commissions or by council members being formed by contacts with these schools of theology.

The Catholic theology faculty of Montréal, Canada, was the formative milieu of Montréal's archbishop, Cardinal Paul-Émile Léger, who during the council became an influential exponent of reform ideas coming from Pope John XXIII. In the pre-preparatory phase, the theologians of Montréal proposed that the council initiate preparation of a new universal Catholic catechism, which would revise the four-hundred-year-old *Catechism of the Council of Trent* to include instruction on doctrines which had become official church teaching since Trent, to treat scripture passages on the basis of solid recent biblical exegesis, and above all to draw amply on the pastorally enriching "kerygmatic theology" then being promoted in Austria and Germany.

The Montréal theologians also called for the council to issue a doctrinal text, *On the Sources of Revelation*, to set forth the Catholic understanding of how God's Word comes to us. The nature of "tradition" needs clarification, as it is a term with various meanings. According to the meaning one uses, there follow different ways of explaining the interrelation of tradition with scripture. On the biblical source of revelation, the council should aim to reconcile two different attitudes, namely, the church's religious veneration of the inspired books of the Bible and the technical study of the words, style, and historical background of the biblical books that is proper to exegesis. In scholarly study of the Bi-

---

teaching—deviations, that is, deserving to be censured by Vatican II. Two helpful studies, in part identical, of the broader background of proposals like that of Piolanti are by Joseph A. Komonchak, "The Enlightenment and the Construction of Roman Catholicism," *Annual of the Catholic Commission on Intellectual and Cultural Affairs* 4 (1985): 31–59, and "Modernity and the Construction of Roman Catholicism," *Cristianesimo nella storia* 18 (1997): 353–85. The latter is also available at https://jakomonchak.wordpress.com/category/Vatican-II.

ble, new methods were becoming widely used, which prompted the Montréal theologians to suggest that the council should move Catholic teaching beyond the directives given in the two papal encyclicals on biblical studies, Leo XIII's *Providentissimus Deus* (1893) and Pius XII's *Divino Afflante Spiritu* (1943).[18] In Rome, the Pontifical Biblical Institute, with its staff of Jesuit professors, became influential during the council by circulating memoranda in evaluation of the use of scripture in draft-texts under discussion. Among the Institute's alumni were Cardinals Bernard Alfrink (Utrecht, The Netherlands) and Albert Gregory Meyer (Chicago). The rector of the Institute, Fr. Ernst Vogt, a Swiss Jesuit, had taught in Brazil and the large episcopal conference of Brazil regularly took over the memoranda of the Institute as bases of their interventions commenting on draft-texts. Also, a major player in the council, Cardinal Augustin Bea, SJ, president of the Secretariat for Promoting Christian Unity, was a long-time professor of the Institute and served as its rector before Fr. Vogt.

In the preparatory phase of Vatican II, the Biblical Institute offered a five-point proposal for the council agenda regarding scripture. (1) The council should explain how both scripture and the tradition initiated by the apostles come from a single source, namely, the Gospel of Christ, and in the further life of the church, scripture and tradition are never separated but stand in close mutual interrelation. (2) From the letters of St. Paul, the council should underscore how faith in the good news of Christ is central in our acceptance of salvation, for such teaching is of considerable ecumenical importance. (3) To show the basis of the church's esteem of scripture, the council should teach about the saving efficacy of the proclaimed Word of God, which scripture records. (Here the Biblical Institute echoed, without knowing it, the proposal from Münster.) (4) In teaching on the Gospels as historical documents about Jesus, the council should remind Catholics that

---

18. The Montréal faculty proposal is given in *Acta et Documenta* I, 4.2:461–62.

after Easter, before the Gospels were composed, the Holy Spirit was guiding the apostles and their associates to a progressively deeper understanding of the person and work of Jesus, an understanding which the Gospels express in various ways. (5) The Institute, where the scriptures of Israel were studied intensively, called for the council to mince no words in condemning all forms of anti-Semitism.[19]

Finally, among the theology faculties, one should hear from Louvain, in view of the huge influence on Vatican II exercised by Cardinal Leo Josef Suenens, with other Belgian bishops such as Andre-Marie Charue of Namur and Emiel-Jozef De Smedt of Bruges, as well as by the Louvain theologians associated with the conciliar commissions, like Gerard Philips, Lucien Cerfaux, Charles Moeller, and the canonist Willy Onclin. In early 1960, the Louvain proposal for Vatican II followed the outline of the attributes of the church, which the council should set forth in a way that would show the true face of the church to the world. As "one and catholic," the church should actively promote ecumenical relations with other Christians. As "holy" the church should look optimistically upon the world, not seeing it as the source of myriad errors, but as God's good creation which Christ has redeemed.

Louvain gave the note of "apostolic" special treatment, beginning by urging a renewed Catholic fidelity to scripture, which combines the sacred books of Israel, which served Jesus and his apostles as their own Bible, with the New Testament books coming directly or indirectly from the apostles. Second, as the bishops of today are successors of the apostles, the council should formulate a doctrine of the episcopate, to complete Vatican I, which treated only the pope. The new teaching should present bishops not only as chief pastors of individual dioceses but also as together forming the universal episcopal college, which will be in action in the council itself. Finally, to make clear that it is "apostolic," the

---

19. *Acta et Documenta* I, 4.1:125–36.

church should receive from the council a concentrated teaching on Jesus Christ himself, and this should go beyond treating Jesus as the supreme mediator and communicator of revelation about God and human life, to treating his very person and work as the revelation itself of God. Therefore, in Christ himself the church finds the deep roots of every dogma and doctrine that it teaches. He is the founder of the church in his past actions, is its present-day guide, and in the final consummation God plans to unite all things under his headship (Eph 1:10).[20]

The studies sent in from theology faculties in 1960 showed notable differences, especially contrasting with the Lateran University proposals. During the Vatican II's working periods (1962–65), both in the council hall and in the commissions, these burst forth in disputes between their exponents.

Vatican II's Preparatory Phase (1960–62)

On Pentecost Sunday, June 5, 1960, Pope John XXIII declared the end of the pre-preparatory phase and instituted the bodies with responsibility for drawing up draft-texts for Vatican Council II. He created ten preparatory commissions, roughly corresponding to the congregations of the Roman Curia, making the cardinal prefect of the congregation the president of the respective commission.[21] In an action of far-reaching impact, John XXIII also founded the Secretariat for Promoting the Unity of Christians, which was also to function in ways still undefined in preparing the council. Its first president was Cardinal Augustin Bea, SJ.[22]

---

20. *Acta et Documenta* I, 4.2:223–26.

21. Preparatory commissions were founded for these areas: theology, bishops and the governance of dioceses, the clergy and Christian people, religious orders, the sacraments, liturgy, seminaries and studies, the Eastern Catholic churches, missions, and the lay apostolate. Their work is analyzed in *History of Vatican II*, ed. Alberigo and Komonchak, 1:167–356.

22. On the Secretariat and the council, see chapters 4–5, below. M. Velati related the founding and conciliar action of the Secretariat in *Una difficile transizione: Il cattolicesimo tra*

From September 1959 to March 1960, the Pre-Preparatory Commission analyzed the proposals sent in by the future members of the council and organized them under the headings of current systematic theology, moral teaching, and the Code of Canon Law. Many of the proposals were easy to group together, but others lost their biblical and spiritual content by adaptation into pre-established categories. Mimeographed summaries of the proposals from the different geographical areas were prepared and sent to the Vatican congregations in anticipation of the work of actual preparation of draft-texts. A two-volume *Analyticus Conspectus*, detailing roughly nine thousand individual proposals, was printed in early 1961 for use by the preparatory commissions.[23] Based on further summaries, Pope John XXIII formulated topics which each of the preparatory commissions should treat in preparing draft-texts based on the proposals and on their own further perceptions of needed council actions.

One of the last actions of the pre-preparatory group, working under Cardinal Tardini in spring 1960, was to draw up lists of possible members and consultants whom the preparatory commissions could well invite to take part in their work. Tardini foresaw the problem posed by the close relation between the Curia's congregations and the conciliar preparatory commissions, and so he urged the commission presidents to gather bishops and competent experts from the whole Catholic world, not just from those associated with the Curia's congregations. But this did

---

unionismo ed ecumenismo (1950–1964) (Bologna: Il Mulino, 1996), chaps. 8–13, and more recently Velati documented its work during the preparation period in *Dialogo e rinnovamento: Verbali e testi del segretariato per l'unità dei cristiani nella preparazione de concilio Vaticano II* (1960–1962) (Bologna: Il Mulino, 2011), which I presented in "Still More Light on Vatican Council II," *Catholic Historical Review* 98 (2012): 467–502, at 477–89. One of Cardinal Bea's first co-workers told the story from his personal experience: Thomas Stransky, "The Foundation of the Secretariat for Promoting Christian Unity," in *Vatican II Revisited by Those Who Were There*, ed. Alberic Stacpoole (Minneapolis, Minn.: Winston, 1986), 62–87.

23. The *Conspectus* is an appendix to *Acta et Documenta* I. Fouilloux studied the process by which the proposals were filtered into established schemes of thought and law. See his account in *History of Vatican II*, 1:140–49.

not prevent some of the commissions from being dominated by Vatican congregation members and consultants. In fact, in June 1962, an astute observer of the council's preparation called the near identity of the preparatory commissions with the curial congregations the "original sin" of the Vatican II preparation. Then, in the preparation itself there followed several "actual sins," such as the claim and practice of autonomy by the commissions, especially that for theology, which refused to collaborate with other commissions and with the Unity Secretariat on topics of common responsibility, such as the liturgy, theological education, and the Catholic understanding of the sacraments and life of the Eastern Orthodox and Protestant churches.[24]

But along with the individual preparatory commissions, John XXIII also created a large Central Preparatory Commission, with over a hundred members, including numerous presidents of the episcopal conferences of the world. This group was to receive the draft-texts of the preparatory commissions and to evaluate them with a view to recommending either their further revision or passing them on to the pope for distribution to all the future members for deliberation in the council itself.[25]

Theologians Working for Individual Preparatory Commissions (1960–62)

Regarding the preparatory commissions that prepared the draft-texts for Vatican II, it seems important not to be carried along by an easy generalization based on a partial perception of their

---

24. Cardinal Carlo Confalonieri, speaking at the June 19, 1962, meeting of the Central Preparatory Commission, when draft-texts, sharply differing from each other, were presented by the Theological Commission and the Unity Secretariat on the question of church-state relations. *Acta et Documenta* II, 4:731.

25. The narrative of the sessions of the Central Commission includes more than a few moments of sharp debate. Antonino Indelicato, *Difendere la dottrina o annunciare l'evangelo: Il dibattito nella Commissione centrale preparatoria del Vaticano II* (Genoa: Il Mulino, 1992).

work. To be sure, there were groups such as the Commission on Clergy and the Christian People and the Commission on the Sacraments that were controlled by individuals closed to new directions, proposing that Vatican II simply confirm the doctrine and law then in force. Also, among the ten bodies, the Theological Commission was a special case, which I will treat below.

The Preparatory Commission on the Liturgy had an excellent group of members and theological experts oriented to the renewal of Catholic worship, such as Josef Andreas Jungmann, Theodor Klausner, Francis McManus, Bernard Botte, Godfrey Diekmann, Cipriano Vagaggini, Johannes Hofinger, and Johannes Wagner. They gave Vatican II in 1962 a model draft-text based on fifty years of liturgical research and pastoral experience that flowed together with a fresh perception of the Christian community as the priestly people called through Christ to worship the Father in the Holy Spirit. The Commission for the Lay Apostolate included well-informed progressive bishops such as Emilio Guano (Livorno, Italy), Franz Hengsbach (Essen, Germany), and Gabriel Garrone (Toulouse, France), with the social thinkers Pietro Pavan and Agostino Ferrari Toniolo, and had consultors such as Ferdinand Klostermann, Johannes Hirschmann, SJ, and Roberto Tucci, SJ, all of whom in time made solid contributions to the Pastoral Constitution of the Church in the Modern World, *Gaudium et Spes*.

Clearly the Secretariat for Promoting the Unity of Christians was a special case, as it was newly established in 1960. It was prepared by the Catholic Conference led by Frs. Willebrands and Thijssen, and it had the extraordinary leadership of Cardinal Bea, who was supported by Bishops Lorenz Jaeger (Paderborn, Germany), François Charriére (Lausanne-Geneva, Switzerland), and Emiel-Jozef De Smedt (Bruges, Belgium), with competent theologians like Hermann Volk, Johannes Feiner, Eduard Stakemeier, Gustave Thils, Christoph Dumont, OP, Jerôme Hamer, OP, Maurice Bevenot, SJ, and George Tavard, AA.[26] This group prepared excellent texts for Vatican II, such as its draft of a pastoral decree *The Word of God*, and it added new co-workers during the council for the taxing labors of seeing three significant documents through successive revisions to completion, namely, the Decree on Ecumenism, the Declaration on the Church and Non-Christian Religions, and the Declaration on Religious Liberty. But during the preparatory phase of 1960–62, the Secretariat had to struggle to establish itself as a body with competence to contribute draft-texts.

Some theologians found themselves unable to contribute much to the preparatory commissions with which they were associated. The historian of the Council of Trent, Hubert Jedin, was in a minority on the Commission on Seminaries, with his ideas for reform of seminary studies.[27] Karl Rahner was not a consultant of the Theological Commission, but rather of that on sacraments, for which he was only asked to prepare a document on the restoration of the permanent diaconate, to which married men could be ordained. This was a topic requested with some frequency by bishops in the proposals of 1959–60, and Rahner prepared a written text in collaboration with Bishop Franjo Šeper (Zagreb, Croatia), which in time became the basis of no. 29 of the Dogmatic Constitution on the Church *Lumen Gentium*.[28]

26. Chapter 4, below, tells of several contributions of the Secretariat's theologians during the preparatory period, for example by Alberto Bellini (Bergamo) and Hermann Volk (then Münster). Chapter 5 relates the roles of Gérard Philips (Louvain) in clarifying the issue of membership in the church and of Jan Witte, SJ (Gregorian University), in proposing a key modification of *Lumen Gentium*, no. 15, in recognition of the non-Catholic churches and ecclesial communities.

27. Jedin related in his autobiography that in Commission discussions, his proposals for reform joined with suggestions made by Fr. Paolo Dezza, SJ, and Fr. Pierre Girard, General Superior of the Sulpicians, but Rome-based members of the Commission regularly outvoted them. H. Jedin, *Lebensbericht*, ed. Konrad Repgen (Mainz: Grünewald, 1984), 200–201.

28. Early in 1961, the archbishop of Munich, Cardinal Julius Döpfner, proposed Rahner as a consultant of the Preparatory Theological Commission, but the president, Cardinal Alfredo Ottaviani, was reluctant, as the Holy Office, which Ottaviani headed, was then processing

The Preparatory Theological Commission often dominates perceptions of the preparations of 1960–62.[29] Cardinal Alfredo Ottaviani presided over its work along with his main collaborator from the Holy Office, Archbishop Pietro Parente. Fr. Sebastian Tromp, SJ, long-time professor of fundamental theology at the Gregorian University and Holy Office consultant, was chosen by Cardinal Ottaviani as the Commission's secretary. Tromp played a central role in coordinating contact with the Commission members, parceling out assignments, preparing meetings, and overseeing the movement of draft-texts through the stages of composition.[30] Of the thirty-three members, thirteen were bishops and twenty were veteran theologians like Antonio Piolanti, Salvador Garofalo, Lucien Cerfaux, Joseph Fenton, Franz Hürth, SJ, Luigi Ciappi, OP, and Karel Balić, OFM. But the thirty-six consultants did include major figures of twentieth-century theology, such as Yves Congar, OP, Henri de Lubac, SJ, Bernard Häring, CSSR, and Joseph Lécuyer, CSSP.

The Preparatory Theological Commission prepared six draft-

---

accusations against Rahner as deviating from Catholic doctrine. Klaus Wittstadt, *Julius Kardinal Döpfner (1913–1976)* (Munich: Don Bosco, 2001), 183. Rahner threw himself into research on the diaconate and gathered thirty-eight contributions from all over the Catholic world for publication in what became a basic text of reference on the diaconate, *Diaconia in Christo: Über die Erneuerung des Diakonats* (Freiburg: Herder, 1962). Herbert Vorgrimler, "Karl Rahner: The Theologian's Contribution," in *Vatican II Revisited*, ed. Stacpoole, 32–46, at 39–40.

29. On this body, see Joseph Komonchak, "The Preparatory Theological Commission," available at https://jakomonchak.wordpress.com/category/Vatican-II. This text documents the Commission's assertion of hegemony over the other commissions and it cites Henri de Lubac's incisive observations on the theology dominating the Commission. See the latter's *Vatican Council Notebooks*, ed. Loïc Figoureux, trans. Andrew Steffanelli and Anne Englund Nash (San Francisco: Ignatius Press, 2015), 1:77–78, 93–94, 113, 119–20, and 122–24.

30. Tromp's diary recording the work of the Commission during the preparatory period has been published as *Konzilstagebuch Sebastian Tromp SJ mit Erläuterungen aus der Arbeit der Theologischen Kommission*, ed. Alexandria von Teuffenbach, vol. 1, *Commissio praeparatoria theologica (1960–1962)* (Rome: Gregorian University Press, 2006). This 965-page publication gives (with helpful annotations) Fr. Tromp's day-by-day record of the Commission's activities in 1960–62, both in the original Latin with a German translation, adding letters and other documents from the Vatican Archive on the Commission's work.

texts which in time were distributed in their completed form to the members of Second Vatican Council: "The Sources of Revelation" (drafting coordinated by Salvatore Garofalo); "Guarding the Purity of the Deposit of Faith" (Luigi Ciappi, OP); "The Christian Moral Order" (Franz Hürth, SJ); "Chastity, Matrimony, the Family, and Virginity" (Ermenegildo Lio, OFM); "The Church" (Rosario Gagnebet, OP); and "The Blessed Virgin Mary" (K. Balić, OFM).

However, none of these six drafts made its way successfully through the phases of the council's procedure of open discussion, written comments by the members, revision, a second discussion, further revision, and voting with the possibility of offering final amendments, followed by promulgation as a constitution or decree of Vatican Council II. All six documents of the Preparatory Theological Commission were either replaced by new drafts made during the council or were dismantled for partial inclusion in other draft-texts. Thus, the Preparatory Theological Commission was a failure, and for understanding one of the basic theological problematics of Vatican II, much light comes from identifying the reasons for this failure. Fortunately, Congar and de Lubac were acute observers who saw the problems besetting the Commission, and jotted them down in their diaries, well before they came to the notice of the council and the wider world.

(1) Congar noted that the mentality that dominated the Preparatory Theological Commission of 1960–62 was deeply formed by the style of work of the Holy Office, the Curia's office of doctrinal vigilance and correction of error, where priorities differed greatly from what John XXIII was proposing, in his own way, as goals of the council.[31] A clear sign was the draft-text, "Guarding the Purity of the Deposit of Faith," which went out to all the council members before the council opened in 1962. The text

---

31. Congar, *My Journal*, 47 (Council preparation for Cardinal Ottaviani is an extension of the Holy Office, August 24, 1961), 72 (Holy Office atmosphere dominating the Commission, March 5, 1962). De Lubac found the concerns of the Commission typical of "the milieu of the Holy Office." *Vatican Council Notebooks*, 1:77.

had ten chapters, each of which set out to correct an erroneous belief or theological tendency, for example, on human knowledge of truth, creation and evolution, God's objective word of revelation spoken to human beings, the right distinction between the supernatural and natural orders, original sin, and other points. The first impression of this text on quite a few readers was that of a "Syllabus of Errors," like the list of modern ideas which Pope Pius IX declared alien to Catholic truth in 1864. Those who were reading the discourses of Pope John XXIII during 1961–62 came to sense a serious disconnect between his expressed hopes for Vatican II and this extensive document, on protecting the deposit of faith, produced by the Preparatory Theological Commission.

(2) For drafting texts, the Commission divided its consultants into sub-commissions, in which a designated presider asked individuals to prepare short sections. Much of this work went on between the plenary meetings of the Commission, when only those residing in Rome had easy contact with each other and with Fr. Tromp. This impeded the proposals made earlier by the Biblical Institute and the Louvain theologians from influencing the overall direction of work. Congar noted that he was asked only for comments on short sections of the drafts that were developing. In 1962, when criticisms of the theological drafts began circulating and Congar joined his voice to them, he had to defend himself against an accusation by Cardinal Ottaviani of disloyalty to the Commission. Congar told the cardinal that the method of preparatory work never gave him an occasion for speaking to the overall orientation of the documents or even to single points on which he had done research and published, like the role of Mary, the nature of tradition, and the fundamental nature of the church itself.[32]

---

32. Congar, *My Journal*, 34 (fragmentation of work, November 16, 1960), 221–22 (accusations by Cardinal Ottaviani with Congar's response, November 30, 1962). De Lubac makes the same contrast between the ideal of theology drawn from works of the great tradition and the assembling of material from the ecclesiastical texts of the past century. *Vatican Council Notebooks*, 1:93–94.

(3) Congar was formed in the tradition of the Dominicans of northern France, in the school of Saulchoir, which prized returning to the early Christian sources where the Christian mystery was expressed more simply, more concretely, and more vigorously than in recent scholastic theological manuals. This orientation alerted Congar early in the preparation of Vatican II to a method that dominated the Theological Commission, namely, that of composing draft-texts which assembled positive teaching and censure of errors from encyclicals and discourses of the popes of the previous seventy years, from Leo XIII through Pius XII.[33] Congar's diary entry registers his profound disturbance at seeing the source of teaching not being the word of God addressed to the church, but instead the word of the church itself, in the limited form of recent papal documents.[34] Compared with the classics of Christian theology from the early Church Fathers through the medieval masters like St. Thomas and St. Bonaventure, the Preparatory Theological Commission was in fact introducing an innovation quite discontinuous with the great tradition of Catholic thought nourished from the authentic sources.[35]

(4) Finally, there was the refusal of the Preparatory Theological Commission of 1960–62 to form mixed commissions with other preparatory bodies like the Liturgy Commission or the Unity Secretariat. Concerns over the church's life of worship or ecumenical issues were not allowed to disturb work in the sealed-off doctrinal area. Congar saw the absence of ecumenical sensibili-

33. Cardinal Ernesto Ruffini, who had been rector of the Lateran University and secretary of the Congregation for Seminaries, but after World War II became archbishop of Palermo, had expressed just this hope for Vatican II's work in a discourse in October 1959. The council would render definitively valid the principal teachings of the popes from Leo XIII through Pius XII, by adding to their own magisterial authority the greater authority of an ecumenical council, to raise these doctrines above any possible questioning. Ernesto Ruffini, "Il Santo Padre Giovanni XXIII nel primo anno di pontificato," *Divinitas* 4 (1960): 7–28.

34. Congar, *My Journal*, 78 (the Magisterium, not scripture and tradition, as the source in drafts, March 10, 1962).

35. Ibid., 46–48 (drafts out of the encyclicals, August 21, 1961), 52–56 (ecumenical concerns missing in doctrinal drafts, September 21–22, 1961), 78.

ties in the Theological Commission posing a threat to Pope John's frequently expressed hopes that Vatican II would pave the way to future reunion with the now separated churches. In July 1961, he wrote to the pope about this narrowness of the Preparatory Theological Commission, and some months later he heard from Cardinal Bea that Pope John was very disappointed over the absence of cooperation in preparing the council between the bodies headed by Cardinals Ottaviani and Bea.[36] But there was also the large Central Preparatory Commission to which the Preparatory Theological Commission began submitting its draft-texts in November 1961.

Theologians Consulted by Members of the Central Preparatory Commission

The Central Preparatory Commission met for sessions of several days' work on the prepared draft documents from early autumn 1961 into June 1962. Some members were pleased with two of the draft-texts of the Theological Commission, namely *The Sources of Revelation* and *Guarding the Purity of the Deposit of Faith*, but other members were not satisfied. In fact, at the meetings of this Central Commission a critical opposition gradually formed, especially against the texts of the Preparatory Theological Commission and against the mentality of their drafters.[37] Cardinal Bea exercised an increasing influence over many members because he arrived at some meetings with detailed criticisms that he had worked out with the theologians of the Secretariat before sessions of the Central Commission. On the draft-text *The Sources of Revelation*, Bea said it should be withdrawn, because in treating the topics of biblical inspiration and interpretation it issued

36. Ibid., 45n5. See also 46–48 (refusal of mixed commissions, August 24, 1961) and 67–68 (exclusion of ecumenical concerns, November 22–23, 1961).

37. In March 1962, the members and consultants of the Theological Commission heard of the Central Commission's critical reception of the first theological drafts that it reviewed. Congar, *My Journal*, 71, which Congar also heard from Cardinal Bea (73).

censures of positions held by a few Catholic exegetes, but by so small a number that Vatican II should not even take notice. But most of all, when the draft-text spoke of interpretation of the Bible, it gave only admonitions and no signs of appreciation and encouragement for the work of the great majority of Catholic exegetes and biblical theologians.[38]

Other critical opponents of the drafts of the Preparatory Theological Commission spoke out during meetings of the Central Commission, such as Cardinals Joseph Frings, Bernard Alfrink, Julius Döpfner (Munich, Germany), Franz König (Vienna, Austria), with Bishop Dennis Hurley, OMI (Durban, South Africa), and Patriarch Paul Cheikho of the Chaldean church. On November 10, 1961, the Central Preparatory Commission took a vote on *The Sources*, revealing that sixty-one of the seventy-seven members present associated themselves with the sharp criticisms voiced by Cardinal Bea. This was eleven months before Vatican II opened, and it signaled division among leading members of the coming council over the work of the Preparatory Theological Commission. The wider world was informed of this a year later, when many of the criticisms of "The Sources" were voiced in open sessions during Vatican II's first working period.

Cardinal König prepared his interventions for meetings of the Central Preparatory Commission by obtaining evaluative comments from Karl Rahner on the draft-texts.[39] Using comments

38. It was an open question how the coming council would address itself to Catholic scripture scholars. The approach of admonition and censure of error, because of new opinions about the kind of history given in Genesis and in the Gospels, had been in effect urged by Monsignor Antonino Romeo, in a long article published in the Roman journal *Divinitas* at the beginning of 1961. Romeo offered a scathing criticism of the professors and graduates of the Pontifical Biblical Institute, accusing them of undermining the Catholic faith, which led to two of them being temporarily suspended from teaching. See, on this, Joseph Fitzmyer, "A Recent Roman Scriptural Controversy," *Theological Studies* 22 (1961): 426–44. Another account, relating as well the repercussions in the U.S., is Gerald P. Fogarty, *American Catholic Biblical Scholarship: A History from the Early Republic to Vatican II* (San Francisco: Harper and Row, 1989), 281–96.

39. Rahner's often devastating comments have been published: "Konzilsgutachten für

coming from Rahner, König lamented that "The Sources" begins by treating *our knowledge* of God's word, from scripture and tradition, and not by an account of God's word *itself*, which should be the true "source" of Vatican II's renewal of doctrine and church life. Further, the draft goes to such lengths to defend the role of tradition as a source that it leaves scripture in the shadows, while in fact the church places scripture first, which it venerates as a sacred and inspired text. Also, the draft should show appreciation for the work of Catholics in the hard work of biblical exegesis instead of laying down admonitions about their work. König concluded that the Theological Commission should have an exchange with the Pontifical Biblical Commission to get input by experts in the biblical field, and then the draft could be presented a second time to the Central Preparatory Commission. In January 1962, König used arguments coming from Rahner in criticizing the draft on the deposit of faith, because it offers apologetic arguments against ideas considered wrong, when what is needed by contemporaries is a positive synthetic presentation of revealed truths, with attention to the difficulties that sincere people have with some of the intricacies of Catholic doctrine.

During the time of the Central Commission's work, Cardinal Frings was consulting with Joseph Ratzinger, then in Bonn. This was especially necessary because Cardinal Frings was nearly blind, which was compensated by his total recall of what he heard. From these consultations, Frings prepared numerous incisive interventions both before and during Vatican II. In another consultation with a Bonn professor, Frings heard from Hubert Jedin a reminder of the great importance, once the council began, of the new commissions that would oversee revisions of texts in the light of the council members' interventions. This led

Kardinal König," in Rahner, *Sämtliche Werke*, vol. 21, *Zweite Vatikanum: Beiträge zum Konzil und seiner Interpretation*, ed. Günther Wassilowsky (Freiburg: Herder, 2013), 1:37–214. Selections came out earlier in *Sehnsucht nach dem geheimnisvollen Gott*, ed. Herbert Vorgrimler (Freiburg: Herder, 1990), 95–149.

to Frings's intervention on the first working day of Vatican II, October 13, 1962, seconding the dramatic call of Cardinal Achille Liénart (Lille, France) for a postponement of the elections of the council's commission members, so the members could get to know who were the most competent on the various council topics among the bishops from other nations.[40]

Theologians Working during and between the Council Periods (1962–65)

When the council opened, two hundred *periti* were named as official consultants to the council. Many other theologians came to Rome as personal advisers of individual bishops or of episcopal conferences. For many, what began in October 1962 was a singular experience of intense theological work in exchanges with colleagues from around the world and in response to requests by the pastoral leaders of the church for help based on their theological competence. The diaries of two Jesuit experts, Otto Semmelroth and Pieter Smulders, contain expressions of amazement over the number of other theologians they were meeting each day to exchange news and receive stimulating ideas about the topics the council would be discussing. It was also deeply satisfying to be actively involved in an undertaking of such magnitude and long-range importance as an ecumenical council of the Catholic church.

Otto Semmelroth taught dogmatic theology at the Jesuit faculty of Sankt Georgen in Frankfurt, Germany, and was called to Rome for the council to assist Bishop Hermann Volk of Mainz. During his years of teaching in Münster, Volk had given lectures and held seminars in German and so he regularly asked Semmelroth, who used Latin at Sankt Georgen, to prepare Latin analyses of the draft-texts and to put into good Latin the interventions

40. *Acta Synodalia*, 1.1:207–8. Jedin reports his advice to Cardinal Frings in his *Lebensbericht*, 203.

Volk wanted to make. Semmelroth's Vatican II experience was intensified by his living at the German College, a residence for seminarians and student-priests, where Cardinal Döpfner and Karl Rahner also lived during the council.[41]

Pieter Smulders taught dogmatic theology and patristics at the Jesuit faculty of Maastrict in The Netherlands, from which he was called to Vatican II by a former student, the Jesuit Archbishop Adrianus Djajasepoetra of Jakarta, Indonesia, who made Smulders part of a four-man "brain trust" for the thirty bishops of Indonesia. Smulders lived at a Franciscan sisters' hostel on Via Cassia, along with some Indonesian bishops and with a group of bishops and their experts from Brazil.[42]

First, I will sketch something of the myriad services given by theologians to the council members and the episcopal conferences. A following section will relate the specialized work demanded of the theologians who were taken on as co-workers of the different council commissions.

Theologians Serving Council Bishops and Episcopal Conferences

Before Vatican II formally opened on October 11, 1962, a powerful stimulus to theological work came by the mailing during August to the council members of a booklet containing seven draft-texts for conciliar discussion, of which four came from the Preparatory Theological Commission. Many bishops quickly called on theologians to study and evaluate these texts proposed for discussion at the first working period of Vatican II.

41. I read Semmelroth's unpublished diary, *Konzilstagebuch*, in the Archive of the Jesuit Province of Germany at Berchmans College in Munich.

42. I draw on Smulders's collection of papers documenting his Vatican II activity, especially his letters to the Maastrict Jesuit community, which are kept in the Smulders-Archive of the Katholiek Documentatie Centrum, Nijmegen, The Netherlands, where the staff was very helpful in assisting my Vatican II research.

Karl Rahner continued his consultative help of Cardinal König after the arrival of the first draft-texts, and Cardinal Döpfner asked for copies of Rahner's remarks.[43] In a similar way Yves Congar gave his critical comments on the drafts to Archbishop Jean Julien Weber of Strasbourg.[44] Jean Daniélou evaluated the drafts for the Coadjutor Archbishop of Paris, Pierre Veuillot, who had Daniélou's critical remarks translated into Latin, which he then sent to the Council Secretariat before Vatican II opened.[45]

In Freiburg, Germany, Archbishop Hermann Schäufele got from Professor Friedrich Stegmüller thirty-three pages of analysis and criticism of the drafts, along with an alternative draft-text on what was lacking in the preparation, namely, a text on God as sovereign creator and Lord. Stegmüller thought it urgent to counteract what he sensed underlay them, namely, a spirituality too absorbed in personal psychology and horizontal relations in the church.[46] In The Netherlands, Pieter Smulders, of the Maastrict Jesuit theologate, studied the seven first draft-texts at the request of the papal nuncio, Archbishop Giuseppe Beltrami, for whom he wrote sixty-seven pages of evaluations. Smulders praised the draft on the nature and renewal of the liturgy, but expressed serious reservations about the content and tone of the four drafts from the Preparatory Theological Commission.[47]

---

43. A sample is given in *Sehnsucht nach dem geheimnisvollen Gott*, 149–63. On the four theological texts, Rahner commented: "Here there's no radiance at all of the victorious power of the Gospel" (155). The text protecting the deposit of faith is, in Rahner's view, asking the council to treat many topics well below the dignity of an ecumenical council of the Catholic church.

44. Congar, *My Journal*, 79–80.

45. Pietro Pizzuto, *La teologia della rivelazione di Jean Daniélou: Influsso su Dei Verbum e valore attuale* (Rome: Gregorian University Press, 2003), 32–39, giving the texts on 505–23.

46. I am grateful to Fr. Paolino Zilio, OFM Cap., for copies of material by Stegmüller which he found in the Freiburg Diocesan Archive. The draft-text, entitled *Schema de Deo*, is in the Vatican Secret Archive, *Concilium Vaticanum II*, Box 124, *Animadversiones Patrum ante Concilii Initium*, as Bishop Schäuffele's contribution sent in a month before the council opened.

47. I presented this in "Pieter Smulders and *Dei Verbum*: A Consultation on the Eve of Vatican II," *Gregorianum* 82 (2001): 241–97, giving texts of Smulders's critical analyses on 283–97.

As the opening of the council drew near, some theologians enlarged the scope of their critical work on the first draft-texts.[48] In The Netherlands in late August, Bishop Willem Bekkers (Den Bosch) had asked for comments on the draft-texts from Eduard Schillebeeckx, OP, of the University of Nijmegen's Theology Faculty. In mid-September Bishop Bekkers brought together seventeen missionary bishops of Dutch origin to whom Schillebeeckx made an oral presentation of his criticisms. This prompted the secretary of the Dutch Episcopal Conference, Fr. Jan Brouwers, to initiate action with a view to bringing Schillebeeckx's evaluations to the attention of the whole body of 2,400 council members. Schillebeeckx composed a fifty-page text in Dutch, incorporating some of the analyses that Smulders had sent to Nuncio Beltrami. Brouwers got translations made from Schillebeeckx's Dutch into Latin and English and then had the two texts typed onto mimeograph stencils. In Rome, at the residential college for Dutch student-priests, Brouwers ran off some 2,700 copies of the text in Latin and English, which circulated widely in October 1962 among groups of bishops and the theologian-experts.[49]

Among other points, Schillebeeckx said that the draft *The Sources of Revelation* lacked a necessary first chapter on God's revelation itself in the history of salvation. The Preparatory Theological Commission also shows no sign of having followed the pre-preparatory proposals of the future council members, which the Preparatory Commission on Liturgy did do, to the enrichment of the draft-text on liturgy. Where *The Sources* deals with the word of God, it takes this as God's speaking (*locutio*) which evolves into true propositions concerning God and human life, while seriously neglecting the revelation of God in events and

48. Chapter 3, below, treats in more detail selected texts on God's revelation circulated by theologians in the council's early stages.

49. Jan Brouwers, "Vatican II, derniers préparatifs et priemière session. Activités conciliares en coulisses," *Vatican II commence ... Approaches francophones*, ed. Étienne Fouilloux (Leuven: Bibliotheek van de Faculteit der Godgeleerdheid, 1993), 353–78.

the "real tradition," beyond the oral, through the worship and practice of believing Christians in their communities. At a fundamental level, the texts on the sources and on guarding the deposit of faith have an inadequate notion of God's revelation, which comes to supreme expression in the incarnation of the Son of God, for Christ *is* the revelation of God well before he opens his mouth to teach. To be sure, oral communication is necessary, but it is narrative and explanation of the living truth present in Jesus. The texts of the Preparatory Theological Commission suffer greatly when set beside the text on liturgy, which for Schillebeeckx is "an admirable piece of work."[50]

To keep this chapter within reasonable limits, I will simply mention three other texts by theologians that were circulated as alternative draft-texts in first weeks of Vatican II. Joseph Ratzinger and Karl Rahner composed an exposition of the revelation in Christ of God and of humans in a text which was mimeographed and read widely in November 1962.[51] Congar's "conciliar creed" gave vital reaffirmations of the central Christian truths.[52] Congar also contributed a beautiful short text on tradition and scripture, as an alternative to "The Sources," for the bishops of western France, who gladly accepted Congar's emphasis on the

---

50. [E. Schillebeeckx], *Commentary on the "prima series" of "Schemata Constitutionum et Decretorum de quibus disceptabitur in Concili sessionibus"* (1962). A photocopy was given me by E. Schillebeeckx, to whom I am grateful for this help and our discussions during my visits to Nijmegen. The *Commentary* has been published in its English version in Sebastian Tromp, SJ, *Diarium Secretarii Commissionis de fide et moribus Concili Vatican II*, ed. Alexandra von Teuffenbach, vol. 2, *Commissio Conciliaris (1962–1963)* (Nordhausen: Verlag Traugott Bautz, 2011), 948–91.

51. *De Revelatione Dei et Hominis in Jesu Christo Facta*, distributed in roughly two thousand copies. It is given in B. Dupuy (ed.), *La Révélation divine*, Unam Sanctam 70b (Paris: Cerf, 1968), 2:577–87, and in Rahner, *Sämtliche Werke*, 21.1:217–36. An English translation can be found in Brendan Cahill, *The Renewal of Revelation Theology* (Rome: Gregorian University Press, 1999), 300–317. I treat it, along with the text that Ratzinger contributed to the collaboration with Rahner, in "The Fullness of Revelation in Christ in *Dei Verbum*," *Josephinum Journal of Theology* 23 (2016): 176–204, at 184–89.

52. Published in the original Latin, with a German translation, in *Glaube im Prozess, Festschrift K. Rahner*, ed. Elmar Klinger and Klaus Wittstadt (Freiburg: Herder, 1984), 51–64.

living tradition of the believing community, by which the church becomes the corporate subject that passes on its own faith and life to successive generations.[53]

Along with these writings created under the stimulus of the council's beginning, theologians gave numerous lectures around Rome to groups of bishops during the first working period. On October 10, the day before the opening liturgy, Joseph Ratzinger spoke to the German-speaking bishops on the serious problems in the draft-text, "The Sources of Revelation." Difficulties begin with the title itself that shows more interest in the places where we come to know God's word than in God's own action which comes before any human effort to pass on the witness that we find in scripture and tradition.[54] Congar's diary records that he lectured during the first weeks of the council on scripture and tradition before the French bishops, the Melkites, the French-speaking bishops of Africa, and the Episcopal Conference of Argentina.

The Indonesian bishops lived during Vatican II in houses scattered around Rome, but they came together one afternoon each week to discuss council topics, especially in the light of presentations by experts, such as Hermann Schmidt, SJ (Gregorian University) on the liturgy, Ignace de la Potterie, SJ (Biblical In-

---

53. Published in *Acta Synodalia*, 3.3:902–4, in which nos. 3–5 already have the structure and many contents of what will become *Dei Verbum*, Chapter II, nos. 7–10.

54. "Bemerkungen zum Schema De fontibus revelationis," in a sixteen-page copy in the Smulders-Archive (note 42, above), in folder no. 100. I published it, with the author's permission, in "Six Texts by Prof. Joseph Ratzinger as *peritus* before and during Vatican Council II," *Gregorianum* 89 (2008): 233–311, at 269–85 (English) and 295–309 (original German). Ratzinger told how classical Catholic figures such as Thomas Aquinas and Bonaventure held that all the truths of faith are in some way present in the inspired scriptures, a notion that *The Sources* proposed to condemn as a Protestant error now infiltrating Catholic theology. Further, the draft-text wants to raise to the level of dogma the theory that the textbooks teach about how God's inspiration affects a biblical author. The theory, however, is now outdated by what we know about the lengthy genesis, through many revisions, of the biblical books. In speaking of Old Testament revelation, *The Sources* works with the outdated six-thousand-year view of human history, which must be corrected by the evidence of paleontology for the long span of time between the first humans and the call of Abraham.

stitute) on Gospel interpretation, and Frans Thijssen (Unity Secretariat) on ecumenism. The American Passionist, Barnabas M.
Ahern, give the U.S. bishops lectures on the methods and results
of contemporary scripture studies, which raised their awareness
of the narrowness of *The Sources* in its passages on biblical interpretation.

Personal contacts between theologians from different countries stimulated the circulation of theological ideas and new proposals during the first working period of Vatican II. Many council
members, individually and in their episcopal conferences, added
to the intensity by the welcome they gave to experts who offered
them theological updating. The texts under discussion were also
stimulating, but in many cases this called for the formulation
of concise alternatives grounded in the early sources. It was no
time for the theologians to offer brilliant personal insights, but
instead texts with potential to find wide acceptance among the
council members because of what they could contribute to renewing Catholic doctrine, catechesis, and preaching.

During Vatican II's first period of autumn 1962, Smulders was
not yet an official expert of the council and so he could not go to St.
Peter's to hear the oral interventions at the morning sessions.[55]
But this left him free to move around Rome to gather information for the Indonesian bishops on positions emerging in other
episcopates. On October 30, Smulders went to see Cardinal Bea,
who was glad to pass on advice through Smulders to the bishops.
Bea urged them to discuss thoroughly the upcoming draft-texts
until they reached a consensus, and then to choose one member
to speak in the Aula in the name of the whole group of thirty. Bea
advised against urging any of the alternative texts then in circulation, as there was no realistic chance for them to be officially proposed. The "brain trust" should study carefully Pope John XXIII's

---

55. What follows here and in the following section on Smulders comes from his council
diary and other papers in his archive in the Catholic Documentation Center in Nijmegen.

opening discourse of October 11, as citations of this by Indonesian bishops would have a wide impact.

Some of the council members were good Latinists and could easily prepare concise interventions, like Cardinal Ruffini of Palermo, the man who made the most oral interventions of any council member. But others needed help, given by their theologians, in drafting correct and forceful Latin addresses, limited to ten minutes. On the first day of debate on *The Sources of Revelation*, November 14, 1962, Archbishop Gabriel Manek, SVD (Endeh, Indonesia), spoke in the name of all the Indonesian bishops, giving both general and specific reasons for rejecting the draft-text. The intervention had been written by Smulders and lightly revised at the November 9 meeting of the Indonesian bishops.[56] The Italian Franciscan Umberto Betti recorded in his diary four different times that the archbishop of Florence, Ermenigildo Florit, had delivered in the Aula "the comments that I drafted," which was also the case for Archbishop Florit's important introductory presentation before the council, on September 30, 1964, of the emended text on revelation, which had replaced "The Sources of Revelation."[57]

As the council proceeded, the draft-texts were revised in the light of the oral and written interventions of the members. In time, the revisions came up for vote, when a council member voting in favor of the text could ask for a further amendment (called a *modus*) which he thought would improve the text without changing its substance. Numerous theologians actually drafted these proposed amendments, often at the request of members, but also on their own in the hope that a council member would adopt it and append it to his favorable vote. In the last votes on the Constitution on the Church in 1964, Congar circulated among numerous French bishops a text which would add to the document a full Catholic recognition of the episcopate in the Eastern Orthodox

---

56. I related this in "Pieter Smulders and *Dei Verbum*: 2. On *De fontibus* during Vatican II's First Period," *Gregorianum* 82 (2001): 559–93.

57. Betti, *Diario del Concilio*, 22–25.

churches, both in terms of their orders and their jurisdiction over their dioceses.[58]

Theologians as Consultants and Redactors of Draft-Texts for the Commissions

With the opening of the council, the ten preparatory commissions ceased to exist, and new conciliar commissions of twenty-five members each were chosen from among the council fathers, with sixteen being elected and nine, including the president, appointed by the pope. The work of these conciliar commissions began slowly, but for the members and the co-opted theological experts of some commissions this changed toward the end of the first period of 1962. A crucial event was the rejection by the council, in early December 1962, without need of even taking a vote, of the draft-text from the Preparatory Theological Commission, "The Church." Within a few weeks, at the request of different episcopates, no less than five new draft-texts of ecclesiology were worked out by groups of theologians, along with four further texts on individual points of doctrine on the church.[59]

After the first period, at the end of January 1963, Congar went to Mainz where Bishop Hermann Volk called together the German theologians who were working on a new draft on the nature of the church. Alois Grillmeier had composed this alternative text with considerable input from Karl Rahner, but Congar found it more academic than conciliar, hardly such as to build consensus in the

58. I related in "Congar's Doctrinal Service of the People of God," 537–38, how Congar saw the gestures of Pope Paul VI during ecumenical encounters with Orthodox bishops as being equivalent to recognition of them as bishops in the full and proper sense. But Congar's *modus* on this, after discussion in the Doctrinal Commission, was not accepted, although it was not denied outright, as we read in the final paragraph, introduced by "N.B.," of the "Preliminary Explanatory Note, appended to *Lumen Gentium*. See, for example, the revised edition of *Vatican II Documents*, ed. A. Flannery (Northport, N.Y.: Costello, 1996), 94–95.

59. J. Grootaers presents this turning point in *History of Vatican II*, 2:391–410.

council.[60] But the French bishops had not asked Congar to work on a text, and besides he had not yet been called into service of a conciliar commission. But this changed on March 1, 1963, when Congar was urgently called to Rome to become an expert of the council's Doctrinal Commission, which was holding the first of its many working sessions between the autumn gatherings of the whole council.

When Congar arrived, the Commission had just decided to take as the basis of a new working-text on the church the draft composed, at the request of Cardinal Suenens, by the Louvain systematic theologian, Gérard Philips.[61] Congar became one of the seven theologians, along with seven Commission members, who formed a sub-commission to amend the Philips draft by incorporating useful ideas and texts from other proposed drafts that had come in from France, Germany, Rome, and Chile. Congar's diary is a record of intense work with other *periti*, such as Rahner (Innsbruck), Rosario Gagnebet, OP (Rome, Angelicum), Gustave Thils (Louvain), Charles Moeller (Louvain), Pierre Lafortune (Montréal), and G. Philips (Louvain). The Belgians came to the meetings well prepared, and within three days the first two chapters of the new draft could be presented to the full Commission.

Congar, now a Commission *peritus*, began attending the meetings of the Doctrinal Commission and recording in his diary his experiences and perceptions of this significant Vatican II body. In

60. The draft-text produced by the German theologians and bishops is given in Francisco Gil Hellín, *Concilii Vaticani II Synopsis . . . Constitutio dogmatica de ecclesia Lumen gentium* (Vatican City: Libreria editrice Vaticana, 1995), 716–50. Congar wrote in his diary after the January meeting that the German text was too long, too scholarly, too much like a short university course than a conciliar text (*My Journal*, 253–55). The draft is studied in its depth and further influence on the council by Guenther Wassilowsky, *Universales Heilssakrament Kirche: Karl Rahners Beitrag zur Ekklesiologie des II. Vaticanums* (Innsbruck: Tyrolia Verlag, 2001).

61. Congar, *My Journal*, 261–83, relates the work of March 1–13, 1963, of the Doctrinal Commission, especially on the opening chapters of the new draft *De ecclesia*. On G. Philips's drafting of a new *De ecclesia*, see 131–38, below.

a hall in the Papal Palace, the twenty-five members had seats at a quadrilateral of tables in the center, with Cardinal Ottaviani at the head, and the Commission's secretary, Fr. Sebastian Tromp, at his side. The theologians sat on simple chairs around the wall, mainly as observers, but they could speak if invited to do so by a commission member.

At one point during the review of the new draft on the church, Congar was asked to contribute, and he suggested that the paragraph on the church's Magisterium could well contain a phrase taken from the papal definitions of the Immaculate Conception (Pius IX, 1854) and Assumption of the Blessed Virgin Mary (Pius XII, 1950), namely, that church teaching arises from a *conspiratio*, or consensus, existing between the church's pastors and the body of the faithful. But Cardinal Ruffini objected that such a *conspiratio* is not an essential and universal factor in the development of magisterial teaching. Congar answered that the notion had biblical backing, on the need of two or three witnesses (Dt 19:15), but the president, Cardinal Ottaviani, questioned whether such a biblical rule had juridical force in the church. Sitting next to Congar was Monsignor Salvatore Garofalo, scripture teacher and rector of the Urban University in Rome, who supported Cardinal Ottaviani with the assurance that the text in question, in its setting in the Old Testament, comes from a wholly other context.[62]

At the end of the meeting, during which the full Commission reviewed quite positively the work of the ecclesiology subcommission of seven members and seven experts, Fr. Tromp told the members to hand in to his office their proposed amendments in writing, which would be examined by the sub-commission and its theologians, before a new version would be presented to the full Commission for its approval with a view to distributing the new draft-text on the church to all the council members.

---

62. Congar, *My Journal*, 266–67, describing the Commission meeting of March 4, 1963.

During the second council period in autumn 1963, Smulders was named a council expert, at the request of the Indonesian episcopate, in the hope that by his attending the morning sessions in St. Peter's he could better assist the bishops. But he also was called to work for the Doctrinal Commission, which found itself inundated with hundreds of comments by the council members on the new draft, *The Church*, the topic of discussion through most of October 1963. Smulders was assigned to a sub-commission working on the paragraphs treating priests and deacons, which in time became nos. 28–29 of *Lumen Gentium*. The members were Archbishop Maurice Roy (Quebec City, Canada), Bishop Frane Franić (Split, Croatia), and Archbishop Vicente Scherer (Porto Alegre, Brazil). The other theological experts were the Jesuits Alois Grillmeier and Otto Semmelroth, who handled proposals for revision of the paragraphs on priests, while Smulders worked with the Brazilian Franciscan Boaventura Kloppenburg on a new text on deacons.

Smulders first studied the cards on which the Commission's secretarial staff had recorded each of the 120 interventions, oral or written, regarding deacons, on their roles as church ministers, on the reintroduction of the diaconate as a permanent order of the Latin church, and on whether married men could become permanent deacons. Smulders worked in his room at the hostel on the Via Cassia, classifying the positions taken. He found forty-five interventions favoring restoration of the permanent diaconate, but because a good number of these were made in the name of groups of bishops, he counted 714 council members favoring the restoration. Twenty-five had spoken against this innovation, with a further sixty-seven signing on to their negative vote. In fact, an orientation vote taken on October 30, 1963, showed 1,588 favoring restoration of the diaconate, but a sizeable minority of 525 against it, mainly, it seemed, because the permanent deacons would be men given sacramental ordination but not obliged to celibacy.

On November 15–16, Smulders typed a ten-page single-spaced

analysis of the arguments, indicating the names the proponents or opponents after each consideration. Out of these, Smulders formulated five questions for the three episcopal members of the sub-commission to decide before he and Kloppenburg could write the draft of a revised text incorporating many views of council members. On November 19, the three bishops reached a partial agreement that the council should not decree the restoration, but only the *possibility* of such a change, as they had different ideas on the roles of episcopal conferences and the Holy See in any future process of making the diaconate a permanent feature of the Catholic church. After this, Smulders rewrote his analysis to show the backing present for the views of the three sub-commission members, and he composed a first proposal of a revised paragraph for the draft-text.

In the meetings, Bishop Franić, a dogged opponent of having permanent deacons, criticized Smulders for inserting into his analysis some of his own ideas not documented by what the council members had proposed. So, when Smulders reworked his text, he took pains to give the name of a bishop or conference as responsible for every point introduced into the text. On November 21, the three episcopal members of the sub-commission approved Smulders's analysis and new text, and on November 30 the full Doctrinal Commission followed suit, but they also introduced some modifications of Smulders's wording when two-thirds approved proposed amendments. So, Smulders typed out once more the text of the paragraph on deacons that first went into the second complete draft-text of *The Church*, which remained with slight modifications as *Lumen Gentium*, no. 29.

December 1, 1963, was a Sunday and Smulders brought his typed text, with the cards, to the Belgian College to return them to Gerard Philips, who was overseeing the revision. Later he went to the Gregorian University to visit Fr. Tromp, an older fellow Dutch Jesuit. He found Tromp tired and depressed, but quite ready to talk, mainly with laments over the preponderant influence of the bishops and theologians connected with Louvain on the Doctrinal Commission. Tromp had lost influence even with Cardinal Ottaviani, who now was following the suggestions of Philips and Archbishop Parente.

On the next day, December 2, 1963, the new configuration of the Commission was confirmed by the election of Bishop André-Marie Charue (Namur, Belgium) as second vice-president and of Gérard Philips as adjunct secretary who would take over some of the work done to this point by Sebastian Tromp.

At the end of the Commission meeting of December 2, Smulders was told to come to Rome in February–March to work for the Commission. This led to him being named to assist a new sub-commission on divine revelation, where in March–April 1964 he worked on what would later become the first chapter of *Dei Verbum*, on revelation itself, similar to his work on the diaconate for *Lumen Gentium*.[63] In the fourth period of 1965, Smulders had a similar task of studying interventions and composing a new text proposed for what became Part I, chapter III, on human activity in the universe, in the Pastoral Constitution.

In early 1964, Congar noted in his diary that the council was overloading its experts, who already had their regular work as teachers and writers. Nonetheless, Congar accepted further requests to assist conciliar commissions. In February 1964, he helped the Unity Secretariat revise the text on ecumenism in the light of interventions by council members commenting on a first draft during the second period.[64]

---

63. I treated Smulders's work on the 1964 revision of the first chapter of *De Revelatione* in "*Dei Verbum* Developing: Vatican II's Revelation Doctrine 1963–64," in *The Convergence of Theology, Festschrift Gerald O'Collins*, ed. Daniel Kendall and Stephen Davis (Mahwah, N.J.: Paulist Press, 2001), 109–25. I sketched his remote preparations for work on *De Revelatione* in five articles in *Gregorianum*, published in 2002, 2003, and 2005. He also appears in my study, "*De revelatione* under Revision," 461–94, and in "The Fullness of Revelation in Christ in *Dei Verbum*," *Gregorianum* 23 (2016): 194–206.

64. On Congar aiding the Unity Secretariat, see *My Journal*, 481–87.

In March–April 1964, Congar was with the sub-commission on revelation, where he made important contributions, in collaboration with Karl Rahner and Umberto Betti, to the account of tradition in chapter II of the future *Dei Verbum*.[65] Congar was in a good position for this, as among the council members' interventions he found a three-paragraph text which he had himself written in 1962. The text had been submitted to the Commission over the signatures of a group of bishops of western France as a good way to fill out the undeveloped idea of tradition in the draft, *De Fontibus Revelationis*.[66] It also helped that the sub-commission on revelation had as members some bishops with backgrounds in theology like A.-M. Charue, Georges Pelletier (Trois Rivières, Canada), and Joseph Heuschen (Liege, Belgium), along with Abbot Christopher Butler, OSB (Downside Abbey, England).[67]

In September 1964 Congar joined the sub-commission responsible for the chapter on human dignity in the future *Gaudium et Spes*. Earlier, he had made critical comments on the draft-text on the life and ministry of priests, and so he was drawn into revising this text as well, over which he later complained that the bishop-members of the Commission on priests were a do-nothing lot, while all the work on the future decree *Presbyterorum Ordinis* was done by three *periti*, Joseph Lécuyer, Willy Onclin, and himself. Another weak draft-text was the one treating the missions, whose first draft reflected more the approach of the Vatican Congregation for the Propagation of the Faith than that of an ecclesiology renewed from the Christian sources. When invited to help, Congar threw himself into this work, becoming appreciative of his fellow *peritus* Joseph Ratzinger. Their work led to the Vatican II decree on missionary activity *Ad Gentes* being a mature ec-

65. Betti treated the development of Chapter II of *Dei Verbum*, with many accounts of input by the experts, in *La dottrina del concilio Vaticano II sulla trasmissione della rivelazione* (Rome: Pontifical Athenaeum Antonianum, 1985).

66. *Acta Synodalia*, 3.3:902–4.

67. On Congar at work with these men on *De Revelatione*: *My Journal*, 503–4 and 516–21.

clesiological text, little affected by the turmoil that accompanied the genesis of *Lumen Gentium*.[68]

Congar knew well what Smulders learned while working on the diaconate, namely, to subordinate his own ideas to what the council members proposed. Every amendment had to rest on a council member's intervention and not be contradicted by that of another council member. Compositional work by the *periti* had to produce texts that would win wide adherence among the council members, and on doctrine this meant near-unanimity.

In October 1964, Congar saw the revised draft-text on religious liberty, and right away he recognized numerous ideas of the principal expert-redactors, Pietro Pavan (Lateran University) and John Courtney Murray, SJ (Woodstock College). For Congar these were improvements, but many of the introduced changes were from the two experts, without any cited backing in interventions on the topic by the council members. The revision was good, but the members should have an opportunity to react to it, at least in writing. Thus Congar agreed with the decision of Paul VI in November 1964 to postpone voting to the fourth period, an action that infuriated the U.S. bishops.[69] In the intersession of early 1965, new comments came in and Congar worked on a further revision, which turned out so well that the opponents of this initially controversial document were reduced to less than 5 percent of the council members.[70]

---

68. Ibid., 563–66 (contributing toward *Gaudium et Spes*, September 10, 1964); 624–25 (critical observations on the schema on priests, October 14, 1964); 645–73 (repeated references, October 26 to November 12, 1964, to drafting revised sections on priests); 670 (request that Congar draft sections of the decree on missions, November 11, 1964); 698–706 (drafting on missions, December 1964, with January 1965 work at the Commission meeting at Nemi, Italy); and 709–27 (notes on the crucial Ariccia and Rome meetings on the church in the modern world, January 31 to February 13, 1965).

69. Ibid., 626 and 688–89.

70. Ibid., 727–36 (two weeks' work at the Unity Secretariat on revising *De Libertate*, the future declaration *Dignitatis Humanae*, February 18 to March 2, 1965).

Concluding Reflections

Recalling the limitation imposed at the beginning, namely, to omit interventions at Vatican II by Popes John XXIII and Paul VI, and by council members of major influence, I have presented some wide-angle views of the contributions of the theologians to the council.[71] According to the perspective taken, the perceptions differ notably.

Looking at the council from the early preparations in 1959 and pondering its step-by-step development, a contrast emerges between dominant mentalities among the theologians involved. On the one hand, the militantly antimodernist orientation of the early twentieth-century Catholic church deeply formed some council theologians, who envisaged a council in continuity with Pius XII's cautionary encyclical *Humani Generis* of 1950 (A. Piolanti; the drafters of "Guarding the Purity of the Deposit of Faith"). But other theologians worked with conviction toward a wide-ranging renewal based on more ancient sources. They wanted to help formulate a Catholic teaching which would be more biblical, more coherent with fundamental liturgical structures, and better able to ground an ecumenical engagement (Congar; proposals from the Biblical Institute; topics suggested from Münster and Louvain).

During the preparation of the council, 1960–62, the advocates of renewal were dispersed, even isolated. Only their con-

71. One group of considerable theological significance at Vatican II, also omitted here, is the corps of delegated observers and ecumenical guests from the other churches and ecclesial communities. Thomas Stransky introduced them and noted their influence on the council's Decree on Ecumenism in "Paul VI and the Delegated Observers/Guests to Vatican Council II," in *Paolo VI e l'ecumenismo* (Brescia: Istituto Paolo VI, 2001), 118–58, esp. 146. See also Carmen Aparicio, "Contributo di Lukas Vischer alla *Gaudium et spes*," in *Sapere teologico e unità della fede*, ed. Carmen Aparicio Valls, Carmelo Dotolo, and Gianluigi Pasquale (Rome: Gregorian University Press, 2004), 3–19. More recently, Mauro Velati published a comprehensive study, *Separati ma fratelli: Gli osservatori non cattolici al Vaticano II (1962–1965)* (Bologna: Il Mulino, 2014), which I present in "Yet More Light on Vatican Council II," *Catholic Historical Review* 102 (2016): 97–117, at 107–17.

fluence in Rome in October 1962 allowed their lines of thought to unite in an intense and fruitful exchange, leading to the alternative drafts of 1962 that helped focus opposition to the draft-texts of the Preparatory Theological Commission. The impact of this opposition came to dramatic expression on November 20, 1962, when 1,368 council members voted to remove "The Sources of Revelation" from the immediate agenda. But one should not forget that this was foreshadowed a year earlier in the Central Preparatory Commission (Cardinals Bea and König) and grew once the council members had before their eyes in late summer 1962 a clear contrast, namely, the official draft-text from the Preparatory Commission on Liturgy, which had been assisted by a notable corps of liturgical theologians.

Theologians helped the currents of renewal from original sources to flow more forcefully by their texts which circulated during the Vatican II's first weeks (the *Commentary* of Schillebeeckx; Ratzinger and Rahner on revelation) and by their lectures to groups of bishops. Numerous episcopates, like that of Indonesia, resonated with the critical and constructive points made by their theologian-advisers and this occurred in sufficient numbers so that by the end of 1962 the council had defined itself as an organ of broad renewal of the Catholic church.

The new purpose and the themes of renewal, however, did not pass directly from the theologians into the published documents of Vatican II. The theologians drew on scripture and classic sources to put into circulation numerous valuable ideas. The conciliar situation forced them to concentrate on themes clearly grounded in the sources, but still their proposals had to be accepted positively by the council's members and then had to mature into texts that would gain the wide acceptance needed to ground a properly conciliar teaching or decree. The members of the council had to study the theological proposals, recognize their value, and judge them worthy of conciliar adoption. Here theology and the Magisterium were working in their characteristic manners.

But the general perception is different when one looks back from the end of Vatican Council II in 1965, especially with an eye to the sixteen documents that Vatican II gave to the church and the world. Developing these texts demanded countless hours of work from the theologians of Vatican II, as they helped prepare the members' interventions on the draft-texts and their successive revisions. Many theologians assisted individual bishops or national episcopates by explaining the theology behind the draft-texts and proposing directions to take in assessing them (Betti with Archbishop Florit; Smulders with the thirty bishops of Indonesia). Once the members decided the line they would follow, their theologians at times worked out concise Latin texts for delivery in the Aula or longer ones to hand in, over the bishops' signatures, as written comments on drafts under discussion.

Consideration of the breadth of topics taken up at Vatican II makes one grow in esteem for the council's theologians. They had to quickly become experts in areas outside their own theological specialty. Smulders taught theological anthropology at Maastrict and had just written a well-received book on Teilhard de Chardin, but for the Indonesian bishops he had to first analyze the problematic of scripture/tradition in 1962 and in the following year give accounts to the bishops on the episcopate as a universal college, on ecumenism, and on the role of the bishop as head of his diocese. Soon, work for the Doctrinal Commission forced him to study the diaconate and God's revelation.

Theologians working for the conciliar commissions had to analyze exactly what the council members said on every point of the draft discussed in the council hall, which for the Doctrinal Commission's experts meant studying the note-cards prepared for G. Philips. They had to give an accurate report on the overall configuration of the members' thinking, taking care not to omit any intervention, whether substantive or more attentive to particular wordings (Smulders on the diaconate in 1963; Congar, Betti, and Rahner on tradition in early 1964).

When a sub-commission found the analysis by the experts to be accurate, the theologians moved on to compose a revision of their part of the draft-text, trying where possible to introduce the very wording that the council members had used, but not in a way that might set off opposed reactions from bishops who differed. Texts revised by experts had to pass through two approvals, first by a relevant sub-commission and then by the full Commission. At these stages, further changes could be introduced before the theologian retyped the text for delivery to the Commission's secretary who would pass it on to the central secretariat for delivery to the Vatican printers who prepared the booklets with revised texts for the council members.

Vatican II demanded immense labors from its theologian-experts, which made up a component, not of secondary importance, of the ecclesial event of the council. The theologians worked well with the bishops and religious superiors who were the voting members of Vatican Council II. One can see here a well-functioning epistemological duality between (1) the consultative thought of the theologian-experts, that is, their perceptions and concepts drawn from the sources, leading to proposed formulations, and (2) the deliberative judgments by the council members, who discerned and evaluated, and then voted to adopt or reject the experts' proposals, and so became the responsible authors of Vatican II's teaching and decrees.

This collaboration at Vatican Council II shows well one component in the relationship between theologians, with their research and intellectual explanations, and the church's Magisterium, with both being bound by the normative contents of the word of God and the tradition of faith and life in the church. An adequate understanding of this common work by two different components of the church must take account, also, of the singular situation created at the beginning of the council by its complex but problematic preparation and by the simple fact that the council's working periods brought together in intense daily contact so many persons from the Catholic world. The stimulus to reflection and dialogue among the theologians was enormous. This complex conversation is surely one of the reasons why the overall results of the Second Vatican Council far surpass the aims and purposes set for it as it began and even go far beyond the expectations that emerged and found formulation in late 1962.

3

Vatican II on Revelation

Behind the Scenes

The previous chapter illustrated that an enriched understanding of Vatican II can be had by studying the writings of the theological experts (*periti*) who assisted at the council. Work with texts prepared by these expert-consultants can lead to fresh appreciation of particular teachings of Vatican II.[1] Today, we can follow some of the experts in their day-by-day experiences of contributing to the council, as the diaries of Yves Congar, Henri de Lubac, Umberto Betti, and of the little-known but hugely influential Lou-

This chapter was originally published as "Vatican II on Revelation—From Behind the Scenes," *Theological Studies* 71 (2010): 637–50. Published by SAGE Publishing, all rights reserved. https://doi.org/10.1177/004056391007100306. It was intially given as an address at my receiving the Johannes Quasten Award at the Catholic University of America, School of Theology and Religious Studies, December 3, 2009.

1. I draw in this chapter on work by doctoral candidates I directed at the Gregorian University, who will be cited below where appropriate. My own studies of the *periti* include five articles under the general title, "Pieter Smulders and *Dei Verbum*," in *Gregorianum* 82 (2001): 241–97 and 559–93; 83 (2002): 225–67; 85 (2004): 242–77, and 86 (2005): 92–134. See also "Dei verbum Developing: Vatican II's Revelation Doctrine 1963–64," in *The Convergence of Theology*, ed. Kendall and Davis, 109; "Six Texts by Prof. Joseph Ratzinger as *peritus*"; "*De revelatione* under Revision," 460–94; "Theologians at Vatican Council II" (chapter 2, above); and "The Fullness of Revelation in Christ in *Dei Verbum*."

vain theologian, Gérard Philips, have been published.[2] To illustrate the richness of these sources, I will below take the case of *Dei Verbum*, especially the prologue and the first chapter on revelation itself.

The *periti* contributed all along the timeline of Vatican II, beginning with scattered cases in 1959 of future council members consulting with theologians and taking over their ideas to submit in response to Pope John XXIII's request for suggestions about council topics. During the preparation of the council in 1960–62, senior theological scholars such as Hubert Jedin and Gérard Philips were members of preparatory commissions, while some two hundred expert consultors of the commissions worked out draft-texts, redrafted them in accord with the members' preferences, and then polished them to the point where they could be distributed to all the council members as draft schemas on doctrine and on the renewal of the church's worship, ministries, and relations *ad extra*. During the four working periods of Vatican II from 1962 to 1965, the bishops, both as individuals and as groups in their national or regional conferences, learned much from the *periti* whom they heard lecturing, who circulated texts, and who composed many of the bishops' oral and written evaluative comments on the schemas. During and between the four working periods, many *periti* rendered a hidden but essential service to the commissions made up of council members, as these theologian assistants culled the interventions, discovered convergen-

2. Yves Congar, *My Journal of the Council*, presented by Jared Wicks in "Yves Congar's Doctrinal Service of the People of God"; Henri de Lubac, *Vatican II Notebooks*, presented by Jared Wicks in "Further Light on Vatican Council II," *Catholic Historical Review* 95 (2009): 546–69, at 546–62; Gérard Philips, *Carnets conciliaires de Mgr. Gérard Philips, Secrétaire adjoint de la Commission doctrinale*, trans. Karim Schelkens (Leuven: Peeters, 2006), which I presented in "More Light on Vatican Council II," *Catholic Historical Review* 94 (2008): 75–101, at 76–80. Umberto Betti was personal *peritus* for the influential Archbishop Ermenegildo Florit of Florence and for the Doctrinal Commission Betti worked with Congar and Rahner on the major revision of 1964 of chap. II of *De Revelatione*. Betti published *Diario del Concilio*, as well as an account, with appended documents, of the genesis of chap. II of *Dei Verbum* in *La dottrina del Concilio Vaticano II*.

ces, weighed their cogency, and formulated revised texts of the draft schemas, with the aim of bringing back to the council members emended texts in which many members would be satisfied to find results of their previous comments and proposals.[3]

Yves Congar wrote three times in his diary that this many-sided service by theologians was essential to the council's production of its documents and to the depth and freshness these texts would be giving to Catholic teaching and attitudes.[4] These might seem to comprise Congar's *apologia pro vita sua*. Or is it an accurate perception by one who was deeply immersed in the council and so has pointed out an aspect that should be emphasized in a complete and accurate understanding of "what happened at Vatican II"?

Another witness to the impact of the theologians is Dom Helder Camara, bishop of Recife, Brazil, in his 293 letters from the council during its four working periods.[5] The letters record how much Dom Helder gained from the late afternoon lectures on council topics given during the four working periods for the bishops by the *periti*. The letters also pass on his insights from reading on liturgy, the laity, ecumenism, biblical theology, and spirituality in various books by theologians, both those present at the council and others exerting influence from afar. Dom Helder also observed that the episcopates with most assurance in their council work were those which brought their own conference-*periti* with them to Vatican II. We turn now to a case study of different *periti* at work behind the scenes at the council.

---

3. Chapter 2, above, develops this sketch in greater detail.

4. *My Journal of the Council*, 529, 800, 835.

5. Dom Helder Camara, *Lettres conciliaires (1962–1965)*, ed. José de Broucker (Paris: Cerf, 2006), which I presented in "More Light on Vatican II," 81–86.

Vatican II's Transformation of Catholic Doctrine on Revelation

The First Vatican Council issued in April 1870 the Dogmatic Constitution on the Catholic Faith, *Dei Filius*, which deeply influenced the notion of God's revelation that was held by generations of Catholic theology teachers and students.[6] I would characterize this teaching as terse and correct, but in its presentation, it was in fact concerned less with *what* God says to humankind and more with aspects which qualify and surround God's revelation. The text said that it pleased God's wisdom and goodness "to reveal to the human race Himself and the eternal decrees of His will." God did this (1) in a *supernatural manner*, conveying some truths beyond the reach of our reason, but this fits with our supernatural calling. The giving of this revelation has been (2) *accompanied by the outward signs* of miracles and prophecies showing revelation's credibility as God's word. The content, although supernatural, is nonetheless, once given and received in faith, (3) *open to believers' rational inquiry and investigation* for gaining beneficial insights into its meaning. Thus God's revelation of himself and of what he has decreed is qualified by its supernatural character, its credibility, and its penetrability by intellectual investigation of its meaning. On actual revealed content, Vatican I said a bare minimum, while emphasizing three qualities that mark God's revelation—whatever it might say about himself and whatever might be the eternal decrees of the divine will about which revelation informs us.

But *Dei Verbum*, issued by Vatican II on November 18, 1965, is much different. It gives in its prologue and first chapter an account of God's revelation, which in its ample content is soterio-

---

6. *Dei Filius* is provided in *Decrees*, ed. Tanner, 2:804–11. I treat it in *Doing Theology*, 17–20, giving in English the paragraphs on revelation, faith, and the faith/reason relation on 172–79.

logically focused on God-with-us, in Christ, to free human beings and lead them into communion with himself. The apostles' witness (no. 1), following 1 John, gathers hearers into *koinonia* with the apostles and so with the Father and the Son. In its unfolding across history, God's revelation combines deeds and words, for it is history narrated and proclaimed, with events of "mystery" anchoring the linguistic communication and doctrinal meaning. Jesus himself is God's truth for us, mediating it and summing it up (no. 2) by recapitulating all that God reveals (no. 7). Christ shows God to the human family, in his presence and epiphany, in words and works, in signs and miracles, and especially in his death, resurrection, and sending of the Spirit—all of which reveal God to the human family as Emmanuel, with us to liberate us from sin and death and raise us to eternal life (no. 4). Such revelation can and should be more deeply understood under the benign care of the Holy Spirit, who fosters and deepens the "Yes" of faith through which revelation comes to its term and finds a dwelling place to exist over time in believing hearts and minds.[7]

Vatican II stated revelation's evangelical content in its opening six paragraphs. One can argue that in the overall logic of the council documents, this passage stands first, as the Gospel amply stated here is the word by which the church is assembled as *congregatio fidelium* and the priestly people for worship. This is the Gospel that all church ministries and apostolates serve and promote. The same Gospel creates the horizon of understanding within which Catholic Christians view the world and its struc-

---

7. The last sentence goes beyond the text itself of *Dei Verbum*, no. 5, to state the insight voiced by Cardinal Julius Döpfner on September 30, 1964, that faith is primarily God's work in humans to make his word of revelation effective, so that "in faith the very essence of revelation is completed." Beyond a dialogue, faith is *participative* of and in what God reveals. *Acta Synodalia*, 3.3:146. This came out in the Gregorian dissertation of Gianluca Montaldi, *In fide ipsa essentia revelationis completur. Il tema della fede nell'evolversi del Concilio Vaticano II: la genesi di DV 5–6 e i suoi reflessi su ulteriori ambiti conciliari* (Rome: Pontifical Gregorian University, 2005), 355–60. Below, 87n2 indicates that Joseph Ratzinger had found in St. Bonaventure such a concept of revelation and faith.

tures for the unfolding of the human vocation. Because of this, Vatican II's Doctrinal Commission once said that the Constitution on Revelation is in a certain way (*quodammodo*) the first of all the council's constitutions.[8] Some editions place *Lumen Gentium* at the head of the Vatican II Constitutions, but the conciliar ecclesiology would be better contextualized if it were placed *after* the council text starting with "hearing the word of God reverently and proclaiming it confidently ..." and ending with "the word of God ... stands forever," as does *Dei Verbum*.[9]

Early Contributions to Vatican II's Revelation Doctrine

This is not the place to trace the itinerary that led from the Preparatory Theological Commission's schema *De Fontibus Revelationis* of 1962 to the Constitution of 1965, *Dei Verbum*, but a few selected moments of early influence by the *periti* can be theologically enlightening about this most important teaching.

(1) Vatican II formally opened on October 11, 1962. But some six weeks earlier, Cardinal Josef Frings received his copy of the booklet containing the first seven official draft schemas. The cardinal was nearly blind and so he sent the book to his theological *peritus*, Joseph Ratzinger, who at the time taught in the Catholic theology faculty of the University of Bonn, just south of Cologne. Frings had already taken critical positions on some of the published texts when earlier drafts of them had come before the

8. The Commission said this in its *relatio* accompanying the late 1964 revision of *De Revelatione*. The Commission was defending the formulation of the final clause of no. 1, which expresses the grand intention of promoting faith, hope, and charity in the whole world. This ambitious claim can stand here, so the Commission argued, because it is introducing not just *Dei Verbum*, but the whole body of Vatican II's main documents. *Acta Synodalia*, 4.1:341.

9. My view amounts to taking a critical difference from the position that the Constitution on the Liturgy has not only a chronological but also a theological priority in the Vatican II corpus of documents, as Massimo Faggioli advanced in "*Sacrosanctum Concilium* and the Meaning of Vatican II," *Theological Studies* 71 (2010): 437–52.

Central Preparatory Commission in 1961–62 for evaluation and possible emendation before being sent on to Pope John XXIII for his *nihil obstat* for distribution to the bishops of the council. Now Frings wanted help from Ratzinger in formulating reactions to the initial batch of official texts, so that he, Frings, might respond to a request by the papal secretary of state for a letter, due in the Vatican by September 15, giving an initial evaluation of the seven texts. This evaluation would help in selecting the first texts to put on the council's agenda for deliberation in the council hall, the transformed Basilica of St. Peter. Frings asked Ratzinger to read the texts and note where they had—or had not—been modified over the earlier drafts on which the Central Preparatory Commission had made its critical observations. Also, which of the schemas should simply be rejected as council texts? And, further, for which parts does Ratzinger have suggestions for revisions to improve the texts?[10]

Ratzinger, realizing that time was short, composed and typed a Latin letter evaluating the seven schemas. When Cardinal Frings received Ratzinger's letter, he found the contents helpful and he simply added the date, the proper salutation to the cardinal secretary of state, and his signature and sent the letter on to the Vatican.[11] The letter judged that only two of the seven texts were fit for conciliar deliberation, namely, the schema on the liturgy and another on ecumenical openings to the Orthodox churches. The other five texts do not measure up to the standards of conciliar teaching, nor are they likely to attract separated Christians to seeking unity, as Pope John XXIII has been emphasizing as one of the aims and purposes of Vatican II. One schema in the booklet, the Prepa-

---

10. Norbert Trippen relates this Frings/Ratzinger exchange in detail in his biography of Frings, *Josef Kardinal Frings (1887–1978)* (Paderborn: Schöningh, 2005), 2:308–13. A photographic reproduction of Cardinal Frings's letter to Ratzinger requesting his evaluation of the initial schemas is given in the *Mitteilungen* of *Institut Papst Benedikt XVI* 2 (2009): 177.

11. The Frings/Ratzinger letter is in *Acta Synodalia, Appendix* (Vatican City: Tipografia Poliglotta Vaticana, 1983), 74–77; English translation in Jared Wicks, "Six Texts by Prof. Joseph Ratzinger as *peritus*," 264–68, with an introductory analysis at 239–41.

ratory Theological Commission's draft-text "Guarding the Purity of the Deposit of Faith" is so diffuse that it must be set aside, with some parts possibly considered for transfer to other schemas. Also, its several censures of theological positions allegedly held by Catholics do not fit with the aims of the council as stated by Pope John. The first text in the booklet, "On the Sources of Revelation," treats scripture and tradition, biblical inspiration and inerrancy, and the Bible in the church. This, states Ratzinger, has to be revised so as to avoid speaking authoritatively on issues of dispute among Catholic theologians in good standing. Ratzinger added that the text on the sources also needs to have an initial chapter added before it, presenting the nature and processes of revelation itself, that is, on the Word of God. Scripture and tradition are means of transmitting and communicating to us the Word, that is, what God has revealed. Teaching on the communication of revelation has to be introduced by an account of revelation itself.[12] For this needed first chapter, Ratzinger mentioned that some ideas could well be taken over from chapter 4 of the otherwise inept text "Guarding the Purity of the Deposit."

12. Today we know more about Joseph Ratzinger's thinking on revelation at the time of Vatican II. See Ratzinger, *Offenbarungsverständnis und Geschichtstheologie Bonaventuras: Habilitationschrift und Bonaventura-Studien*, ed. Marianne Schlosser, in his *Gesammelte Schriften*, vol. 2 (Freiburg: Herder, 2009), containing the full text of Ratzinger's 1955 dissertation submitted at Munich to qualify as a chair-holder in a theology faculty. Ratzinger set forth Bonaventure's conception of revelation in the opening section of this work, which because of the criticisms of Professor Michael Schmaus was withdrawn and not published at the time. On this, see J. Ratzinger, *Milestones: Memoirs 1927–1977* (San Francisco: Ignatius Press, 1998), 106–13, which also indicates the relevance of the Bonaventurian insights at Vatican II. One insight is that revelation is complete only with the arrival of God's action at that action's term and outcome, that is, in faith, a graced enlightenment of the believer (*Offenbarungsverständnis*, 88–102, 218–21). Faith is from hearing, but this is a graced interior hearing *per aurem cordis* (153–55). Revelation itself is always more than its formulation in scripture. Scripture gives a fixed and normative witness, but this remains the material principle of revelation, which exists as a vital reality only when God has brought it about in living subjects. "By definition, revelation requires someone who apprehends it" (*Milestones*, 108). Professor Schmaus certainly took note of the accentuated personalism, or actualism, of this notion and could well have found it infected with modernist thinking, as such revelation was not complete with the apostles.

As a matter of principle, Ratzinger stated that the council texts "should not be treatises in a scholastic style, as if they were taken over from textbooks of theologians, but should instead speak the language of Holy Scripture and the holy Fathers of the Church." Furthermore, the council has to speak in ways that will attract separated Christians and will give fresh witness to Jesus Christ in a world in which many people find Christian faith an alien reality.[13] Thus, a letter penned by *peritus* Ratzinger and signed by Cardinal Frings was an early call for Vatican II to give to the church and to the world an updated account of Catholic teaching on God's revelation.

(2) As noted above, Ratzinger had suggested taking ideas from the schema "Guarding the Purity of the Deposit," that is, from its chapter 4 on revelation and faith. However, another *peritus*, Pieter Smulders, a Dutch Jesuit professor at the Maastrict theologate, had already composed serious criticisms of that passage. In August and September 1962, the same booklet of schemas that Ratzinger evaluated for Cardinal Frings was also the object of Smulders's study, as requested of him by the papal nuncio to the Netherlands, Archbishop Giuseppe Beltrami.[14]

In chapter 4 of the schema on preserving the deposit, Smulders perceived such an insistence on revelation as *locutio divina* that the account places divine works, God's *opera magnalia*, outside revelation itself. The events thus serve only to show the credibility of the message or doctrine given in words. Smulders judged that the drafters of this chapter had not drawn on recent biblical theologies of revelation which highlight the combination of works or events with words or doctrine. The schema is impov-

---

13. "Six Texts," 266. Later, on October 10, 1962, the vigil of Vatican II's inauguration, Ratzinger addressed the German-speaking bishops on *De Fontibus*, subjecting it to incisive criticism of its account of revelation and of scripture/tradition. I give this lecture in the German original in "Six Texts," 295–309, and in English on 269–85.

14. See my "Peter Smulders and *Dei Verbum*: 1. A Consultation on the Eve of Vatican II," 288–97, giving Smulders's critique of *De Deposito Fidei*, chap. IV, on revelation.

erished because it lacks important themes developed by authors like Josef Rupert Geiselmann, Romano Guardini, Karl Rahner, Jean Daniélou, Jacques Dupont, and Jean Mouroux, who all hold that the revelatory "word" comprises both God's saving deeds and verbal communication through God's spokespersons. The events include the liberation of God's people from slavery in Egypt and above all the person and deeds of Christ, culminating in his passion, death, and resurrection. In him, as crucified and risen, "the grace of God our savior has appeared" (Ti 2:11, well known from the Christmas lectionary). God reveals himself as close to humans in his grace, as Emmanuel who frees from servitude and gives life to the dead. *"Deus Salvator se revelat salvando."* The words announcing God's saving deeds are for Smulders essential, but the schema is extreme in excluding revelation-in-deed, because it fears the reduction of revelation to human experience, as allegedly held by Catholic modernists.

The drafters of "Guarding the Deposit," in Smulders's analysis, overreact against the excesses of modernism and see deviations in the more recent cultivation of a biblically grounded conception of revelation both in history and in words of narrative, proclamation, and derived doctrine. They have not sensed that the very person of Christ, in the totality of his earthly being, is God's self-manifestation, as is clear from the opening of 1 John, which Smulders cited to much the same effect as it would later have in *Dei Verbum*, no. 1.

Smulders's critical positions in his notes for Nuncio Beltrami in time became significant. First, Smulders was called to serve as *peritus* of the bishops of Indonesia, for whom he composed conciliar interventions. Two interventions came on November 14, 1962, the opening day of debate on the draft on the sources of revelation. In a text prepared by Smulders, Archbishop Gabriel Manek, SVD, spoke for the bishops of Indonesia to call for the council to reject *De Fontibus* because of its low theological level, its insinuated censure of good Catholic theologians, and its creation of obstacles to dialogue with separated Christians. After Manek, Archbishop Albert Soegijapranata, SJ, used a Smulders text to expand the horizon of debate by a critique of the three theological schemas that followed "The Sources" in the initial booklet, arguing that they clashed with the pastoral aims of the council.[15]

Later, in June 1963, during a visit to Indonesia, Smulders met with the bishops at Jakarta and with them prepared an evaluation of the revised text *De Divina Revelatione*, which had been distributed to all the Vatican II bishops in May 1963.[16] This Indonesian text was constructively critical, as it offered some of Smulders's favorite formulations, in order to bring out the salvific message and Christological concentration of God's revealing word to us. Smulders's ideas on revelation became even more important in March 1964, after he had been co-opted to serve Vatican II's Doctrinal Commission in revising the draft of *De Revelatione*. When the Commission apportioned the work, Smulders was commissioned to write, based on the council members' interventions, including the one from Indonesia, a first sketch of a revised prologue and first chapter of *De Revelatione*. In this, Smulders was not to propose his own theological ideas, but had to revise the text in line with what the episcopal members of the council had said in their written comments. But these interventions included his own text from Jakarta and he quite properly worked its ideas into the new draft, which the council received with considerable satisfaction during its third period of 1964.[17]

---

15. *Acta Synodalia*, 1.3:55–57 (Manek) and 58–59 (Soegijapranata), giving the written texts handed in, to which nineteen bishops of Indonesia appended their signatures. Since cardinals spoke first, these were the thirteenth and fourteenth interventions of the day and the tenth and eleventh which declared *non placet* on this first day of debate on *De Fontibus*. The second speech referred to the other texts of the Preparatory Theological Commission, on guarding the deposit of faith in its purity, on the moral order, and on chastity, marriage, and the family. I treated the genesis of these interventions in "Pieter Smulders and *Dei Verbum*: 2, On *De fontibus revelationis* during Vatican II's First Period, 1962."

16. *Acta Synodalia*, 3.3:913–17. I studied the evaluation in "Pieter Smulders and *Dei Verbum*: 5, A Critical Reception of the Schema *De revelatione* of the Mixed Commission (1963)," *Gregorianum* 86 (2005): 92–135, at 105–11 and 124–26.

17. I treated this work of revision in "*Dei Verbum* Developing," in *The Convergence of*

(3) Amid the daily routines of the council's first period in 1962, an unexpected happening was the circulation of systematic critiques of the prepared doctrinal texts and even of alternative texts as substitute schemas offered by individuals or groups of *periti*. From the Dutch College, 2,700 mimeographed copies went out to the bishops of Schillebeeckx's critical *Animadversiones* (Comments) on the seven initial schemas.[18] Rahner also put in circulation a critical *Disquisitio brevis* (Short Critical Essay) on scripture and tradition.[19] Congar wrote an eight-page profession of faith which he offered as an introduction to all the eventual council documents.[20] The Belgian exegetes Jacques Dupont and Beda Rigaux put out a short draft *De Scriptura* to improve passages in "The Sources."[21] Some mimeograph machines worked overtime in October–November 1962.

The best known alternative schema of 1962, given the fame and eventual authority of its two authors, Rahner and Ratzinger, is *De Revelatione Dei et Hominis in Jesu Christo Facta*, in three chapters, which circulated in November, in two thousand copies, just before the council began discussing the schema "On the Sources of Revelation."[22]

Theology, 109–25, which indicates fourteen changes which Smulders lifted from episcopal comments for the revision. Charles Moeller (Louvain) also contributed a detailed written analysis of possible modifications proposed by the council fathers, as I related in "*De revelatione* Under Revision (March–April 1964)," in *The Belgian Contribution*, 461–94.

18. Jan Brouwers, secretary of the Dutch Episcopal Conference, told of the origin of Schillebeeckx's work in "Vatican II, derniers préparatifs et première session: Activités conciliares en coulisses," in *Vatican II commence ... Approches francophones*, 353–78. The text of nearly fifty pages, which circulated in Latin and English, is published in English in Tromp, *Diarium Secretarii*, ed. von Teuffenbach, 2:948–91.

19. Hanjo Sauer made Rahner's Latin text available among the appendices of *Erfahrung und Glaube: Die Begründung des pastoralen Prinzips durch die Offenbarungskonstitution des II. Vatikanischen Konzils* (Frankfurt: Peter Lang, 1993), 657–68.

20. Congar presents the whole divine economy as springing from God's love. The text is given in *Glaube im Prozess: Christsein nach dem II. Vatikanischen Konzils. Festschrift Karl Rahner*, ed. Elmar Klinger and Klaus Wittstadt (Freiburg: Herder, 1984), 51–64.

21. *De Scriptura* is unpublished, but present in archives (e.g., those of Vatican II participants held in both Leuven and Louvain-la-Neuve).

22. The original Latin was published in *Glaube im Prozess*, ed. Klinger and Wittstadt, along with a German translation, on 33–50. Brendan Cahill gives the Latin with an English

The Rahner/Ratzinger schema offered a grand vision of God's saving economy, a vision which would show the light of the Gospel from a lampstand from which it will console suffering humans and guide their steps in the way of peace. Chapter 1 is a basic anthropology, telling of human beings made in God's image and called to share in his gratuitous love. Humans long to live in communion with God and this aspiration constitutes the deepest truth of being human. Christ reveals God's intent, namely, to give the truth that frees from falsehood, the love that draws us out of solitude, and the grace that overcomes sin. God's gratuitous love pervades human existence, which cannot be grasped without this dimension.

Chapter 2 explains God's universal saving presence in history, because God's will to save embraces every human being. Some natural insight into this is possible but remains obscure, while world religions have some truth, of which Christ is the fullness. Christian faith esteems the religions and wants to purify them, bringing their positive aspects to Christ and the church. The call of Israel is fundamental, for "whatever was written previously was written for our instruction ... that we might have hope" (Rom 15:4).

Chapter 3 treats God's revelation in the church, which transmits the way, truth, and life coming from Christ, as attested to by scripture in fixed and inspired texts. The New Testament authors

---

translation in *The Renewal of Revelation Theology* (Rome: Gregorian University, 1999), 300–317, after his study of the text on 172–80. Rahner wrote to Herbert Vorgrimler on October 19 that he was working on a text that he would present at a meeting of German and French theologians convened by Bishop Hermann Volk of Mainz. On October 25, Cardinal Frings met at his residence with six other cardinals, including Suenens and Montini. Frings argued that because the schema *On the Sources* was sure to divide the council fathers and cause an impasse, a remedy was needed. He had a fresh approach in the work of his *peritus* Ratzinger on revelation and scripture, which was read to the cardinals. The efforts by Rahner and Ratzinger fused in *De Revelatione Dei et Hominis*, for which Frings got backing for circulating it from the presidents of the Austrian, Belgian, Dutch, and French bishops' conferences. It was a greatly reduced compendium of the first two schemas, in a positive and pastoral style. On the key events in these crowded days, see Wicks, "Six Texts by Prof. J. Ratzinger," 250–52, and "The Fullness of Revelation in Christ," 184–89.

served the church by their inspired writing, from which God's word resounds in the assembly. The church recognizes scripture as expressing its own life, discerns the limits of the canon, and in its teaching, worship, and life makes the biblical message come alive. On the one hand the church is bound to the scriptures of which it is not master but servant. Scripture gives the church its message and the bread it offers to human wayfarers. On the other hand, the church has a magisterial authority and the Holy Spirit's guidance for explaining what scripture contains, of which Christ is the key. In the community, Christ's words take on relevance for today, that is, for revealing human reality in the light of God—for the kingdom in which all God's works are fulfilled.

This text suggests something of the stimulus given to the theologians by their assembling and first exchanges in Rome in 1962 as they began serving at Vatican II. Their diaries tell of amazement at the end of these days over their many conversations on substantial topics for the benefit of such a grand undertaking as a general council of the Catholic church.

But some bishops looked realistically to what could be done by the heterogeneous assembly of 2,300 Catholic bishops, who had first to deal with what came to them through official channels from the council's preparatory commissions. The Rahner/Ratzinger text opened a grand horizon, stirring hopes for wide-ranging doctrinal renewal, but it could not be easily fitted into the task at hand in Vatican II's opening weeks.

(4) Archbishop Gabriel Garrone of Toulouse played a central role in turning Vatican II toward its eventual teaching on God's revelation. During the November 1962 debate on the sources of revelation, Garrone joined two other French bishops in speaking in the council hall of the need of adding to the schema's treatment of tradition and scripture an opening passage on God's gracious deeds and words in the economy of revelation, just as Ratzinger had proposed earlier for Cardinal Frings.

November 21 marked a turning point when Pope John XXIII

removed the draft, "On the Sources of Revelation," from the immediate agenda of the council. He created a mixed doctrinal and ecumenical Commission for a thorough revision of the text. Archbishop Garrone was on the Commission, and as he had proposed adding a new opening section, he was asked to supply the Commission with the draft of a new prologue. Garrone turned to another *peritus*, Jean Daniélou, the patristic scholar and professor at the Institut Catholique of Paris.

Daniélou composed for Garrone a draft of seven paragraphs, "On Revelation and the Word of God," which Garrone presented to the mixed Commission on November 27, 1962. The text was, at that time, conceived as an introduction (*prooemium*) to the Commission's eventual revision of "On the Sources." The Daniélou/ Garrone text took important steps toward the eventual nos. 1–6 of *Dei Verbum*, promulgated three years later.[23]

Daniélou's nos. 1–2 enrich Vatican I on revelation by stating how the transcendent God—omnipotent, most wise, most loving—conveys two great truths of revealed content, namely, his own triune life and the human vocation to share in God by grace and glory. A gratuitous gift, this revelation exceeds our creaturely reach and comes only because God first seeks us out. Christ opens the otherwise sealed book of God's plan. As savior, he carried out redemption; as revealer, he conveys the good news for understanding salvation. Christ reveals the truth of God turned to us in the three persons. He reveals the truth of humans, chosen for adoption as God's children for God's glory. Daniélou wrote that in Christ are all the treasures of wisdom and knowledge: *in ipso . . . tota Revelatio continetur* (all of revelation is contained in him).

In nos. 3–4, Daniélou sketched the stages of revelation, beginning with the witness to God given to all humans from the be-

---

23. Pietro Pizzuto treats Daniélou's alternative text in *La teologia della rivelazione di Jean Daniélou*, 21–26, after which he notes changes introduced into the text. Pizzuto's appendices give the text on 525–32 in the three known stages of its development.

ginning, as Paul remarked at the Areopagus (Acts 17:14). This cosmic witness to God's being and justice can be received in faith, as shown by the "holy pagans," Abel, Henoch, and Noah (Heb 11:6). Israel's scriptures are an advance, showing God as holy and living, who freed his people, dwelt in their Temple, established the covenant, and announced a coming definitive presence of God's glory. Revelation culminates in Christ, in whom the Father shows himself perfectly. Because Christ realized the purposes of the whole divine project, namely, glorifying God and divinizing human nature, Christianity is ultimate among religions. Because of its perfection, it cannot be just a stage in human development.

No. 5 tells how revelation takes place, namely, by God's words of address and his saving deeds. These must be taken as closely related, even perceived *simul*, in a view contrasting with the official schema "Guarding the Purity of the Deposit." For Christ manifested himself in words vindicating his divine prerogatives along with actions attesting to his divine authority. He spoke words instituting a new law and declared himself Lord of the sabbath, while his deeds confirm that his witness is authoritative. On the other hand, what our Lord says makes clear the mystery otherwise concealed in his works.

Daniélou's no. 6 restates Vatican I's *Dei Filius* on the naturally knowable truths that revelation also conveys, that is, God's personal nature and our human dignity, which cohere with our supernatural vocation. Revelation thus not only shows how humans reach their supernatural goal, but also casts light on a truly humane life in time.

Finally, Daniélou, in no. 7, contrasted the objectivity of God's deeds and words about God and humans with the revealing word's interior impact as "effective and sharper than any two-edged sword" (Heb 4:12). The word is powerful in converting hearts and gently attracting them. In eliciting faith, the internal testimony of the Holy Spirit joins the outer witness of speech. The Spirit's action continues as well for the deepening of faith by gifts which enhance the believer's understanding of God's revelation.

We can list the points of Daniélou's draft that eventually found their way, after a further conciliar journey, into *Dei Verbum*'s teachings. Daniélou had articulated (1) the Christological concentration of revelation, (2) a statement of revelation's content in its main foci, (3) the dual revelation of God and of the human reality, (4) revelation in words and deeds intimately interrelated, (5) revelation in Christ as unsurpassable, on intrinsic grounds of its content, (6) revelation both for attaining our supernatural end but also for the coherence of our temporal-earthly life, and (7) the Spirit's role both in eliciting faith and in its development toward deeper grasp of God's word.

In the mixed Commission, objections were raised to the Daniélou/Garrone text as being too long for a prologue to the revised chapters on tradition/scripture, inspiration, the two Testaments, and the Bible in the church's life. Consequently, it was considerably abbreviated in the schema *De Revelatione* distributed to the council members in May 1963. But the agenda for the council's second period did not include the new text on revelation, because the initial written observations of the bishops treated this draft quite critically. Thus, it was held back for further development in the revision on which Smulders worked in early 1964. But the Daniélou/Garrone ideas were in the air and many of them returned to have their place in *Dei Verbum* on revelation.

Conclusion

Interpretations of Vatican II commonly portray the removal of the schema "The Sources of Revelation" from the immediate agenda on November 21, 1962, as the major turning-point in the early phase of the council.[24] From the selection given here of texts by

---

24. O'Malley, *What Happened at Vatican II*, 141–52.

the theological experts, we learn that beyond the many expressions of dissatisfaction with that schema, there were also several quite positive theological proposals circulating at the time. The *periti* were making ready the elements of a much improved conciliar teaching on revelation, as formulated in *Dei Verbum*, promulgated in 1965.

More generally, as I concluded in the previous chapter on varied contributions of *periti* from 1959 through 1965, Vatican II was a unique case of cooperation between the theologians, who serve by research and intellectual explanation, and the church's episcopal and papal Magisterium.[25] The opening of Vatican II was a singular situation because aspects of its preparation were problematic and this was noted by several of the theologians who found themselves in intense daily contact as the council opened. The stimulus from the prepared texts and from the interaction was enormous. Major theological talents were having their impact, both directly, through texts by Ratzinger, Rahner, and Daniélou, and indirectly, through works refreshed by biblical theology which Smulders diligently consulted.

The conversations among and the writing by the *periti* turn out to be, when seen from our vantage point, reasons why the overall results of the council, such as *Dei Verbum*, far surpass what could have been expected in mid-1962. The work of the *periti* was quite significant in this, as we have seen in their proposals for a revised account of God's word of revelation that the church receives in faith. They took the lead in proposing a movement well beyond what Vatican I and the manuals had taught. From their proposals, eventually accepted by the council, came a stirring evangelical account of God's saving communication to our human family.

---

25. See above, 76–79, and Wicks, *Doing Theology*, 187–223, at 222–23.

4

Cardinal Bea's Unity Secretariat

Engine of Renewal and Reform at Vatican II

At the daily meetings of Vatican II, called "congregations," the general secretary began proceedings by reading out the list of those who were scheduled to speak that day on the draft-text then being considered. When Cardinal Augustin Bea was on the list, his name came toward the middle, after other cardinals and before bishops, as he had low seniority among cardinals, having become a cardinal only recently, that is, in Pope John XXIII's creation of cardinals in December 1959. But it is a commonplace that when Bea's turn to speak did come, the coffee bars were empty and most of the council members were at their places to hear his interventions. Many council members expected important contributions from Cardinal Bea because of his role as president of the Secretariat for Promoting the Unity of Christians, which made him the ecumenical conscience of Vatican II.[1]

This chapter was originally published as "Cardinal Bea's Unity Secretariat: Engine of Renewal and Reform at Vatican II," *Ecumenical Trends* 41, no. 12 (December 2012): 1–5. The text expands a lecture given on September 20, 2012, at the colloquium "The Spirit of Vatican II, Then and Now" at the Hank Center for the Catholic Intellectual Heritage, Loyola University Chicago.

1. I sketched Augustin Bea's early services of the church and his pre-conciliar

The present chapter does not go through Cardinal Bea's council discourses in St. Peter's, as information on them is accessible in Stjepan Schmidt's biography of Bea.[2] Also they are all mentioned in the context of the council debates in the five volumes of the *History of Vatican II*, edited by Giuseppe Alberigo and Joseph A. Komonchak.

The point of departure in this chapter is the publication in 2011 of Mauro Velati's nine-hundred-page compilation of texts and minutes of meetings of Bea's Secretariat for Promoting Christian Unity from late 1960 into early 1962, when the Secretariat was functioning as one of the preparatory bodies producing drafts texts for the council.[3] Velati presents, with helpful introductions, the genesis of texts—through initial drafting, a critical review by members and consultors, and final polishing—which the Secretariat sent on to one of two destinations, that is, either to other preparatory bodies, such as the Preparatory Theological Commission, as ecumenically helpful suggestions for the work of the other body, or to the Central Preparatory Commission as draft-texts proposed by the Secretariat for eventual adoption by the whole council.

This newly accessible record of the Secretariat fuses with earlier studies of the Secretariat to show even more convincingly that

---

ecumenical formation, along with his influential roles during Vatican II, in "Augustin Cardinal Bea, Biblical and Ecumenical Conscience of Vatican II," at a Boston College conference of September 26, 2013, published in *The Legacy of Vatican II*, ed. Massimo Faggioli and Andrea Vicini, SJ (Mahwah, N.J.: Paulist Press, 2015), 185–201.

2. *Augustin Bea, the Cardinal of Unity* (New Rochelle, N.Y.: New City, 1992), 536–70, gives testimonies to the impact of the cardinal's nineteen interventions and relates what he said on draft-texts other than those in the care of the Secretariat. Schmidt's second appendix, 774–76, catalogues these interventions by Bea.

3. *Dialogo e rinnovamento*, ed. Velati. This work is unique, as a documentary record of the genesis of all the texts of a Vatican II preparatory body. Karim Schelkens presents the genesis of one text among the several preparatory drafts of the Preparatory Theological Commission, i.e., *De Fontibus Revelationis*, in his work treated below in chapter 10, at 236–57. For the many other drafts of the commissions, the published record begins with their submission to the Central Preparatory Commission during its meetings from November 1961 to June 1962.

it was a significant engine of renewal and reform in the council. Cardinal Bea had a central role here, being Pope John XXIII's appointee as the Secretariat's first president upon its founding in June 1960, from which a remarkable communality of intention developed between the pope and Bea.[4] Bea began the Secretariat's work in concert with the "chief operations officer," Johannes Willebrands, by appointing the Secretariat's members and consultors. The two leaders then plotted the creation of sub-commissions to treat the topics by which the ecumenical cause would be honored—and not impeded—by the council.[5] Furthermore, Bea was an active member the Central Preparatory Commission, and he intervened in ways critical and influential in the 1961–62 meetings at which the Central Commission evaluated the texts coming out of the individual commissions.[6]

This chapter will relate, first, selected highlights of *ressourcement* theology in the Secretariat's initial proposals for the council.[7] Second, I will treat Bea's role in the Central Preparatory Commission, where he became allied with a small but significant group of critics of many of the prepared schemas, especially of texts com-

4. On the founding of the Secretariat, see Jerome-Michael Vereb, CP, *"Because He Was a German!" Cardinal Bea and the Origins of Roman Catholic Engagement in the Ecumenical Movement* (Grand Rapids, Mich.: Eerdmans, 2006).

5. Willebrands was a key figure as he had coordinated the Catholic Conference on Ecumenical Questions, which since 1952 had brought together in yearly meetings the Catholic ecumenical experts, several of whom became members or consultors of the Secretariat. Velati treats the Conference in the first four chapters of *Una difficile transizione: Il cattolicesimo tra unionismo ed ecumenismo (1952–1964)*. See also Peter De Mey, "Johannes Willebrands and the Catholic Conference for Ecumenical Questions (1952–1963)," in *The Ecumenical Legacy of Johannes Cardinal Willebrands*, ed. Denaux and De Mey, 49–77.

6. Velati gives a full listing of the members and consultors in *Dialogo e rinnovamento*, 103–10, adding the makeup the Secretariat's initial fourteen sub-commissions on 173–74.

7. *Ressourcement* indicates the process, flourishing in Western European Catholic centers in the period 1945–60, of drawing upon Christian sources of scripture, Church Fathers, and early liturgies, to adopt from them more vital formulations than were common in the doctrine and theology of the day. It is linked with *aggiornamento*, updating or modernizing, and with "development," the progressive drawing out of implications from current teaching, to designate changes in Catholic teaching and practice brought to the fore by Vatican II. See O'Malley, *What Happened at Vatican II?*, 36–43.

ing from the Theological Commission. Third, I will reflect on the ongoing historical significance of the documents that Bea's Secretariat saw through the process leading to their approval. These texts include not only the Vatican II Decree on Ecumenism, but also—and especially—the Declaration on Religious Liberty and the Declaration of the Relation of the Church to Non-Christian Religions, especially to Judaism.

The conclusion will be that Bea's Secretariat deserves a central place in any satisfactory global interpretation of Vatican II, (1) because it was a site of proposed and appreciated *ressourcement* theology during the preparation, (2) because Bea voiced early critical judgments which in time echoed in influential interventions at Vatican II in the following months, and (3) because Bea's Secretariat saw through the council's complex process documents which embody in unmistakable ways the reforming character of Vatican II. The council documents on religious liberty, *Dignitatis Humanae*, and on non-Christian religions, *Nostra Aetate*, along with the Pastoral Constitution on the Church in the Modern World, *Gaudium et Spes*, are part of what Joseph Ratzinger called a "counter-syllabus" reversing salient Catholic attitudes of critical opposition toward major developments of modern cultural, political, and religious history. Today the significance of the Secretariat's documents is emphatically underscored by Sacerdotal Society of St. Pius X, that is, the followers of Archbishop Marcel Lefebvre, which takes them as prime examples of Vatican II's rupture with the age-old Catholic tradition.

Bea's SPCU as Proponent of *ressourcement* during Vatican II's Preparation

In the first volume of *History of Vatican II*, Joseph Komonchak works out basic contrasts that emerged during Vatican II's 1960–62 preparation between the Preparatory Theological Commission, led by Cardinal Alfredo Ottaviani and Fr. Sebastian Tromp, and the Bea/Willebrands Unity Secretariat.[8] There is no need to belabor the broad fissure that separated these two Vatican II preparatory bodies. The Theological Commission's schemas massively referenced the papal encyclicals from Leo XIII to Pius XII, while drawing minimally on biblical and patristic theology. In the Commission's *De Ecclesia*, the church originates in decisions by God and by Christ, the divine founder, who instituted offices and conferred powers for directing the earthly ecclesial society. Today, from Velati's volume, we can identify the alternative to these traits that the Secretariat offered in its documents, notably those on the church's hierarchical offices, on the priestly people, and on the word of God in the life of the church.

First, we have the proposal in twelve points that the Unity Secretariat completed on April 20, 1961, and gave to the Theological Commission as an aid toward treating in an ecumenically positive manner the church's structures of hierarchy and ministerial offices.[9] The proposal begins by setting forth a Christology selected out of the range of New Testament possibilities. This drew especially on Ephesians and Colossians to show ecclesial offices and authority existing in subordination to the exalted Christ. The Christological starting point had the effect of setting ministries and hierarchy in a relation of derivation from and dependence

8. See the sections on the SPCU and on "Doctrine and Dialogue" in *History of Vatican II*, ed. Alberigo and Komonchak, 1:263–300. Chapter 10, below, contrasts features of the Preparatory Theological Commission's draft constitution, "The Sources of Revelation," with the promulgated Dogmatic Constitution *Dei Verbum*, in which ecumenical concerns have been honored in promoting scripture in theology and Christian life—as the Secretariat sought to bring into the council's texts from the beginning of its work.

9. Velati, *Dialogo e rinnovamento*, 342–46. The Secretariat's second sub-commission prepared the proposal, under the direction of Archbishop Lorenz Jaeger, with an important oral comment on the primacy of Christ made by Alberto Bellini of Bergamo (225). Even though the Theological Commission made little, if any, use of the proposal, its contents eventually entered Vatican II's *Lumen Gentium* during its successive revisions, as shown by Eduard Stakemeier in "Leimotive der Kirchenkonstitution in einem Votum des Einheitssekretariats vom 20. April 1961," in *Martyria Leiturgia Diakonia. Festschrift für Hermann Volk*, ed. Otto Semmelroth, SJ (Mainz: Grünewald, 1968), 386–98.

upon Christ exalted. He is the present Head of the body, who has a wide-ranging saving influence to reconcile all things in himself, making peace on earth and in the heights (Col 1:18–20). The exalted Christ works through the Holy Spirit, who is the principle of church unity and the source in it of growth in life, faith, and charity. Christ is not only founder by historical decisions giving his followers a durable social structure, but he remains the influential Head as well as the cornerstone from whom the Temple and house of God grows (Eph 2:20–22). The risen and exalted Christ does not retire once the apostles and their successors begin their mandated services. This is *ressourcement* ecclesiology, taken over from biblical theology, for example, from the works of Lucien Cerfaux on the church and Christ in the Pauline letters.[10]

Second, the Secretariat promoted a specific kind of "people of God" ecclesiology which it also forwarded to the Theological Commission.[11] Believers are united by faith and charity into a "sphere of the action of the Holy Spirit" in which separated Christians also move and act. But taking account of Protestant criticisms led the Secretariat to draw out the dignity and responsibilities of the "royal priesthood," which this people is, as affirmed in 1 Peter, Hebrews, and Revelation. They are a people implanted in Christ and sanctified for priestly service amid all peoples. The ministerial priesthood serves the priestly people which has from Christ their roles of "spiritual worship" and bold witness to the truth of God's word. Amidst creation, the royal priesthood carries out a redeeming, unifying, and humanizing

10. See Lucien Cerfaux, *The Church in the Theology of St. Paul* (New York: Herder and Herder, 1959; originally published in 1942), 300–356, on the "mystery of Christ" and the church in this mystery in the letters to the Ephesians and Colossians. See also Cerfaux, *Christ in the Theology of St. Paul* (New York: Herder and Herder, 1959; originally in French, 1954), esp. 397–432.

11. Velati, *Dialogo e rinnovamento*, 369–72. Again, Lucien Cerfaux contributed a base from which to work, namely, "Regale sacerdotium," in *Recueil Lucien Cerfaux* (Gembloux: Duculot, 1954), 2:283–315, originally published in 1939. The text came from the SPCU's fourth sub-commission, chaired by Bishop De Smedt and based on a consultation with the Louvain theologians Gustave Thils, Gérard Philips, and L. Cerfaux himself.

mission to the glory of God. The glorified Christ continues his own priestly, prophetic, and royal office or task in and through the people who participate in his work and action.

Third, the Secretariat aimed to promote a pastorally comprehensive biblical movement among Catholics. The effort was concentrated in a concise and elegant text, "The Word of God: Schema of a Pastoral Decree," for submission to the council itself, a text aiming to ground and foster a biblically enriched spirituality and care of souls permeated by God's word.[12] By this word the content and saving power of God's revelation enters minds and hearts. This word has its witnesses in written, oral, and vital forms, from which it echoes constantly in the church's worship and life. By its power, it truly becomes for believers in Christ a vital source of sturdiness in faith and of a characteristic spirituality, to give the church support and strength—as *Dei Verbum* will say in its chapter VI on scripture in the life of the church. Theological work should be done in the closest possible proximity to scripture, while pastors must lead their people in the frequent practice of devout scripture reading, from which the whole church will receive new spiritual impulses.

Here are three theological positions articulating biblical *ressourcement* theologies for the enrichment of ecclesiology and Christian life. This is a part of the Vatican II reality, both in the conciliar event and in its documents—a part which deserves to be raised up for fresh consideration and emphasis as we re-receive the council over fifty years after its close.

---

12. Velati, *Dialogo e rinnovamento*, 872–83 (longer draft in French), 883–89 (condensed Latin draft, with changes introduced). The main drafter was Hermann Volk of Münster. The text received by the Central Commission in June 1962 is "De verbo Dei Schema decreti pastoralis," given in *Acta et Documenta* II, 2.4:816–19. My English translation is in "Scripture Reading Urged *vehementer* (DV, No. 25)," 573–77; reprinted in *50 Years On*, ed. Schultenhover, 382–87.

Cardinal Bea's Impact on the Central Preparatory Commission, November 1961–June 1962

Beginning in November 1961, the Central Preparatory Commission of about ninety cardinals and archbishops evaluated each draft-text that the preparatory commissions and secretariats had completed.[13] This was a moment of judgment on the adequacy of these drafts for distribution to the future council members and their formal treatment in sessions in St. Peter's. Cardinal Bea made several incisive interventions on necessary ecumenical considerations (not found in the drafts) and on improving the use of scripture in the texts.[14] Bea's contributions linked him with nine other Commission members who regularly intervened critically on many drafts. They remained a dissatisfied minority on the Central Commission, but became during Vatican II leaders of the reforming majority.[15] In two dramatic confrontations, Bea anticipated many criticisms that would later rain down on two schemas of Cardinal Alfredo Ottaviani's Preparatory Theological Commission, that is, those on the sources of revelation and on the nature of the church, during Vatican II's first period in November and December 1962.

13. The work of the Central Preparatory Commission has been surveyed in detail by Antonino Indelicato in *Difendere la dottrina o annunciare l'evangelo*. In presenting the preparatory commissions and their draft-texts, J. Komonchak regularly tells of the individual commissions' submission of their drafts to the Central Commission (*History of Vatican II*, ed. Alberigo and Komonchak, 1:179–300), treating directly the Central Preparatory Commission on 171–75 and 300–318.

14. Bea's biographer Stjepan Schmidt gives an account of Bea's Central Commission interventions in *Augustin Bea, the Cardinal of Unity*, 363–79, adding that the Commission met on sixty mornings from November 1961 to June 1962, and that Bea missed only five meetings because of other commitments. Schmidt's appendix 2 lists thirteen interventions by Bea (773–74), to which can be added his many brief remarks when he voted on the texts, that is, either to approve, reject, or approve with reservations.

15. These included Cardinals Alfrink, König, Frings, Döpfner, Liénart, Léger, and Suenens (Malines), who were joined by Patriarch Maximos IV and Archbishop Hurley. On two occasions, Cardinal Montini (Milan) spoke forcefully against schemas of the Preparatory Theology Commission, namely *De Ordine Morali* and *De Tolerantia* on church and state.

On November 10, 1961, Bea treated incisively the Theological Commission's dogmatic schema, "The Sources of Revelation" (*De Fontibus Revelationis*), offering nineteen corrections of inept formulations in the schema, critiquing its treatment of biblical inspiration and interpretation, and then giving a general evaluation which concluded that the text must go back for a revision, both to make it agree more completely with Pius XII's biblical encyclical, *Divino Afflante Spiritu* (1943), and to relate it to issues of the day by consultation of Catholic exegetes of France, the United States, Germany, and Austria.[16]

During further meetings of the Central Commission, Bea intervened less provocatively to call for reformulations introducing considerations of separated Christians, for example, by presenting the moral order in a way more intelligible to them and by urging pastors to include them in some way in their pastoral care.[17] The schema on seminary studies was unilateral in its recommendation of St. Thomas, especially in consideration of the Eastern churches. Bea reminded the Commission that Vatican II will be an ecumenical council, not "a general synod of the Latin Church."[18] Bea joined the chorus of praise for the schema on renewal of the liturgy, while adding specific backing for introducing communion under both forms and concelebration, while calling for a revised lectionary to let the people hear much more of the Bible at Mass.[19]

A second Bea/Ottaviani confrontation came on May 8, 1962, when the Theological Commission presented its schema on the nature of the church and on church membership.[20] Bea first re-

16. *Acta et Documenta* II, 2.1:541–48. In the subsequent voting on the schema, fifty-five other members of the Central Commission indicated their backing for Bea's critical intervention. On December 15, 1961, Bea sent to the head of the sub-commission on amendments a further statement on *De Fontibus*, adding criticism on its proposals on scripture/tradition and on the Bible in the life of the church. *Acta et Documenta* II, 4.3:33–45.

17. *Acta et Documenta* II, 2.2:85 and 606 (with a ten-line proposal of reformulation).

18. *Acta et Documenta* II, 2.2:792–93, and 4:190 (cited).

19. *Acta et Documenta* II, 2.3:96 and 140.

20. Bea's incisive comments are in *Acta et Documenta* II, 2.3:1012–16.

marked that these topics were of importance both for Catholics and for separated Christians and so the Secretariat for Promoting Unity had treated them in detail and even requested the formation of a mixed Commission with the Theological Commission in order to collaborate on that Commission's dogmatic schema on the nature of the church. When this was refused, the Secretariat sent over its proposals, but the schema before the Central Commission shows that the proposals received no serious consideration by the Theological Commission. Therefore, to inform the Central Commission and gain backing for amendments, Bea recalled certain of the Secretariat suggestions not adopted by the Theological Commission.

The proposed schema deals extensively with the internal essence of the church, but treats minimally Christ and his intentions, which is fundamental in discussion with Protestants and the Orthodox. Similarly, there is much on the hierarchy, but little on roles of the Christian people, which does come later in chapter IV on the laity, but in fact pertains to the whole people of God, both members of the hierarchy and the laity. The title of chapter I, "The Church Militant" (*De Ecclesia Militante*) obscures several essential ecclesial activities which go beyond battling Satan and the world. A far better title would be "The Pilgrim Church on Earth" (*De Ecclesia Peregrinante in Terris*). The schema moves too quickly to treat juridical bonds within the church, neglecting the communication of life in the Lord. These and other revisions would make the schema more biblical and more intelligible to separated Christians.

On the *De Ecclesia* schema's chapter II, on church membership, Bea began with the commonplace observation that a majority of human beings living today can be saved outside the Catholic church. Where the schema attributes their salvation to their having a sincere desire (*votum*) of doing God's will, this is ambiguous, as the desire will have quite different forms and meanings among non-Christian pagans, among Jews, among Protestants, and among Orthodox Christians.[21] The account neglects the objective means of saving communion with Christ given to other Christians by baptism and by other means of grace, which the separated bodies share with Catholics.[22] This part of the schema is fixated on the notion of "member," because it sees the church only as a *corpus* or mystical body. But the New Testament presents other designations, such as kingdom, vine, family, house, etc. In any event, the schema's distinction between membership "in reality" or "by desire" (*in re / in voto*) is not a matter of full consensus in Catholic theology, and so is out of place in a draft of a dogmatic constitution of a council.

At the last meeting of the Central Preparatory Commission in June 1962, Cardinal Bea finally presented the Secretariat's schemas intended for treatment by the council, namely, on religious liberty, on the Catholic practice of ecumenism, on prayer for unity, and on the word of God in the church's life.[23] The first two draft-texts were presented in tandem with chapters of the Theological Commission's *De Ecclesia* and so they occasioned further clashes between Bea and Ottaviani in the closing hours of work by the Central Preparatory Commission.[24]

21. This is drawn from the work of the Secretariat's first sub-commission, in which Jerôme Hamer, OP, had formulated the basic text on different ways of being related to the church and on the elements of union with Christ. See Velati, *Dialogo e rinnovamento*, 326–29. The position became foundational for *Lumen Gentium*, nos. 14–16, and for *Unitatis Redintegratio*, no. 3 and chap. III.

22. Cardinal Bea cited, without giving the author's identity, the criticism of the *votum* concept and lament over Pius XII's non-consideration of non-Catholic baptism voiced by the Heidelberg professor of Lutheran dogmatic theology, Peter Brunner. *Acta et Documenta* II, 2.3:1014, for which S. Schmidt supplied the source in a 1961 article by Brunner. *Augustin Cardinal Bea*, 366.

23. Indelicato, in *Difendere la dottrina*, relates these presentations and discussions in 290–313.

24. Concluding his book, Indelicato offers a final reflection, on 315–39, on the "open problems" left by the Central Preparatory Commission which the council had to resolve. The problems arose from the Central Commission's methods, the fragmentation between many drafts presented to it, and the narrow horizons of many of that Commission's members. But still the Commission's minority articulated significant orientations which became central in the drama of the council's first period in late 1962.

In the Central Preparatory Commission, Bea emerged as a major contributor well before the council's formal opening in October 1962. His interventions gave evidence which weakened the credibility of the Preparatory Theological Commission in the eyes of many cardinals and archbishops from the world beyond the Roman Curia. He revealed that that Commission had refused to cooperate with the Secretariat—which Pope John had founded. Furthermore, Bea contributed, along with others, portions of *ressourcement* theology, which were alternatives to the Theological Commission's schemas on the sources of revelation and on the church, which were both held by that Commission to be essential texts of its contribution to Vatican II.

Once discussion of draft-texts began in the meetings of the council, Bea appointed members and theologians of the Secretariat, as individuals and small groups, to attend carefully to ecumenical issues and questions raised by the texts and interventions of the council members. This work of critical observation and evaluation led to oral and written comments by the bishops of the Secretariat on ways to promote "ecumenicity" in revising the council drafts. This occurred most strikingly in the discourse, made in the name of the Secretariat, by Bishop Emiel-Jozef De Smedt on October 19, 1962, during the debate on "The Sources of Revelation." De Smedt gave the council fathers an elementary lesson on teaching in an ecumenically constructive manner—which was sorely lacking in the draft then under discussion.[25]

The Secretariat's Documents in Vatican II's "Counter-syllabus"

In a passage seldom cited, Joseph Ratzinger linked Vatican II's Pastoral Constitution on the Church in the Modern World, *Gaud-*

25. *Acta Synodalia*, 1.3:184–86. See chapter 6, below, on De Smedt's intervention in the debate of November 14–20, 1962.

ium et Spes, with two other council texts, those on religious liberty, *Dignitatis Humanae*, and on world religions (especially Judaism), *Nostra Aetate*. The latter two arose in the Bea Secretariat
and were with no little effort shepherded by it through the council's process to the conclusion of their being approved as council
declarations.[26] Ratzinger said that this set of texts constitutes the
Catholic church's "revision of the *Syllabus* [*of Errors*] of Pius IX,"
and they make up "a kind of counter-syllabus."[27] Ratzinger ascribes to Vatican II a corrective and reforming action by contrasting the council's work with Pius IX's encyclical of 1864, *Quanta
Cura*, which included an appended list, a "syllabus," of eighty
erroneous views on doctrine, philosophy, ethics, political and
social policy, and especially on the rights of the Catholic church.
This emblematic Catholic text of the mid-nineteenth century
did not state new censures and condemnations, but instead it
collected and listed censures already expressed in Pius IX's discourses and encyclical letters of the previous seventeen years.[28]
Ratzinger explained that "the *Syllabus* established a line of demarcation against the determining forces of the nineteenth century: against the scientific and political world view of liberalism."
But much had changed between 1864 and 1965, and during this
time Catholics gradually corrected the one-sidedness of the *Syl-*

26. On *Dignitatis Humanae*, Silvia Scatena has related the tortuous itinerary from preparatory work in the Secretariat through several Aula debates and text revisions to its final
approval. *La fatica della libertà: L'elaborazione della dichiarazione "Dignitatis humanae" sulla
libertà religiosa del Vaticano II* (Bologna: Il Mulino, 2003), which I presented in "New Light
on Vatican Council II," *Catholic Historical Review* 92 (2006): 609–28, at 621–28. *Nostra Aetate* awaits a complete monographic treatment of its genesis.

27. *Principles of Catholic Theology*, 381. The passage cited is from the essay, "Church and
World: An Inquiry into the Reception of Vatican Council II," which Joseph Ratzinger first
published in *Internationale katholischen Zeitschrift Communio* 4 (1975): 439–54. Chapter 9,
below, treats this analysis by Ratzinger in connection with the vociferous objections to the
texts of the counter-syllabus, which were made in 1964 and 1965 by the *Coetus internationalis Patrum*, led by Archbishop Marcel Lefebvre.

28. Pius IX's *Quanta Cura* and *Syllabus* were well known and taken as normative by
Archbishop Marcel Lefebvre. See the citations given by Gilles Routhier, "The Hermeneutic
of Reform as a Task for Theology," *Irish Theological Quarterly* 77 (2012): 219–41, at 221.

labus through practical adaptations to the modern world. While this was done "along the road of actions" (*via facti*), it remained for Vatican II to make a basic statement of the changed relationship—which it did in its three texts on *ad extra* issues of the modern world, including two on which the Secretariat functioned as the responsible commission.[29]

The two topics of the religions (with Judaism) and of religious liberty extended the original conception of a Secretariat for Promoting the Unity of Christians. Yves Congar wrote in his diary that to give religious liberty its proper doctrinal context the place to treat it was not in conjunction with ecumenism, where it started, but instead with the sections on human dignity in the schema on the church and the modern world. Similarly, a council statement on the Jewish people would have its proper theological place in the early part of *De Ecclesia* on "the people of God."[30] But the Secretariat took over both topics over when it was asked to do so. First, Pope John XXIII asked Cardinal Bea to have the Secretariat review Catholic doctrine on the church's relation to Jews and to prepare for the council a condemnation of anti-Semitism.[31] Second, the doctrine and practice of religious freedom was urged upon Vatican II through the Secretariat by the World Council of Churches, which saw a Catholic development in this area as an essential condition for Catholic participation in the existing ecumenical move-

---

29. Ratzinger's "counter-syllabus" thesis of 1975 harmonizes well with what he said as Pope Benedict in the widely discussed discourse of December 22, 2005. The later text offers "the hermeneutic of reform" (combining discontinuity with a deeper continuity) as an adequate global reading of Vatican Council II. See the text in *Origins* 35, no. 32 (January 26, 2006): 534–39, and the recent analyses by John W. O'Malley, "'The Hermeneutic of Reform': A Historical Analysis," *Theological Studies* 73 (2012): 517–46, and Joseph Komonchak, "Interpreting the Council and Its Consequences," in *After Vatican II: Trajectories and Hermeneutics*, ed. James L. Heft with John W. O'Malley (Grand Rapids, Mich.: Eerdmans, 2012), 164–72, at 164–69.

30. Congar, *My Journal of the Council*, 484, entry of February 6, 1964.

31. The pope requested Bea to take up the Jews and anti-Semitism on June 18, 1960, shortly after the institution of the Secretariat. On the Secretariat's first steps in this area, see Velati, *Dialogo e rinnovamento*, 46–55.

ment. So the Secretariat worked on these questions and recruited teams of experts to develop them adequately into Vatican II declarations.

Ratzinger's original idea of Vatican II's "counter-syllabus" was principally focused on the Pastoral Constitution *Gaudium et Spes*, which speaks, in a manner sharply contrasting with Pius IX's *Syllabus*, about mutually helpful relations of church and world, saying for example that the Catholic church "is convinced that there is a great variety of help that it can receive from the world in preparing the ground for the gospel, both from individuals and from society as a whole, by their talents and activity" (*Gaudium et Spes*, no. 40). Shortly after, this statement expands into a fifty-line account of "What the Church Receives from the Modern World" (no. 44).

Today, we can read Vatican II documents synchronically in their interrelations, and it is easy to show the close relation between *Gaudium et Spes* and *Dignitatis Humanae*. The latter's affirmation of the inviolability of conscience and the limits of government has obvious roots in *Gaudium et Spes*'s account of the dignity of the human person, especially on conscience as "the most secret core and sanctuary of the human person" (no. 16). The next paragraph expands this to speak of the excellence of actions done out of free choice and not by blind impulse or by external constraint (no. 17). The latter threat to religious freedom is of course a main concern of the Declaration on Religious Liberty.

Nostra Aetate obviously expands upon *Lumen Gentium*, no. 16, which treats those who have not yet accepted the Gospel in their various relations to the people of God, with brief mention of Jews, Muslims, and followers of other religions. But there is a *Gaudium et Spes* connection too. For when *Nostra Aetate* urges Catholics to enter respectful dialogue with followers of other religions, it begins with a foundational affirmation of the single human community of all peoples (*Nostra Aetate*, no. 1) and ends with an expanded repudiation of discrimination against any group of persons, for all are created in God's image (no. 5). At its beginning and end, *Nostra Aetate* is applying the Pastoral Constitution on the human community and the essentially social character of human life and development (*Gaudium et Spes*, nos. 26 and 28).

If the Secretariat gave Vatican II two parts of Ratzinger's "counter-syllabus," we can also ascribe a "counter" and "corrective" character to *Unitatis Redintegratio*, the council's charter for Catholic engagement in the ecumenical movement. This decree clearly revises the Catholic approach to separated Christians expressed in papal encyclicals, namely, Pope Leo XIII's *Satis Cognitum* (1896) and Pope Pius XI's *Mortalium Animos* (1928), both of which envision Christian unity solely as the return to the Catholic communion of those Christians whose forebears sadly departed into schism and heresy—which the Vatican II Decree on Ecumenism thoroughly reconceptualizes within an ecclesiology of communion.

Finally, the profoundly reforming character of the Vatican II documents cared for by the Unity Secretariat gains confirmation by their place in the texts central to Archbishop Lefebvre's 1985 explanation of the dissenting position of his Sacerdotal Society of Pius X. "Accepting that the Declaration of Religious Freedom is contrary to the Magisterium of the church, we demand a total revision of this text. Equally indispensable is a significant revision of documents such as: The Church in the World, Non-Christian Religions, Ecumenism, and clarifications in numerous texts which lead to confusion."[32]

A few years after huge majorities of the Vatican II bishops approved these documents as Catholic teaching, Pope Paul VI

---

32. "Lettre de Mgr Lefebvre au cardinal Ratzinger," of April 17, 1985, cited by Routhier, "The Hermeneutic of Reform," 229. Cardinal Ratzinger declared this unacceptable in his answer of May 29, 1985. The present superior of the Sacerdotal Society of Saint Pius X, Bishop Bernard Felley, spoke of the newly elected Pope Benedict XVI in an interview of June 13, 2005, as marked by a principal failing of being attached to the council. "For us, our position on the council is that one finds errors in it, ambiguities which lead to other errors which are worse" (ibid., 236–37).

countered Archbishop Lefebvre's views of them in his theological letter of October 11, 1976. The archbishop's dissent from these Vatican II teachings rests, according to the pope, on the mistake of not attributing to the church an ability to discern the possibilities of developing its message and life. The teaching office is equipped to do this and then, without surrendering foundational components of the deposit of faith, it may adopt better ways to communicate the faith in new historical circumstances. Lefebvre's dissent proceeds from a theology of the church "that is warped in essential points." This includes a "false" concept of the church's tradition—false, because bereft of the historical dynamism of adaptation in transmitting its faith and life.[33]

Cardinal Bea and his Secretariat for Promoting Christian Unity thus gave to Vatican II a small complex of texts, one decree and two declarations, which today make defining contributions to authentic Catholic identity—as acknowledged from both sides of the divide across which Joseph Ratzinger (Pope Benedict XVI) and the Sacerdotal Society of Pius X once faced each other. Both implicitly admit, while evaluating the results in diametrically opposed ways, that the Secretariat of Cardinal Bea was an important Vatican II "engine of renewal and reform." When one re-receives Vatican II after more than fifty years, accuracy demands an awareness of central contributions to its body of doctrine and prescribed practices made by the Secretariat for Promoting the Unity of Christians, initially led by Cardinal Augustin Bea.

---

33. See below, chapter 9, 228–29, for the majorities affirming these texts during the council, and 232–35, for Paul VI's letter to Archbishop Lefebvre.

5

Vatican II's Turn to Ecumenism

The Foundations Laid in 1962–64

In June 1964 Prof. George Lindbeck visited Monsignor Johannes Willebrands in the office of the Vatican Secretariat for Promoting the Unity of Christians (SPCU). Lindbeck was in those years representing the Lutheran World Federation (LWF) as a delegated observer at the Second Vatican Council. He came to inform Willebrands, Cardinal Bea's chief assistant in the Secretariat, that he was proposing to the LWF leadership that the Federation undertake, after the council, a theological dialogue with the Catholic church.[1]

From that starting point there came the Lutheran–Roman Catholic bilateral dialogues, with their many and wide-ranging documents, which reached a highpoint of ecumenical relevance in 1999 with the *Joint Declaration on the Doctrine of Justification*. Two recent texts are signs of the ongoing vitality of this dialogue: *From*

This chapter was originally published as "The Turn to Ecumenical Dialogue: Foundations Laid in 1962–1964," *Concordia Journal* 39 (2013): 296–309.

1. In his appointment book for June 11, 1964, Willebrands recorded the visit of Lindbeck about "further development of the dialogue," and added, "Conversation très intéressante." *Les agendas conciliaires de Mgr. J. Willebrands*, trans. Leo Declerck (Leuven: Peeters, 2009), 131.

Conflict to Communion, a creative proposal of ways Lutherans and Catholics can in 2017 commemorate together the fifth centenary of the Reformation, and *Declaration on the Way: Church, Ministry, and Eucharist*, which shows how world-level and national Lutheran–Roman Catholic dialogues have in fact ascertained thirty-two points of doctrinal agreement, and identified fifteen remaining differences, which however vary in their church-dividing impact.[2]

But this productive Lutheran–Catholic dialogue is just one of the many interconfessional dialogues of the past half-century which have been sites of remarkable theological activity by hundreds of participants. Major multilateral texts have come out, such as the Faith and Order Commission's *Baptism, Eucharist and Ministry* (1982) and *The Church: Towards a Common Vision* (2013).[3] The bilateral ecumenical conversations of the same decades have given us a huge trove of dialogue reports, with the documentation down to 2005 totaling 125 texts of world-level dialogues, conveniently collected in the *Growth in Agreement* volumes.[4] What can still amaze older observers is the active presence of the Roman Catho-

2. Lutheran–Roman Catholic Commission on Unity, *From Conflict to Communion: Lutheran–Catholic Common Commemoration of the Reformation in 2017* (Paderborn: Bonifatius, 2013). The *Declaration* is published by the Evangelical Lutheran Church of America and the Committee on Ecumenical and Interreligious Affairs of the United States Conference of Catholic Bishops in a booklet of xviii + 124 pages (Minneapolis: Augsburg Fortress, 2016). I listed the previous documents of the Lutheran–Catholic dialogues in the appendix of "Lutheran–Roman Catholic World-Level Dialogue: Selected Remarks," in *Celebrating a Century of Ecumenism: Exploring the Achievements of International Dialogue*, ed. John A. Radano (Grand Rapids, Mich.: Eerdmans, 2012), 73–76.

3. On the first text, see the entry by Max Thurian, "Baptism, Eucharist and Ministry (the 'Lima text')," in *Dictionary of the Ecumenical Movement*, ed. Nicholas Lossky et al. (Geneva: WCC Publications, 2002), 90–93. The ecclesiology text came out as "Faith and Order Paper No. 214" (Geneva: World Council of Churches Publications, 2013) in ten languages to promote study in the churches, e.g., by probing the text's accuracy in reflecting the self-understanding of one's own church or the areas of renewal that the text challenges one's church to undertake.

4. *Growth in Agreement*, ed. Harding Meyer and Lukas Vischer (Geneva: World Council of Churches, 1984), offering twenty-one documents published between 1971 and 1981; *Growth in Agreement II*, ed. Jeffrey Gros, Harding Meyer, and William G. Rusch (Geneva: WCC Publications, 2000), giving sixty-six statements of world-level dialogues concluded between 1982 and 1998; *Growth in Agreement III*, ed. Jeffrey Gros, Thomas F. Best, and

lic church in this ecumenical activity, both by Catholic theologians working on the Faith and Order Commission and by the Catholic church taking part in one-half of the bilateral international dialogues documented in the three volumes of *Growth in Agreement*.[5] This Catholic participation could not have been foreseen in the 1950s and in fact was at that time largely blocked by negative attitudes to ecumenism based on Catholic doctrinal principles. What follows is an investigation of crucial turning-points in Catholic teaching at the Second Vatican Council, by which foundations were laid for the Catholic ecumenical engagement made evident in many of the documents just mentioned.

The Catholic Ecumenical Commitment

The place of the Lindbeck/Willebrands conversation of 1964, the SPCU, was an emblematic component of the Second Vatican Council. Pope John XXIII established the Secretariat on June 5, 1960, along with the commissions created to prepare draft-texts for the council, with the Secretariat being ably led by its president Cardinal Augustin Bea and its secretary and chief operating officer, Monsignor Willebrands. Sixteen individuals, bishops or senior churchmen, comprised the Secretariat, assisted by twenty consultors. By the time Vatican II opened on October 11, 1962, this group had gathered in six SPCU plenary meetings of a few days each for the preparation of texts, both as ecumenically constructive recommendations forwarded to the preparatory commissions and as drafts on particular topics for deliberation by the council itself.[6]

When Vatican II began, it took up first the reform of Catho-

Lorelei F. Fuchs (Geneva: WCC Publications, 2007), containing thirty-eight reports issued between 1998 and 2005.

5. Among the characteristics of this Catholic participation, one notes recurrent referencing of the documents of Vatican II. See Jared Wicks, "Vatican II Living on in the Bilateral Ecumenical Dialogues," *Ecumenical Trends* 41 (2013): 122–25.

6. The SPCU preparatory work of 1960–62 has been abundantly reported by Mauro Velati in *Dialogo e rinnovamento*, referenced in the previous chapter.

lic worship leading to the promulgation of the *Constitution on the Sacred Liturgy* on December 4, 1963. This document states in its opening paragraph the four aims of the council, namely, first, to invigorate the Christian lives of Catholics; second, to adapt more suitably to the needs of our own times the aspects of the church that are open to change; third, "to encourage whatever can promote the union of all who believe in Christ," and, fourth, to enhance the missionary call of the church to reach out to all humankind. Pursuit of the third aim led, on November 21, 1964, to the promulgation of the Vatican II *Decree on Ecumenism*, which begins, "The restoration of unity among all Christians is one of the principal concerns of the Second Vatican Council." In its three chapters the Decree states "Catholic Principles of Ecumenism" (nos. 2–4), describes "The Practice of Ecumenism" which it is making imperative for Catholics (nos. 5–12), and concludes by describing how the church sees "The Churches and Ecclesial Communities Separated from the Roman Apostolic See" (nos. 13–24). The third chapter speaks to the situation of the Eastern churches in nos. 14–18, and to that of the churches and ecclesial communities of the West in nos. 19–24.

The ecumenism document is a "decree" that gives guidelines and mandates for action. It states doctrinal bases, but in doing so builds on the *Dogmatic Constitution on the Church*, promulgated on the same day in 1964. That Constitution states briefly in no. 8 that "many elements of sanctification and truth" are found among Christians outside the visible boundaries of the Catholic church.[7] Shortly after, in its chapter on "the People of God," no. 15 names

---

7. With the term "elements" Vatican II adopted a conception of the 1950 Toronto Statement of the World Council of Churches Central Committee regarding how WCC member churches regard the other member churches. The member churches recognize in each other "certain elements of the true church," such as preaching the word of God, holding to scripture, and administering sacraments. See *The Ecumenical Movement: An Anthology of Key Texts and Voices*, ed. Michael Kinnamon and Brian Cope (Geneva: WCC Publications), 467. Below, I will relate how the term "elements" came to be inserted into Vatican II's Constitution on the Church.

several of these elements, which are among "many reasons for knowing that it [the Catholic church] is joined to the baptized" of other Christian bodies. They have and cherish scripture, faith in God and in Christ the savior, "baptism which unites them to Christ" and other sacraments which they receive "in their own churches and ecclesial communities." No. 15 also speaks of other Christians' interior zeal, spiritual benefits, and sanctification, which give rise to true communion in the Holy Spirit.

The ecumenical orientation and mandate given by Vatican II, both in its constitution on the church's nature and its decree on ecumenical action, have been received and confirmed by various popes, most strikingly by Pope Saint John Paul II, in his encyclical *Ut Unum Sint*, of May 25, 1995, where he states that at the council, "the Catholic Church committed herself *irrevocably* to following the path of the ecumenical venture" (no. 3). He restates major affirmations of the council, for example, on the "elements of sanctification and truth," saying: "To the extent that these elements are found in other Christian Communities, the one Church of Christ is effectively present in them" (no. 10). The elements are not static or passive, for "insofar as they are elements of the Church of Christ, these are by their nature a force for the re-establishment of unity" (no. 49). On these bases, a real but still imperfect communion exists. "Ecumenism is directed precisely to making the partial communion existing between Christians grow towards full communion in truth and charity" (no. 14).

The ecumenical commitment just documented represents a historic change in official Catholic attitudes from the outlook before Vatican II. So, the question arises about just *how* such a transformation took place. To provide a partial answer, what follows is a work of historical and theological backgrounding aiming to identify key moments before and during the Second Vatican Council by which foundations were laid for the Catholic ecumenical commitment.

Ecumenical Issues during the Vatican II Preparation: Church Membership

Beginning in late 1960, the council's Preparatory Theological Commission devoted considerable energy to composing the draft-text for a dogmatic constitution on the nature of the church. The need of this was clear, first, as a matter of unfinished business left from the First Vatican Council of 1869–70, where a complete draft of *De Ecclesia* had been prepared, but when threats of a European war began looming, only parts of the draft, on the primacy and infallibility of the pope, were discussed, emended, and promulgated before the council suspended its work. Second, what Vatican I defined left a one-sided account of the Catholic hierarchy and so in proposals made 1959–60 for the agenda of Vatican II many future members called for the new council to state a complementary doctrine of the episcopate and the episcopal college. Third, in the decades before the convocation of Vatican II, ecclesiology was a topic of intensive theological reflection among Catholics, with a focal point being given in the encyclical of Pope Pius XII, *The Mystical Body of Christ* (1943).[8]

The ecclesiological draft of the Preparatory Theological Commission comprised eleven chapters, of which two chapters were especially pertinent to ecumenical concerns, namely, chapter II, on who is a "member" of the church and how membership relates to salvation, and chapter XI on ecumenism itself.[9] Critical mo-

---

8. Examples of this reflection are Romano Guardini, *The Catholic and the Church* (London: Sheed and Ward, 1935; originally 1922); Émile Mersch, *The Whole Christ* (Milwaukee, Wis.: Bruce, 1938) and *Theology of the Mystical Body* (St. Louis, Mo.: Herder, 1951; originally 1936); Henri de Lubac, *Catholicism: Christ and the Common Destiny of Man* (London: Burns and Oates, 1950; originally 1938) and *The Splendor of the Church* (New York: Sheed and Ward, 1956); Otto Semmelroth, *Die Kirche als Ursakrament* (Frankfurt a.M.: Knecht, 1955); and Cerfaux, *The Church in the Theology of St. Paul.*

9. The rest of the ecclesiology draft treated in nine chapters the nature of the church militant (I), the episcopate as the highest grade of ordained ministry (III), bishops in their dioceses (IV), the status and role of vowed members of religious orders (V), the laity (VI), the Magisterium (VII), authority and obedience in the church (VIII), church and state (IX), and evangelization of the world (X).

ments came for the Preparatory Commission when the chapters of the draft-text on the church were examined by the Central Preparatory Commission, a body of eighty cardinals, archbishops, and heads of major religious orders, whose task was to evaluate the drafts coming out of the particular commissions.[10] A positive assessment by the Central Commission would open the way for texts to go to Pope John XXIII for him to approve putting them before the world's bishops for discussion in the daily sessions of Vatican II's working periods. But when Central Commission members expressed reservations or suggested amendments, the draft went back to its Commission of origin for revision.

The Theological Commission's chapters I–VI of its *De Ecclesia* schema came up for treatment by the Central Commission on May 8, 1962, some weeks after the Central Commission members had received each chapter in a printed booklet. The presenter was Cardinal Alfredo Ottaviani, president of the Preparatory Theological Commission. Chapter I, on the nature of the "church militant" on earth, treated the church as founded by Christ and existing as the body of Christ, before concluding with an affirmation of the identity of the socially organized Roman Catholic church with the mystical body of Christ.

Chapter II then treated church membership in three paragraphs.[11] First, it states that the church is necessary for salvation, in line with the traditional axiom *Extra ecclesiam nulla salus*

---

10. The Central Commission held seven week-long meetings from mid-1961 into June 1962, which are fully documented in the *Acta et Documenta* II, vol. 2.

11. In the Theological Commission, Sebastian Tromp, SJ, the Commission's secretary, had drafted chap. II because of his extensive writing on Pius XII's encyclical *Mystici Corporis Christi*. Tromp composed four drafts of the chapter for discussion by a *De Ecclesia* sub-commission, leading each time to considerable revisions of the text. In late September 1961, a fifth draft went before a plenary meeting of the Theological Commission's members, who approved it, but also asked for further emendations. Tromp entered these into the sixth version that then came before the Central Preparatory Commission on May 8, 1962, for which we have the record in *Acta et Documenta* II, 2.4:990–93 (text of chap. II) and 997–1037 (interventions of the Central Commission members on chap. II, followed by their votes, that is, either approval, or rejection, or approval with a call for amendment).

("Outside the church [there is] no salvation"). A person cannot be saved who knows that the Catholic church was founded by God through Christ, but then refuses to enter it and persevere there. The same holds for being baptized, which incorporates a person into the church as a member. But there is also a baptism *of desire* which can fulfill this requirement. For the church, consequently, there is membership in reality (*reapse*), but also a person can be *ordered to* the church by desire (by a *votum*), which will be explained. Such a relation is necessary but not sufficient for salvation, because for this one must also be by grace united to God in faith, hope, and charity.

In its second paragraph the draft's chapter II went into detail on membership in the church. While every baptized person is connected with the church, being a member in reality (*reapse*) rests on conditions that Pius XII had drawn together in his encyclical on the mystical body. The conditions are baptismal regeneration, profession of the Catholic faith, and acknowledgment of the church's authority, while of course not being expelled from the body for a grievous offense. By these, persons are within the visible church as members and are united with Christ who rules it by his vicar on earth. But, as with baptism, there can also be regarding the church a *votum* (desire), "ordering a person to the church," in the case of persons ignorant of the Catholic church being the true and only church of Christ. This desire can be implicit in wanting to obey Christ's will and intentions or, among non-Christians, it can be implicit in a sincere dedication to fulfilling the will of their God and creator.[12]

In a third paragraph, the chapter fulfills, in part, requests made insistently during the drafting process in the *De Ecclesia* sub-commission, especially by Yves Congar, Michael Schmaus,

---

12. The notes to the passage on membership give as sources four references to Pius XII's *Mystici Corporis*, along with citations of other papal documents from 1595, 1749, 1852, and 1960–61 (three texts from John XXIII).

and Gérard Philips.[13] The text speaks of all those who do not profess the Catholic faith and are not in communion with the pope,
and so are not members, but nonetheless are ordered to the
church by desire. Among these non-Catholics, a special place is
acknowledged for baptized Christians who believe in Christ as
God and savior. This union is greater with Orthodox Christians
who revere the eucharist and love the mother of God. With all
these other Christians, there is a shared faith in Christ, a common participation in prayer and spiritual benefits, and a union
in the Holy Spirit who works effectively by gifts and graces not
only in the mystical body but also beyond. The Spirit seeks to in-
corporate the separated brethren into the body of the church and
for this the church prays incessantly, so that they may share in
the abundant aid to salvation enjoyed by Catholics who are *reapse*
members. But Catholics must keep in mind that their condition
is not by their own merit, but by a special grace of Christ to which
they must respond in thought, word, and deed or be more se-
verely judged.

On May 8, 1962, in the meeting of the Central Preparatory Commission, this text came under heavy fire from influential
members. Cardinal Achille Liénart (Lille, France) opposed a central tenet of the draft, namely, the identification of the Catholic
church with the mystical body of Christ as being one and the same.
For Christ's body includes as well those suffering in purgatory
and the blessed in heaven. Separated Christians are buried with
Christ in baptism so that they might rise in him to ongoing super-

13. The papers of G. Philips, in the Leuven Theological Faculty's Vatican II Archive,
include no. 123, a twelve-page Latin exposition for the sub-commission *De Ecclesia* by
Congar, dated April 2, 1961, on the *nexus* of baptized non-Catholics with the visible church
and the mystical body. The connection is sacramental and by the scriptures and the worship of God in their "communions." In the text, Congar says he agrees with what Professor Schmaus called for regarding baptized non-Catholics. The same archive holds no. 119,
which is Philips's seven-page Latin note of April 7 on the members of the church. For him
a baptized non-Catholic has a real *ratio pertinendi* (ground of belonging) to the church
which, though diminished and incomplete, is not just a *votum* or desire, which suffices for a
non-baptized pagan's relation to the church.

natural life. Sadly, they do not share many supernatural benefits administered by the church, but the cardinal will not say they are not adhering to Christ's mystical body. Cardinal Paul-Émile Léger (Montréal, Canada) said that the distinction between "members" *reapse* and those "ordered to" the church by a *votum* is not satisfactory to account for the connection between the church and non-Catholic Christians on the way to salvation. This is a live topic in theology which has not matured sufficiently for it to be decisively stated by the council. For other Christians, Léger proposed saying not "ordered to," but "belong to" the church (*pertinent ad*). Cardinal Franz König (Vienna, Austria) disagreed with the denial of membership to baptized non-Catholics, as canon 87 of the *Code of Canon Law* (1917) affirms that by baptism one becomes "a person in the Church of Christ." Instead of *reapse* on Catholics' membership, better to say *perfecte*, so that a level of membership can be ascribed to all the baptized, even if in cases the connection is defective.[14]

Another member of the Central Preparatory Commission, Cardinal Julius Döpfner (Munich, Germany) underscored the immense ecumenical importance of this particular chapter, which therefore must be carefully reviewed. Pius XII's *Mystici Corporis* laid a basis, but, Döpfner asked, does the encyclical say all that is needed for explaining Catholic doctrine regarding the separated brethren? Döpfner also appealed to canon 87, which ascribes being a "person in the church" to baptism, which is certainly the same as being a member of the church. Other canons, for example, regarding marriage, refer to baptized non-Catholics in ways implying some kind of membership. Another problem is the text's recourse to "ordering by a *votum*" to the church, which is also true of pagans in good faith. The third paragraph tries to work around this problem, but does not sufficiently distinguish between the baptized and the non-baptized. Döpfner concluded that chapter II

---

14. *Acta et Documenta* II, 2.3:998 (Liénart), 1004 (Léger), and 1005–6 (König).

needs to be thoroughly revised if it is to answer today's questions both about the church and salvation and about incorporation as a member of the church.[15]

Cardinal Bea, president of the Unity Secretariat, told the other members of the Central Preparatory Commission that he had to speak at some length on the texts before them, because the Theological Commission had refused to hold joint meetings with the Secretariat. Also, the Theological Commission had not adopted in chapter II some recommendations forwarded to it in writing by the Secretariat. A first point is that the schema exaggerates the importance of the topic of membership, while neglecting to show *how* the church is a means of salvation for all peoples. Then, it speaks of the *votum* of the true church as possibly present in all non-Catholics, whether pagan, Orthodox, or Protestant. Speaking in this way, Bea informed his fellow Central Commission members, greatly offends non-Catholic Christians, because thereby one takes no account of their valid baptism and the status that this confers.[16] Another approach, beginning with God's universal saving will, would work better, but, in any case, one should avoid the term "member," because in St. Paul's usage this does not refer to the visible church. Also, the New Testament has, beyond the "body of Christ," other images of the church, such as a vineyard, family, house, and people. One can say of Catholics that they are "in a full and proper sense" members of the church, but the elements constituting membership are present more widely than only in the Catholic church, with the effects described in the positive part of

15. *Acta et Documenta* II, 2.3:1006–12. In Munich, Cardinal Döpfner regularly sought the advice of Professor Klaus Mörsdorf, the well-respected canonist of the theology faculty of the University of Munich. Döpfner's appeal to c. 87 could well have rested on Mörsdorf's recent article, "Der Codex Iuris Canonici und die nicht-katholischen Christen," in *Archiv für katholischen Kirchenrecht* 130 (1961): 31–58.

16. At this point, Bea cited, without naming the author, a sharp critique of Pius XII's teaching by the Lutheran Professor Peter Brunner of Heidelberg, in "Die abendlandischen Kirchentrennung und das kommende Konzil," in *Erwägungen zukommenden Konzil*, ed. Karl Forster (Würzburg: Echter, 1961), 35–50. Stjepan Schmidt identified Brunner as author of Bea's citation in *Augustin Bea: The Cardinal of Unity*, 366n119.

the chapter's third paragraph. Other baptized Christians are really our "brethren," even though "separated" and Pope John even calls them "sons."[17]

After a few other comments on the chapter, the sixty-five Central Commission members present at the May 8 meeting voted. Only seven voted an approval (*placet*), while eight voted to reject the draft of chapter II (*non placet*). Fifty voted approval with reservations, calling for further work on the text (*placet iuxta modum*). Fifteen said further work should take account, generally, of the comments of the cardinals and bishops who had spoken, but thirty members identified their reservations specifically with the intervention of Bea. Several agreed with other critics of the draft along with Bea, for example, Döpfner and König (twenty-one references each) and/or Liénart and Léger (fourteen mentions each).[18]

The ecumenical cause made a major advance in this critical handling of the Theological Commission's draft on church membership, just five months before Vatican II formally opened. The critics cited above were soon influencing other Vatican II members, with some exercising leadership in sizeable national conferences of bishops and with Cardinal Bea becoming a speaker in the council to whom great attention was given.

However, the critical interventions of May 8, 1962, on the draft Constitution *De Ecclesia* did not take effect immediately, because in the Central Commission the votes with reservations counted as approvals of the draft submitted, which gave a highly favorable total vote for the draft. On behalf of the Theological Commission, in fact, Tromp contested many of the criticisms and admitted only the most clearly demanded changes. Consequently, the schema of a Constitution *De Ecclesia* distributed in November 1962 to the whole council differed in no substantial way from the earlier text and remained vulnerable to the critical points made in

17. *Acta et Documenta* II, 2.3:1012–16.
18. Ibid., 1025–37.

May by members of the Central Preparatory Commission. Catholics are called (*vocantur*) "members in the true and proper sense," while all others of sincere good will are "ordered to the church." Among the latter, other Christians have a more dense ordination by baptism, faith in Christ, and the spiritual benefits set out in the practically unrevised third paragraph.

In the council assemblies of December 1–7, 1962, seventy-seven members spoke on the draft Dogmatic Constitution, *De Ecclesia*, with many, who often spoke for several or many others, unleashing a crescendo of critical points against the draft. But before reviewing the consequences of this development, another part of the prepared text on the church deserves treatment.

Ecumenical Issues during the Vatican II Preparation: The Separated Communities

In the Preparatory Theological Commission's draft constitution, the concluding chapter XI treated ecumenism. It had evolved through six drafts, with Professor Jan Witte (Dutch Jesuit, Gregorian University) serving as the reporter who composed several revised versions after discussions in the sub-commission *De Ecclesia* and in the plenary Theological Commission.[19]

The 1962 draft chapter on ecumenism developed gradually from late 1961 to comprise eight sections, beginning with an Introduction (no. 1) in which the council declares its commitment to promoting the unity of all Christians. No. 2 states the Catholic church's recognition of the bonds of baptism, confession of Christ, and witness to him before the world, which connect separated Christians, especially those of Eastern rites, with herself—albeit not in full communion.[20] No. 3 briefly mentions the

---

19. The successive versions of chap. XI, *De Oecumenismo*, are in the Archive of the Pontifical Gregorian University, Rome, in the papers of Fr. Jan Witte, SJ.

20. Notes to no. 2 explain full ecclesial communion in terms of "eucharistic communion," which presupposes agreement in faith, a common sacramental life, and union in

church's relation to individual separated Christians, as chapter II already treated this. No. 4 then explains the church's relation to the separated communities, about which more below. No. 5 is a Catholic statement on the existing ecumenical movement, which is inspired by God, but which should aim at unity in faith, sacramental communion, and common governance under Christ's vicar on earth. No. 6 expresses hope that Catholics will be ecumenically active while striving theologically and pastorally for inner renewal of their own church to make it known more clearly as the Father's house. No. 7 speaks to the issue of common worship, giving detailed reasons against and for, but still looking to later practical norms. The final no. 8 admits and even urges social collaboration with other Christians, by which the world will become more humane and by which inter-Christian prejudice may be overcome.

No. 4 on the separated communities, after Witte's two initial versions, gave rise to a sharp clash of positions in the *De Ecclesia* sub-commission on November 21, 1961.[21] Professor Heribert Schauf (Aachen, Germany) held that the separated communities of the West had no religious relation to the Catholic church, because their separation leaves them existing as only natural religious associations. Witte countered that they possess and live from supernatural elements such as God's revelation, scripture, and sacraments of Christ. Tromp agreed with Schauf, whom he had directed in doctoral studies at the Gregorian. Philips argued that, in spite of the separation, the elements remain good and fruitful, which gives

---

ministry. The eucharistic focal point of full communion was being proposed in that era not only by Catholic writers like Ludwig Hertling and Gustave Bardy, but as well by others, like Nicolas Afanassief, John Meyendorff, Max Thurian, and Werner Elert in his *Eucharist and Church Fellowship in the Early Church* (St. Louis, Mo.: Concordia Publishing House, 1966; original German edition, 1954), and in documents of the World Council of Churches. See the references given in the November 1962 version of the ecumenism chapter, *Acta Synodialia*, 1.4:87–88.

21. The minutes of the November 21 argument are in the Vatican Secret Archive, Collection *Concilium Vaticanum II*, Box 745, Folder 190.

a supernatural character to the separated bodies.[22] Their members receive the elements in faith, over which we should rejoice, while lamenting the separation. Monsignor Carlo Colombo (Milan, Italy) asserted that Catholic recognition of the Holy Spirit's influence in stirring non-Catholics to begin and carry on the ecumenical movement constitutes acknowledgment of the work of grace in the communities being discussed. Witte's further arguments, with the interventions of Philips and Colombo for the separated communities' religious character, impressed Tromp, who accepted calling them "Christian communities."

After further revision, review by the plenary Theological Commission, and a last revision by Tromp to gain greater concision and more Catholic emphasis, the passage on the "separated Christian communities" was printed in the longer chapter XI of the draft *De Ecclesia* for the Central Preparatory Commission. The final session of the Central Commission was scheduled for June 12–19, 1962, but the number of texts to evaluate made it necessary to hold a further meeting on June 20, at which the Commission reviewed together the Theological Commission's chapter on ecumenism and a draft pastoral decree from the Unity Secretariat, *De Oecumenismo Catholico*.[23] Only thirty-eight Central Commission members were

22. In his written statement of April 7, 1961, indicated at 123n13, above, Philips concluded that the recognition of many spiritual goods among non-Catholic Christians must apply not only to individuals but as well to their bodies. "Most Protestant confessions profess faith in the Holy Trinity, the Incarnation, and redemption, while conferring baptism, promoting a spirit of prayer, etc." (6). Congar's account, from the same time, urged calling the separated bodies "communions," as Augustine did regarding the Donatists. They are true but imperfect actuations of the church.

23. The drafts presented to the Central Commission are in *Acta et Documenta* II, 2.4:785–92 (SPCU, pastoral decree) and 792–800 (Theological Commission, *De Ecclesia*, chap. XI). The SPCU's pastoral text begins with a brief account of the unity of the church, which is constituted by visible and invisible *elementa*. Some elements can exist and be fruitful outside Catholic unity as means of salvation, although in an incomplete manner. Nonetheless, the separated communities are not deprived of a role in the mystery of salvation. In fact, "The Spirit of Christ does not refuse to use them as means of salvation and to generously pour out on them Himself along with gifts of faith, hope, and charity" (786). The draft decree proposes the exercise of ecumenism by growth in knowledge of separated

present on the added day, but six who had departed gave their votes in writing. Two cardinals had brief remarks to make, Ernesto Ruffini (Palermo, Italy) and Michael Browne, OP (Roman Curia), with both speaking positively about the two texts and saying they could well be combined in one decree, having a doctrinal and pastoral part.[24] In the voting, all the members approved the two texts, with twelve saying they should become one text.[25]

Because of the Theological Commission's refusal to work jointly with the Unity Secretariat, there was no immediate fusion of *De Ecclesia*'s chapter XI with the *De Oecumenismo Catholico* of the SPCU. In the draft Constitution on the Church passed out to the members of the council, in November 1962, chapter XI stated that other Christians are moved toward the unity of the church not only as individuals but in their own communities, which hold and administer "certain elements of the Church," especially scripture and the sacraments, which unite recipients with Christ and which tend toward Catholic unity. Sadly, these elements are received outside the fullness of God's revelation, but the council does not deny their saving effect and promotion of a Christian spiritual life. All Catholics should by word and example show the separated brethren that the fullness of divine revelation is held in truth and purity in the Catholic church alone, so that those now separated may come to possess along with us the full heritage coming from Christ.[26]

During the first period of Vatican II, chapter XI on ecumenism of *De Ecclesia* did not come onto the agenda for specific evaluation, because it had been set aside a few days before the council debated the draft Constitution *De Ecclesia* as a whole. This occurred after a short debate of November 26–29, 1962, on a draft-text on the Eastern Catholic churches which encouraged these churches

---

Christians, prayer for unity, and practical cooperation. Promoting ecumenism also entails renewal within the church, through growing catholicity and conversion of heart.

24. *Acta et Documenta* II, 2.3:806–7.

25. Ibid., 807–12, with four members suggesting rewordings of the texts before them.

26. *Acta Synodalia*, 1.4:82–83.

to become promoters of reconciliation and reunion with the Orthodox. The council members voted on December 1 that a fusion into one text should be made of the council's three ecumenical texts, that is, on the Eastern Catholic churches and the separated Orthodox churches, chapter XI of *De Ecclesia*, and the pastoral text on Catholic ecumenism which was coming from the Unity Secretariat.[27]

Chapters I–X of the Preparatory Theological Commission's draft Constitution on the Church were formally discussed in plenary sessions of the council on December 1–7, 1962, during which incisive objections were made, for example, by Cardinals Liénart, Léger, König, Döpfner, and Bea. The criticism gained momentum and became so strong that no vote was needed to formally register the text's inadequacy. Instead, the draft Constitution came under the general mandate, issued by Pope John XXIII on December 5, 1962, that the council's commissions should thoroughly revise all their existing draft-texts to concentrate them on issues of major importance and orient them to the pastoral and doctrinal renewal which Pope John had called for in his opening discourse of the council, October 11, 1962.[28]

De Ecclesia on a New Basis

Cardinal Léon-Joseph Suenens (Malines-Brussels, Belgium) had participated in the Central Preparatory Commission meetings of May and June 1962 on the chapters of the proposed Dogmatic Constitution on the Church. From the criticisms forcefully expressed by leading cardinals, Suenens knew that this key doctrinal text had not been prepared in a manner corresponding to the

27. *Acta Synodalia*, 1.4:10 (proposal) and 141 (outcome of vote).

28. The pope's December 5, 1962, mandate for further work on the Vatican II draft-texts is given in *Acta Synodalia*, 1.1:96–98. Chapter 6, below, treats the overall dynamic of the council's 1962 period, especially as it led to the normative clarification of council's goals late in that first period.

aims of Pope John XXIII for the council. Shortly after the council opened, Suenens asked Philips to draft an alternative *De Ecclesia* text.[29] Philips should do this privately, but should also involve theologians who were serving as experts of other cardinals and bishops.[30] By this work, those opposed to the Preparatory Commission's text will have ready a substitute *De Ecclesia* text to give the council a basis for advancing positively. Philips's initial text was ready in late October when it was reviewed and only slightly amended by Cardinal Bea and theologians of the Unity Secretariat.

The alternative text opens with a brief statement of its intent, which is to respond to Pope John's opening discourse of the council by stating the main points of ecclesiological doctrine in a fresh way. Central to the method is to draw on themes recently developed in biblical theology, patristic studies, and theological reflection, which when fused together should promote the council's aims, that is, to inspire a more intense religious life among Catholics, to make Catholic doctrine better understood by non-Catholics, and to show the church as merciful and benevolent toward the whole human family.[31]

Finally, on November 23, a booklet containing the draft Constitution on the Church was distributed to all the council mem-

29. In doing this, Suenens was acting on the suggestion made to him orally by Vatican Secretary of State Cardinal Amleto Cicognani in St. Peter's Basilica just after the brief plenary session of the council held on October 13, 1962. This is documented in a letter of that day written by Suenens and cited by Mattis Lamberigts and Leo Declerck in "The Role of Cardinal Léon-Joseph Suenens at Vatican II," in *The Belgian Contribution to the Second Vatican Council*, 61–217, at 91. It seems questionable that Cardinal Cicognani did this on his own. More likely, the orally given suggestion came from Pope John XXIII.

30. Philips narrates his drafting work of October 1962 in *Carnets conciliaires de mgr Gérard Philips*, 83–89. Philips's collaborators of October 1962 in composing a revised *De Ecclesia* were, first, three theologian-consultants of the Preparatory Theological Commission, Yves Congar, Carlo Colombo, and Joseph Lécuyer, and, second, Karl Rahner, Joseph Ratzinger, Otto Semmelroth, Lucien Cerfaux, and Willy Onclin. They worked "on the quiet" as the official text of the Preparatory Commission had not been distributed. Congar's diary gives the initial outline, as shown to him by Philips on October 18, and notes meetings of the theologians assisting Philips. *My Journal of the Council*, 97–98, 122, and 124.

31. An early version of the Philips draft, beginning "Concilium duce Spiritu Sancto," is given by Gil Hellín in *Synopsis . . . de ecclesia*, 707–15.

bers. Philips records that the theologians who had helped in developing his text continued to suggest improvements of his alternative draft, but its future remained clouded in uncertainty.

The first period of the council ended in early December 1962 with the "fall" of the prepared *De Ecclesia* and a mandate given by John XXIII to revise all the prepared texts in line with the aims he had expressed for the council. This stirred bishops and theologians around the world to work intently on texts which could replace the previous *De Ecclesia*. As a result, when the council's Doctrinal Commission gathered for a working session in February 1963 the members found five alternative texts that offered different new bases for a Dogmatic Constitution *De Ecclesia*.[32] These had come from: (1) Archbishop Pietro Parente, of the Roman Curia, a member of the Doctrinal Commission who reworked in a modest way parts of the earlier schema; (2) Philips, in a revision of his October work, now beginning with "*Lumen gentium cum sit Christus*"; (3) the German bishops' conference, which approved in early February a theologians' draft of forty-six paragraphs, beginning with "*Lumen gentium cum sit Ecclesia*"; (4) a group of some sixty French bishops; and (5) a group of Latin American bishops, headed by Cardinal Raul Silva Henríquez (Santiago, Chile).[33]

Philips arrived in Rome on February 23 and heard that seven members of the Doctrinal Commission members had been formed into a *De Ecclesia* sub-commission. Cardinal Michael Browne, OP, would preside, with fellow Cardinals König and Léger as members along with four bishops, each of whom would be the advocate for one of the alternative drafts: Parente (for his own text), André Marie Charue (Namur, Belgium, for Philips's draft), Gabriel Gar-

32. With the opening of the council, the preparatory commissions ceased their work and were succeeded by conciliar commissions made up of council members, sixteen of whom were elected on October 16, 1962, and another nine were appointed by the pope and announced on October 29. The Doctrinal Commission members are listed in *Acta Synodalia*, 1.1:225–26 (elected) and 559–60 (appointed).

33. The texts are given by Gil Hellín, *Synopsis ... de ecclesia*, 681–93 (Parente), 694–705 (Philips), 722–60 (German draft), 751–61 (French draft), and 762–845 (Chilean draft).

rone (Toulouse, France, for the French text), and Joseph Schröffer (Eichstadt, Germany, for the German text). Late in the morning of February 26, while Philips was working on refining his text with theologians at the Belgian College, Bishop Charue called to tell him that the seven had chosen his *De Ecclesia* text as the basis of further work, while the other alternative drafts would be consulted for individual contributions judged useful.[34] The seven members of the sub-commission then chose expert theologians to work on further developing the draft, which led to a remarkable grouping. Cardinal König chose Rahner, Archbishop Garrone named Daniélou who was soon replaced by Congar; and Bishop Schröffer chose the Louvain theologian Gustave Thils who soon gave way to Charles Moeller, also of Louvain and very close to Philips. Bishop Charue naturally chose Philips, who was to preside over the experts' work of preparing a newly minted *De Ecclesia* for the Doctrinal Commission to present to the council.

The theologians went immediately to work on further developing the Philips text, drawing on the other alternative texts, on what they knew many council members desired, and on their own considerable theological expertise. Two points deserve mention regarding the text before them in late February 1963, which had grown from Philips's initial work of four months earlier and would develop further as Vatican II turned resolutely to restating Catholic ecclesiology.

(1) The opening chapter was no longer on "the Church militant" as in the Preparatory Commission's text, but on "the mystery of the Church." This then develops biblically from the plan of the Father and the saving mission of the Son. The Holy Spirit sanctifies the church in which the exalted Christ lives on, nourishing it with the bread of doctrine and the eucharist. The church

---

34. Philips, *Carnets conciliaires*, 92–93, also relating also that on Sunday, February 24, Archbishop Garrone had called together four other sub-commission members (König, Léger, Schröffer, and Charue), who agreed on backing Philips's text as the basis for further work because of its mediating position between Parente's text and the German proposal.

is a temple of the indwelling Spirit and the body of Christ by the one bread (1 Cor 10:17), as well as Christ's beloved spouse.

Philips's draft first chapter closes with a paragraph on the church on earth, which is a structured reality endowed with the means of sanctification and is the true church of Christ confessed in the creed as one, holy, catholic, and apostolic. At this point, Philips's earlier text (*Concilium duce Spiritu Sancto*) of October 1962 had affirmed that the church, animated, unified, and sanctified by the Spirit, "is on earth an organically constituted society, namely [*nempe*], the Roman Catholic [church]," which is to lead all persons to the heavenly kingdom for the glory of the Father.[35] This was in effect the same as the final statement in chapter I of the Preparatory Commission's draft, that is, that the church of Christ *is* the Catholic church.

But the phrase of October 1962, opening with "*nempe,*" had been changed during the Belgian theologians' late February work on the initial Philips draft. Consequently, the text chosen by the Charue sub-commission as its basis-text had been enriched in treating the church on earth by a nine-word Latin insertion, which constituted a significant ecumenical opening. Through amendments which are difficult to trace in detail, the new text (beginning "*Lumen gentium quod sit Christus*") affirms that the church now on pilgrimage on earth, "the true mother and teacher of all, constituted in this world as an ordered society, is [*est*] the Catholic Church directed by the Roman Pontiff and the bishops in communion with him, although [*licet*] certain elements of sanctification can be found outside her complete structure."[36]

35. Gil Hellín, *Synopsis ... de ecclesia*, 708.

36. "Haec igitur Ecclesia, vera omnium Mater et Magister, in hoc mundo ut societas constituta et ordinata, est Ecclesia catholica, a Romano Pontificis et Episcopis in eius communione directa, *licet elementa quaedam sanctificationis extra totalem compaginem inventiri possint.*" Gil Hellín, *Synopsis ... de ecclesia*, 697 (emphasis added). This new clause most likely originated with Gustave Thils, for he was at the Belgian College among the theologians working on Philips's text on February 26. Thils, an SPCU consultor, knew well the Secretariat's draft decree on Catholic ecumenism (129n23) and Thils had written *Histoire*

The "is" of the Catholic self-identification with the church of Christ remains, but it is now modified in the same sentence by a contrasting or adversative clause. An ecclesial identification is made, but the added clause shows the identification is not asserted in a totalizing manner. Coming upon "is," or the later "subsists in," one might think it to be an all-inclusive statement about the God-given ecclesial realities which are in and of the Catholic church, but the added clause corrects this, by affirming the existence of constitutive sanctifying components of the church of Christ on earth which exist and operate beyond the Catholic church in bodies separated from it.

As the draft Constitution developed, the main verb *est* (is) in this sentence was first changed to *adest in* (is present in) by the sub-commission that revised chapter I in the light of council interventions made in October 1963. But this was thought to give a too-generic account of the relationship of the church of Christ with the Catholic church. To improve the statement of identification, *subsistit in* (subsists in) came to replace *adest in* in the draft presented for voting in 1964 and in the final text of *Lumen Gentium*. But *subsistit in* remains elusive as to its precise import. It entered the text at the chapter I sub-commission meeting of November 26, 1963, when Tromp proposed it, but the sub-commission members accepted it with little or no discussion of its significance in this context. The *relatio* accompanying the revised text, to explain to the council members the changes introduced, said only that *subsistit in* cohered better than *est* with the *licet* clause affirming that ecclesial elements are also present elsewhere, which underscores the importance of the *licet* clause in connec-

---

doctrinale du movement œcuménique, originally published in 1955, but about to come out in a new edition (Paris: Desclée, 1963), in which he treats the notion of "elements of the church" on 247–59. On this topic, see Catherine Clifford's recent study, "*Elementa ecclesiae*. A Basis for Vatican II's Recognition of the Ecclesial Character of Non-Catholic Christian Communities," in *La théologie catholique entre intransigeance et renouveau: La réception des mouvements préconciliaires à Vatican II*, ed. Gilles Routhier, Philippe J. Roy, and Karim Schelkens (Leuven: Universiteitsbibliotheek, 2011), 249–69.

tion with *subsistit in*.[37] Not surprisingly, an ample literature has developed, especially in Europe and North America, about the meaning of the term *subsistit in*. [38] But most contributions to the discussion do not give due attention to the earlier addition and continuing relevance of the *licet*-clause for interpreting this significant text.

(2) Above, in treating church membership, we related how Philips dissented from Tromp's construction which entered the preparatory draft on the church. On membership, Tromp proposed a twofold main division based on Pius XII, that is, between those "really" (*reapse*) members of the Catholic church and those "ordered to" it by a sincere desire of obeying God's will.

From the beginning of his new draft-text—and remaining in what became Vatican II doctrine—Philips set up a threefold division among persons in regard to the church.[39] First, Catholics are those who "really and without restriction belong to the church" (*reapse ... pertinent*) who are described, as Pius XII had done in his encyclical, as accepting all the means of salvation present in the church, that is, who are baptized, profess the true Catholic faith, acknowledge church authority, and have not been wholly excluded for a grave offense. Philips avoided the term "member," adding a note on the controversy about this, which makes it better to avoid the term. But key phrase on "really belonging" gave way in early 1964, due to requests from council members, to "being fully incorporated into the society of the church" (*plene incorporantur*).[40]

---

37. Gil Hellín, *Synopsis ... de ecclesia,* 64, gives the terse explanatory *relatio*. Alexandra von Teuffenbach has reconstructed the insertion of *subsistit in* from several partial records of the November 26, 1963, Doctrinal Commission meeting in *Die Bedeutung des subsistit in (LG 8): Zum Selbstverständnis der katholischen Kirche* (Munich: Herbert Utz, 2002), 378–88.

38. See, e.g., Christian Washburn, "The Second Vatican Council, *Lumen gentium*, and *Subsistit in*," *Josephinum Journal of Theology* 22 (2015): 145–75, referencing numerous works on *subsistit in*.

39. Gil Hellín, *Synopsis ... de ecclesia,* 709–10.

40. Ibid., 115–16.

The second group, in Philips's draft, comprises non-Catholic Christians, whose union with the church rests on aspects which earlier had been treated as giving density to their relation by desire (*votum*). No such desire appears here, but the text expresses instead the church's sense of connectedness with them, grounded in the others' faith in Christ, Son of God and savior, in the indelible mark of their baptism, and in their acceptance of some at least of the sacraments. From these, follows communion by the Holy Spirit's work in them, along with the Catholic prayer that they come into the one flock. A third group has not yet come to Christian faith and to rebirth in Christ, but to them the church reaches out in prayer and proclamation, while not excluding they can be saved if they sincerely desire, albeit implicitly, what God has in fact established through Christ in his church.

The treatment of non-Catholic Christians in an intermediate place between Catholics and non-Christians coheres well with the recognition of "elements of sanctification" outside the Catholic church. The elements are objective bases of the Christian identity of individuals with whom the Catholic church knows that it is specially connected in Christ and in the Holy Spirit. But the Philips text has left open the theological status and role of the separated churches and communities which transmit the good news of Christ the savior and the sacraments of new life.

Recognition of the Role of the Separated Communities: The Principle of Ecumenism

The Doctrinal Commission's *De Ecclesia* sub-commission of seven members received the revised chapters worked out by Philips and his fellow *periti* and made them ready for review, emendation, and approval by the full Commission. By mid-March 1963, the revised chapter I on the mystery of the church and chapter II on the church's hierarchical structure, especially the episcopate, were approved by the Doctrinal Commission and on April 22, Pope John XXIII added his assent to them for sending the chapters to the council members. In collaboration with other council commissions, further chapters developed in April and May on the laity and on vowed religious, to which the Doctrinal Commission added a chapter on "the call to holiness in the church." After the pause caused by the death of John XXIII on June 3, 1963, and the election of Paul VI on June 21, the new chapters were sent to the council members on July 23. At the end of August, the Commission on Coordinating the Work of the council determined that the second period, scheduled to begin on September 29, would start with discussion of the new draft of a Dogmatic Constitution *De Ecclesia*.

When the council reopened, after a short discussion, an overwhelming majority voted to accept the revised draft-text on the church as a suitable basis of work, and on October 1–4 forty-five council members spoke on chapter I, with fifty-two handing in written observations.[41] In chapter I, the final sections (nos. 8–10) presented Catholics, non-Catholic Christians, and non-Christians in the manner of the Phillips draft treated above. The council discussion of the further chapters of *De Ecclesia* continued until October 31, from which came a large number of further proposals for its development into a revised text.

The Doctrinal Commission created in late October seven sub-commissions to review the council members' oral and written interventions on *De Ecclesia*, among which the second, headed by Cardinal Rufino Santos (Manila, Philippines), was given the paragraphs on "the people of God," a new chapter II of the draft-

41. Of the speakers, thirteen spoke on behalf of others, such as Bishop Hermann Volk for sixty-six German and Scandinavian bishops, Cardinal Jaime de Barios Camara for fifty-three Brazilian bishops, Bishop Antoine Grauls for fifty-five bishops of Burundi and Ruanda, Archbishop John Heenan for the bishops of England and Scotland, and Bishop Herculanus Van der Burgt for thirty-one bishops of Indonesia. Among the written comments, five were from bishops grouped in episcopal conferences.

text. By the transfer to this chapter of sections from the chapter on the laity, the treatment of how persons belong to the church now comprised nos. 9–16, with no. 15 devoted to non-Catholic Christians. In parceling out the work among the sub-commission's *periti*, Professor Jan Witte (Gregorian University) became the reporter on no. 15, on other Christians.

After his study of the council members' interventions, Witte reported to the sub-commission, first, that several comments added further "elements" to what the text indicated as the grounds of connection of non-Catholic Christians with the church, especially the scriptures taken as the norm of belief and life. Second, several proposals had called for recognition of the communities in which other Christians receive baptism and other sacraments.[42] The Santos sub-commission accepted this, as did the full Doctrinal Commission, which led to revisions of no. 15 that remained in *Lumen Gentium*, promulgated in 1964. Thus, other Christians who are not in the unity of the Catholic communion "hold sacred Scripture in honor as a rule of faith and of life, [and] show a sincere religious zeal.... They are sealed by Baptism which unites them to Christ as they recognize and accept other sacraments *in their own churches or ecclesiastical communities.*"

The sub-commission proposing these changes then drafted brief explanations of them for its report to accompany the next text when it went to the council members. Regarding the communities in which other Christians receive the word and sacraments, Witte suggested the following formulation, which was accepted: "The elements enumerated regard not only individuals, but also the communities. In this precise point is located the

---

42. Those making this proposal included Abbot Christopher Butler, OSB (Downside Abbey, England), speaking on October 2 (*Acta Synodalia*, 2.1:462); Bishop Gerard Van Velsen (Kronstad, South Africa), on October 3 (*Acta Synodalia*, 2.2:57–58); Bishop Vladimir Malanczuk, CSSR (Ukranian bishop in France), in a written comment (*Acta Synodalia*, 2.2:178); Bishop José Pont y Gol (Sergovia, Spain), also written (*Acta Synodalia*, 2.3:525–27); and Bishop Maurice Baudoux (St. Boniface, Canada), speaking on October 4 (*Acta Synodalia*, 2.1:70–71).

principle of the ecumenical movement" (*in hoc praecise situn est principium motionis ecumenicae*).[43]

These then are the foundations of the Catholic engagement in ecumenical dialogue with other Christians, in which dialogues with Lutherans have been especially productive.[44] The Catholic commitment rests on the recognitions made in *Lumen Gentium* of the Christian substance cherished and transmitted in the churches and ecclesial communities that have become dialogue partners with the Catholic church.

43. This was printed in the booklet of the revised *De Ecclesia* text on which the council members voted in September 1964. *Acta Synodalia*, 2.1:231; Gil Hellín, *Synopsis*, 124. Our narrative rests on the minutes of the Santos sub-commission in the Vatican Secret Archive, Collection *Concilium Vaticanum* II, Box 766, Folder 306.

44. In addition to the documents collected in the *Growth in Agreement* volumes and the more recent texts mentioned at the beginning of this chapter, Pope John Paul II, during the twenty-seven years of his pontificate, had numerous contacts with Lutheran Christians. See my survey, "Pope John Paul II and Lutherans: Actions and Reactions," in *The Legacy of John Paul II*, ed. Gerald O'Collins and Michael Hayes (London: Burns and Oates, 2008), 139–202.

Part II

The Council in Session (1962–65)

Outcomes and Global Traits

6

Vatican II in 1962

Taking Hold of Pope John's Council Goals

This chapter's title indicates a historic process that unfolded before and after the formal opening of the Second Vatican Council. This perspective expands the horizon from the memorable single day of October 11, 1962, to include both the month before and especially what followed during the first period of the council. The developments of those weeks of Vatican II led to the "intersession" of early 1963, when the Vatican II commissions worked quite productively. In fact, by June 1963 the council members received by mail twelve revised schemas of constitutions or decrees, to which two more were added in August.[1] This later period, however, was punctuated by Pope John XXIII's death on June 3, 1963, which led to worldwide sorrow and grieving.

This chapter was originally published as "Vatican II in Late 1962: Taking Hold of Its (and Pope John's) Council Goals," *Josephinum Journal of Theology* 19 (2012): 172–86. It began as a public lecture at the Pontifical College Josephinum, Columbus, Ohio, on October 24, 2012.

1. The dozen draft-texts treated seminaries, Catholic schools, priestly ministry, the lay apostolate, bishops and diocesan governance, the pastoral care of souls, religious life, the Eastern Catholic churches, divine revelation, the church (chapters on its mystery and hierarchy), ecumenism, and the Virgin Mary. The two further schemas were on the sacrament of marriage and on the church in further chapters on the laity and religious.

Here we focus on a process of a gradual acceptance, by a significant number of the Vatican II participants, of the council's goals, aims, and orientations originating with Pope John XXIII. October 11, 1962, remains important because of John's keynote address, *Gaudet Mater Ecclesia* ("Mother Church Rejoices"), which set in motion a clarifying process that took place in the minds of many council members. Initial developments, especially in November 1962, showed the pope that his goals and orientations were taking hold in the minds of a growing number of council fathers. The result of this came in early December 1962 when Pope John confidently took charge of the council by ordering a wide-ranging revision of the existing or emerging draft-texts, for which he set down specific criteria coming from his keynote address.

Deep Seeds of Pope John XXIII's Goals for Vatican II

Pope John XXIII sensed that he brought to the council a singular vision of the Catholic church's call to have a transforming impact on world, as he made clear in "Words Spoken on His Sickbed," on May 24, 1963, just ten days before he died. On that day, he said the following:

In the presence of my collaborators, it comes to me spontaneously to repeat the act of faith. This is right for us priests, because the Lord's will inspires us to deal with matters of the highest importance for the benefit of the entire world.

Now more than ever, certainly more than in past ages, we are meant to serve human beings as such and not only Catholics. Above all and everywhere this means to defend the rights of the human person and not only those of the Catholic Church.

Present-day circumstances, such as what has been demanded of us the past fifty years, along with the doctrinal deepening, have placed us before new realities, as I said in the discourse at the opening of the council.

It is not that the Gospel changes, but that we are beginning to understand it better.

One who has lived long and found himself early in this century facing new tasks of social activity benefitting the whole person, one who lived, as I did, twenty years in the East and eight years in France, thus encountering different cultures and traditions, now grasps that the time has come to recognize the signs of the times, to lay hold of present-day possibilities, and look toward the distant future.[2]

This remarkable declaration shows how Pope John, fully aware that death was near, reflected within the horizon of the Catholic faith and its creed on his own priestly calling from God. This ministry, he now grasps, entails work "for the benefit of the entire world," for "humanity as such," beyond a parochial narrowness focused on inner-church issues or on one place or nation. Here "the rights of the human person" are of paramount importance. Six weeks before, on Easter 1963, he had issued the encyclical *Pacem in Terris*, with an extended passage on human rights. That encyclical soon became a bright beacon guiding Vatican II, especially in its formulation of its *ad extra* declarations on religious liberty and on the church's relation to the modern world.

John sensed that the past fifty years have brought the Catholic church face to face with new realities. But with the challenges, the times have given as well new capabilities through the "doctrinal deepening" that he mentions and through a better understanding of the perennial Gospel of Christ—which John expressed for Vatican II in his opening discourse of October 11, 1962.[3]

2. As Pope John spoke, his secretary Fr. Loris Capovilla recorded his words, which the latter published in *Giovanni XXIII: Quindici Letture* (Rome: Edizioni di storia e letteratura, 1970), 475. These words have become the final entry in the revised *Giornale dell'anima* (*Journal of a Soul*), ed. A. Melloni (Bologna: Istituto per le scienze religiose, 2003). The translation from Italian is by Jared Wicks.

3. The "doctrinal deepening" probably does not refer to the currents of the *nouvelle théologie* or the liturgical movement, for which Archbishop Roncalli had showed little sympathy when he was Nuncio in France (1945–53). He found these overly intellectualist. Critical remarks about confusing innovations are scattered through his diaries of those years, *Anni di Francia*, ed. Étienne Fouilloux (Bologna: Istituto di scienze religiose, 2004–6). A

Furthermore, Pope John's own biography contains the seeds of his orientations, which converge and fuse with the aims of the council over which he presided. Experiences during his service of the Holy See "in the East" and in France confirm his belief in opportunities for the good and in being called to take the long view toward the future in confidence—about which he has convinced the council fathers as well.

Following the indications of this declaration by John XXIII, it will help to quickly review parts of his biography to show several seeds both of his convoking of Vatican II and of his expressions of its aims. His actions as pope have their background in his experiences, which were quite different from those of previous popes and from those of the officials in the Vatican in 1958, when John assumed the papal office.[4]

(1) In January 1901, Angelo Roncalli, already a seminarian of the Diocese of Bergamo, began his theology studies in the Roman Seminary. In a notebook of excerpts from his reading at that time, he copied a passage from the bishop of Peoria, John Lancaster Spalding, which for him breathed the freshness of the "new world." Roncalli wrote, "We must exclude sterile attachments to the past and to dead realities. Better things are before us, not behind us. . . . The ancient faith, if it is to be held vitally, we must celebrate with an energy which is wholly youthful." The young Roncalli found this to be "full of life and of a good and holy modernity."[5] Here is a distant and little-known American root of the optimistic hopes with

---

more likely point of reference is his sense of the distinction between the dogmatic substance of the faith and the possible variations in updated explanations and expressions to help make truths of faith sources of personal renewal and rejuvenation.

4. What follows is given with more details in chapter 1, above.

5. Marco Roncalli gives these excerpts in his ample biography, *Giovanni XXIII. Angelo Giuseppe Roncalli: Una vita nella storia* (Milan: Mondadori, 2006), 59–60. The text by Spalding was the lecture he gave in Rome in March 1900, "Education and the Future of Religion," which appeared later that year in Italian in the journal *Rassegna nazionale*. The original English text is a chapter in Spalding's book, *Religion, Agnosticism and Education* (Chicago: McClurg, 1903), 147–92.

which Roncalli approached his priestly ministry and then as pope took the momentous action of convoking Vatican Council II.

(2) Angelo Roncalli was ordained for the Diocese of Bergamo in 1904 and served as secretary for his bishop, Giacomo M. Radini Tedeschi, from 1905 into 1914, while teaching church history in the seminary. He accompanied the bishop's pastoral visitation of the 380 parishes of the diocese. Bishop Radini was for Roncalli an ideal churchman, energetic, close to people, not fearing to undertake pastoral and social projects, and still carrying out the duties laid down for bishops by the Council of Trent. As a historian Roncalli saw Bishop Radini's continuity with Charles Borromeo and Francis de Sales who, three centuries before, had implemented in diocesan and parish practice Trent's decrees on episcopal and pastoral residence, preaching, seminaries, and Catholic sacramental and devotional life.[6] Here is a seed of Pope John's insistence on Vatican II exercising a conciliar Magisterium that is above all "pastoral" in orientation, so as to contribute to the renewal of Catholic life in the dioceses and parishes of the world.

(3) During World War I (1915–18), Roncalli was an army chaplain ministering to the wounded and dying in military hospitals, where he came to appreciate goodness and nobility in the soldiers who, however, were in many cases far from the Catholic church.

(4) The years 1925 to 1944 were Roncalli's "twenty years in the East" as the papal representative in Bulgaria and then in Turkey and Greece—all countries with tiny Catholic communities amidst long-standing hostility to the Catholic church. Consecrated bishop in 1925, he oversaw Bulgarian Catholics in a land officially committed to the Orthodox church, where however he became a friends of the Orthodox Metropolitan, Stefan. In Turkey, he lived

6. Young Fr. Roncalli wrote a biography of Bishop Radini, translated as *My Bishop* (New York: McGraw-Hill, 1969). A long-time project was Roncalli's critical edition of the manuscript records of the pastoral visitation of the Bergamo diocese in 1575 by St. Charles Borromeo, who came to Bergamo along with ten associate visitors, to implement the reform decrees of the Council of Trent. See above, in chapter 1.

in Istanbul amid millions of Muslims. In a characteristic diary entry of July 1936, Roncalli wrote, "I love these dear Turks in Christ crucified and I cannot stand it when Christians speak ill of them."[7] The always reflective Archbishop Roncalli gave long thought to the good qualities he appreciated in Orthodox Christians and in the non-Christians among whom he lived.

(5) Then, from 1944 to 1953, Roncalli was in Paris as papal nuncio to France, at a crossroads of Europe, meeting many French exponents of the aggressively "lay" character of public life. But in France, he also read Yves Congar's *True and False Reform in the Church*.[8]

(6) From 1953 to 1958, as cardinal archbishop of Venice, Roncalli went to the parishes on visits and held a diocesan synod. His 1956 Lenten pastoral letter urged Venetian Catholics to take up regular scripture reading for their personal formation in faith and spirituality, much in the way the council's *Dei Verbum*, no. 25, urges Bible reading upon all Catholics.[9]

Roncalli's vision of history featured remarkable individuals, like St. Charles Borromeo and Bishop Radini, whom he saw as "rejuvenators" of the church. For Roncalli, the church had, from Christ and the Holy Spirit, an inner capacity to meet challenges, to adapt itself to changing times, and by this to show its perennial youthfulness.[10] Here is a seed of the calling of Vatican II, which he

7. Diary entry of July 26, 1936, in *La mia vita in Oriente. Agende del delegato apostolico*, ed. Valeria Martano (Bologna: Istituto per le scienze religiose, 2006–8), 1:204.

8. During Vatican II's fourth period, Yves Congar noted in his diary that Joseph Greco, SJ, a *peritus* of the Commission on the Missions, had told him that in 1952 he, Greco, visited Roncalli in Paris, who spoke about Congar's book, which came out in French in 1950, which he was reading. *My Journal of the Council*, 816, entry of October 19, 1965.

9. The diaries of the Venice years are *Pace e Vangelo: Agende del patriarca*, ed. Galavotti. The 1956 pastoral letter is "La Sacra Scrittura e san Lorenzo Giustiniani. Lettera pastorale per la Quaresima," in Angelo Giuseppe Cardinal Roncalli, *Scritti e discorsi* (Rome: Edizioni Paoline, 1959), 2:329–51.

10. In a retreat note from 1910: "The church contains in itself the eternal youthfulness of truth arising from Christ who belongs to all times." At an episcopal consecration in 1938: "The youthfulness of the church is evident in its ongoing life and the insertion of new pastors into the apostolate of Christ." As he left Venice in 1958 for the conclave which

wanted to be a demonstration of the church as youthful, adaptive, and large-hearted.[11] From John XXIII's ecclesiology of "ongoing rejuvenation," one can understand Vatican II's goal of *aggiornamento* in a much more profoundly spiritual and theological way, beside which the image of "opening the windows to the world" pales into the superficiality of a bumper sticker.

The Pre-Conciliar Loneliness of John XXIII— Broken Only in Moments

Three months after being elected pope, John took a decisive step on January 25, 1959, when he announced that he was going to convoke a council. But he remained for a while quite alone in his vision of a rejuvenating council.

A sobering experience was Pope John's first series of one-on-one audiences with the heads of the Vatican congregations. These had been regularly scheduled, but in the 1950s Pope Pius XII had let them drop. After his election, John XXIII began them afresh. Later, he said that many in the Curia have narrow mentalities, as few of them were ever outside Rome or central Italy, and so they do not see major church issues in a universal perspective.[12]

In late summer and autumn 1959, Pope John had letters sent to the world's Catholic bishops, asking them, the future fathers

---

elected him as pope: "We are not here in the church on earth as custodians of a museum, but instead are called to cultivate a thriving garden, full of life, which has a glorious future." At an audience as pope, September 2, 1962: "The church is the guardian of the ongoing youthfulness of the Gospel."

11. Correspondingly, he was all his life long pained by those, for example, in the Bergamo clergy who see the present as worse than the past and fear new ventures. A diary note of 1918: "I never knew a pessimist who brought a good project to a successful end." Again, in 1938, they "criticize everything, make malevolent interpretations and aggressive condemnations. What an affliction of my spirit."

12. From the diary of Fr. Roberto Tucci, Director of *La Civiltà cattolica*, after his audience with Pope John on February 9, 1963, published in *Giovanni XIII e la preparazione del Concilio Vaticano II nei diari inediti del Direttore della* Civiltà cattolica *Padre Roberto Tucci*, ed. Giovanni Sale (Milan: Jaca Book, 2012), 160.

of Vatican II, to suggest council topics and proposals. The canvass brought in nearly two thousand responses from 77 percent of those asked, but very few of them breathed the spirit of John XXIII. Most were cautious in their concern with modifying canonical fine points. There were calls for the council to define that the Virgin Mary was *Co-redemptrix* and/or *Mediatrix* of all graces. Many gave "isms" for the council to condemn, such as communism, the relativism of situation ethics, or neo-modernism in Catholic theology. Some creative proposals were made, especially by bishops who prepared their proposals in consultation, for example, on restoring the permanent diaconate, renewing the liturgy, or reforming practices of the Curia, but very few of these urged the council to deal with problems of the contemporary world.[13]

In October 1959, a prominent Italian cardinal, the archbishop of Palermo, spoke at the Lateran University on the first anniversary of John XXIII's election. He said that a principal work of the coming council would be to render definitive the teachings of recent popes in the encyclicals from Leo XIII to Pius XII. If Vatican II restated their content with the higher authority of a council, this would raise their enunciated doctrine and their censures of deviance above any future questioning.[14]

But Pope John also had some moments of consolation showing he was not completely alone in wanting a rejuvenation of the Catholic church. In June 1960, when he established ten commissions to prepare draft documents for the council, he also brought into being the Secretariat for Promoting the Unity of Christians, a Vatican ecumenical office. Pope John appointed Cardinal Bea as president of this body, with the mandate to aid the commissions and in time the council itself to make a Catholic contribution to furthering the cause of Christian unity. Even though Bea was, like the pope, seventy-nine years old in 1960, he took up his new

13. Étienne Fouilloux presents the pre-preparatory proposals in *History of Vatican II*, ed. Alberigo and Komonchak, 1:97–132.

14. Ruffini, "Il Santo Padre Giovanni XXIII," 7–28.

mission with alacrity and the Secretariat was soon making creative proposals of theological *ressourcement*.[15]

In early 1962 the pope read the Italian translation of an address by Cardinal Joseph Frings, archbishop of Cologne and president of the German bishops' conference. Frings surveyed changes in the world since Vatican I, ninety years earlier, to show the spiritual and intellectual characteristics of the world in which Vatican II would be held. Consequences follow for the council from the increased sense of human unity, the impact of technology, and the influence of ideologies. When Frings was next in Rome, John called him to the papal residence to thank him for setting forth a vision agreeing with his own concerning the council's situation and tasks. Frings had to explain that his lecture was prepared for him by Prof. Ratzinger, then teaching near Cologne, but still this showed the pope that his hopes were resonating positively in one part of the world episcopate.[16]

As the opening of Vatican II came nearer, Pope John also read the Lenten pastoral letter on expectations of the council, published by the archbishop of Malines/Mechlen, Belgium, Cardinal Leo Josef Suenens. In an audience with Suenens, John expressed his agreement and the two discussed the problem of the huge number—and the mediocrity—of the schemas of the preparatory commissions. At the pope's request, in May 1962, Suenens presented to John a five-page note on organizing the council's work. About 80 percent of the prepared texts should go to postconciliar commissions and to the body entrusted with revising the Code of Canon Law. What remains should be divided between issues *ad extra*, in which the church speaks to the great issues of the world of the day, and issues *ad intra*, internal aspects of

15. On this initiative of long-term impact, see Stransky, "The Foundation of the Secretariat for Promoting Christian Unity," in *Vatican II Revisited*, ed. Stacpoole, 62–87. The early texts produced by the Secretariat are given in *Dialogo e rinnovamento (1960–1962)*, ed. Velati. See above, chapter 4, which presents this work and its impact.

16. I digested the Frings address, with translated excerpts, in "Six Texts by Prof. Joseph Ratzinger as *peritus*," 253–61.

church life, especially on how it becomes effective in its mission. The pope encouraged Suenens to further develop his plan by consulting other cardinals, including Giovanni Battista Montini (Milan, Italy), Achille Liénart (Lille, France), Giuseppe Siri (Genoa, Italy), and Julius Döpfner (Munich, Germany). From this, the pope had Suenens's "plan" in his hands by July 1962.[17] Some points from Suenens, including the structural division of outward/inward directed actions, entered the important September 11, 1962, radio address by John XXIII on the council about to open in a month's time.

Pope John XXIII's "Convocatory" Declarations on Vatican II

On three occasions, Pope John spoke publicly about the topics and aims of Vatican II, namely, in his Christmas 1961 Apostolic Constitution formally convoking the council to meet during 1962; in his radio address of September 11, 1962; and most famously in his inaugural discourse *Gaudet Mater Ecclesia* as Vatican II opened on October 11, 1962.

(1) *Humanae Salutis*, delivered on Christmas 1961, first contrasted crises in society, in which "distrustful souls see only darkness burdening the face of the earth" with John's reaffirmation of trust in Christ "who has not left the world that he redeemed."[18] Much in the world facilitates the church's apostolate: "although the world may appear profoundly changed, the Christian community ... has strengthened itself in unity; it has been reinvigorated intellectually; it has been interiorly purified." Where there is spiritual poverty in the world, this contrasts with the vibrant

17. Suenens wrote on this in "A Plan for the Whole Council," in *Vatican II Revisited*, ed. Stacpoole, 88–105, in appendix I, the outline of March 1962, and in appendix IV, the plan of May. Also, Mathijs Lamberigts and Leo Declerck, "The Role of Cardinal Léon-Joseph Suenens at Vatican II," in *The Belgian Contribution to the Second Vatican Council*, 61–217, at 66–75.

18. *Council Daybook*, 6–9; Latin original in *Acta Apostolicae Sedis* 54 (1962): 5–13.

vitality of the church of Christ. The coming council will concern itself with promoting the sanctification of church members and the articulation of revealed truth. It will turn to the problems and worries of the world, concerned to heighten in people a proper sense of their human dignity, to reaffirm the moral order and Catholic social doctrine, and so to benefit family life, education, and civil society.

(2) A month before Vatican II opened, the pope spoke on the radio about the council.[19] Seven draft documents had gone out to the council's members and Pope John had studied these during his August vacation at Castel Gandolfo. Early in the address, he recalled the symbolism of the Easter candle and the cry *"Lumen Christi"* answered by *"Deo gratias,"* for councils are encounters with the risen Lord in which the church reaffirms her grateful "Yes" to the mission Christ has given it. The council will concern the church's vitality *ad intra*, by presenting the light of its doctrine and the sanctifying power of grace.

But John then spoke expansively on issues *ad extra* in the world, about human aspirations which will have their echo in the council: issues of the family, work, peace among nations, education, culture, social duties, and the freedom that corresponds to human dignity. This longer portion of the address featured topics largely absent from the draft decrees already in the hands of the bishops. The contrast was striking and had to raise questions about John XXIII's readiness to give his backing to the first drafttexts. His heart seemed instead to be reaching out in solidarity to embrace the wider world of the human family.

(3) Then, as Vatican II opened, Pope John gave his address of October 11, 1962, which was cited often in 2012 on its fiftieth anniversary. Instead of condensing its abundance here, what follows will look ahead to the appeals made to it and to how it was cited in the following weeks of council debate. This is to consid-

19. *Council Daybook*, 18–21; Italian original in *Acta Apostolicae Sedis* 54 (1962): 678–85.

er the opening discourse in terms of its effective impact. Pope John's *Gaudet Mater Ecclesia* injected concerns and hopes into Vatican II's first period. As the council went to work, the pope listened attentively to hear echoes of these concerns in the fathers' interventions. In time, he sensed that his aims, orientations, and goals were in fact taking hold in the minds of many, even of most, of the council members.[20]

Four Crucial Days of Vatican II Debate (November 1962)

As is well known, the first schema discussed at the council, for three weeks, was the draft Constitution on Liturgical Renewal.[21] The cardinals and bishops who spoke on it were divided over the schema's proposals of introducing vernacular languages, eucharistic communion under both forms and the concelebration of Mass, and giving key roles to national or regional episcopal conferences in preparing the changes that would be called for. But on November 14 the liturgy debate wound down and the council fathers were asked whether they approved the draft-text in its main lines as the basis of further work, while the Commission would revise details in accord with their suggestions. Surprisingly, of the 2,208 who voted, 2,162 voted *placet*, giving their basic approval to the schema, with only 46 (2 percent) opposed, showing

20. Surveys of Vatican II's first period are Joseph Ratzinger, *Theological Highlights of Vatican II* (Mahwah, N.J.: Paulist Press, 2009; originally published in 1966), 17–54, and O'Malley, *What Happened at Vatican II*, 93–159. The former work gives the account and reflections of a theologian who served as a council expert and wrote on the highlights shortly after each period of the council. The latter work is a historian's account, written later with wide use of the council's published records and interacting with other interpretations in a huge secondary literature.

21. The schema on the liturgy had 105 numbered paragraphs spread through eight chapters. The fifteen council meetings on it, from October 22 through November 13, 1962, included 328 oral addresses in St. Peter's, along with 377 written observations handed in by council fathers who did not speak to the assembly. Mathijs Lamberigts relates this discussion in *History of Vatican II*, ed. Alberigo and Komonchak, 2:107–66, esp. 112–49.

that the critics of the text had spoken only for themselves and had not convinced many others. Something was moving in this huge assembly and Pope John, listening by a private radio connection to what was said in the council hall, was surely pleased that the goal of rejuvenation was taking hold. However, only fifteen of the seven hundred oral and written interventions included appeals to the pope's pastoral and ecumenical aims, with none of these appeals referring explicitly to his addresses on September 11 or on the day of the council's formal opening.[22]

November 14 was also the first day of debate on the draft-text "on the sources of revelation."[23] This came from the Preparatory Theological Commission and treated tradition as a source of revealed teachings that are not in scripture, biblical inspiration, biblical interpretation, and scripture in church life, that is, as read by Catholics, as interpreted by Catholic exegetes, and as serving in Catholic theology as a basis of work. As the fathers read the text of twenty-nine paragraphs, many noted three places issuing censures (*reprobat ... damnat*) of theologians of inspiration and of scholars of the Gospels.[24]

---

22. In *Acta Synodalia*, 1.1–2, scattered fathers argue in favor of the draft because it will promote Pope John's aim of updating, revitalization, and the "*scopus pastoralis*" (pastoral objective) he has given to the council (e.g., Bishop Ancel, 1.1:449; Bishop Zak, 1.2:150; Bishop Hoa Nguyen Van Hien, 1.2:613). On October 27, Bishop Marcos McGrath (Panama) opened his remarks in favor of the draft by recalling that the pope has gathered the pastors, "*ad renovationem Ecclesiae in sua missione et in suo cultu* [for renewing the church in his mission and worship]" (1.1:517). Only two participants appealed to the ecumenical goal of Pope John as a reason favoring adoption of the schema (Bishop Mendes Arceo, 1.1:358; Archbishop Hallinan of Atlanta, 1.2:75).

23. The text is in *Acta Synodalia*, 1.3:14–26; in English in Joseph A. Komonchak, as "On the Sources of Revelation," in the section, *The Council That Might Have Been*, at https://jakomonchak.wordpress.com/category/Vatican-II. Karim Schelkens presents the genesis of the schema in the Preparatory Theological Commission in *Catholic Theology of Revelation on the Eve of Vatican II. A Redaction History of the Schema* De fontibus revelationis (1960–1962) (Leiden: Brill, 2010).

24. In the text, three strong censures drew attention, namely, of any effort to "extenuate" the nature of biblical inspiration ("*Ecclesia omnino reprobat*" [the church thoroughly rejects] in no. 8), of denials of the historical truth of Gospel narratives of the deeds of Jesus ("*Synodus illos damnat errores*" [the council condemns those errors] in no. 21), and of attributions to the

In eighty-two speeches over four days, the council members evaluated the schema *De Fontibus* as a whole, with some sharp clashes, as thirty-two speakers expressed their disapproval of the draft-text and urged their fellow council members to join them in voting it down. Of these thirty-two dissenters, eighteen appealed to Pope John's intentions for the council, especially to *Gaudet Mater Ecclesia*, with which they said the schema did not conform but instead breathed another spirit. Suddenly, the pope's aims and intentions in convoking Vatican II became a crucial factor in the council's development. After four days of such exchanges, a momentous vote occurred on November 20.

In the debate, on November 14, Cardinal Frings said that the tone of *De Fontibus* was that of a professor defending theses, lacking that "pastoral note with which the Holy Father ardently wants council statements to be imbued." Cardinal Paul-Émile Léger (Montréal, Canada) said that fear of errors underlay the text, making it dissonant with "the spirit of positive renewal desired by the Pope in this council." Cardinal Bernard Alfrink (Utrecht, Netherlands) cited Pope John from October 11 on the council's aims: we are not here to repeat settled doctrine, but to enunciate Catholic truths in a way promoting unity with separated Christians. Cardinal Bea repeated this, indicating that the council should penetrate Catholic teaching more deeply and then give it a fresh expression which will affect souls, for as the pope said, our Magisterium is "pre-eminently pastoral." Two bishops from Indonesia said that their conference had compared the schema with what the pope said as the council began, and so they propose a thorough revision of *De Fontibus* and of the three other drafts from the Theological Commission, so that the council may effectively attain its pastoral goal.[25]

---

evangelist or the community of the words given as from Jesus in the gospels' texts ("*Synodus errores damnat*" [the council condemns the errors] in no. 22).

25. *Acta Synodalia*, 1.3:34 (Frings), 41 (Léger), 43–44 (Alfrink), 49 (Bea), and 55–59 (Manek and Soegijapranata, both from Indonesia). But at the end, Archbishop Morcillo Gonzalez spoke for forty-seven Spanish bishops who judged *De Fontibus* to be a valid foundation

On November 16, the second day of the debate, those opposed were outnumbered by those favorable to the schema such as the cardinals of Lisbon, Los Angeles, Buenos Aires, and Manila. For these, the first pastoral and ecumenical duty of a council is to propose the whole of Catholic truth. But the French Cardinal Joseph Lefebvre (Bourges) countered that the schema's lack of any elegance to attract souls makes it dissonant with the pastoral concern of the pope's opening discourse. Cardinal Raul Silva Henriquez (Santiago, Chile) spoke for several Latin American bishops against the document, contrasting its condemnations with "the medicine of mercy," privileged by the pope in *Gaudet Mater Ecclesia*. Abbot Christopher Butler (Downside Abbey, England) saw a clash between the schema and the pope's hope that the council would announce good news to the world. Touching up the present text will not remedy its defects. But because a doctrinal text like this must gain virtually unanimous approval, the council needs another text—an intervention with which several fathers registered agreement in the next two days.[26]

On the third day of debate, November 17, the schema had several backers, but two speakers, Cardinal Döpfner and Archbishop Jean Zoa (Yaoundé, Cameroon), opposed the schema in the name of many bishops who signed on to their interventions—many German fathers with Döpfner and many other Africans with Zoa. Both Döpfner and Zoa added weight to their case by naming those who had already cited *Gaudet Mater Ecclesia* as their criterion for opposing the schema (Alfrink, Bea, Frings, Léger, Silva Henriquez, and Joseph Lefebvre). At the end of the day, Archbishop Julio Rosales (Cebu, Philippines), said that because John XXIII had approved distribution of the text, the council members should hear what he thinks of it.[27]

---

for the council's work (*Acta Synodalia*, 1.3:59–62), as had Cardinals Ruffini (Palermo), Siri (Genoa), and Quiroga y Palacios (Compostella) earlier (37–38, 38–39, 39–41).

26. *Acta Synodalia*, 1.3:74–76 (Lefebvre), 81–82 (Silva Henriquez), and 104–7 (Butler).

27. Ibid., 125–26 (Döpfner), 148 (Zoa), and 155–56 (Rosales). Pope John's answer came on November 21, in his act of removing *De Fontibus* from the agenda and creating a

On the fourth day of debate, November 19, Cardinal Valeri-
an Gracias (Bombay) hoped that a joint group of the backers and
opponents could work together on a new text "which would correspond more with the goal of the council and the intention of
the Pope." Cardinal Albert Gregory Meyer (Chicago) agreed that
the schema did not agree with the aim set by the pope's inaugural
allocution and so a new text was needed, for which Cardinal Bea
had given guidelines. The auxiliary bishop of Caracas, Luis Henriquez Jiminez, cited *Gaudet Mater* as the basis for all the Venezuelan bishops wanting *De Fontibus* to be taken off the agenda. A
highlight of the day was the intervention by Bishop Emiel-Josef
De Smedt (Bourges, Belgium), speaking on behalf of the Unity
Secretariat, to explain what would be an ecumenically constructive style of Catholic teaching—in which *De Fontibus* was defective—but which Pope John wants in documents of the council.
Archbishop Denis Hurley (Durban, South Africa) said that John
XXIII had specified the goal as pastoral, but for this just defining
the truth is not enough, for the mode of speech must show revelation's expansive power and bring the reader or hearer to experience delight in the truth.[28]

Finally, on November 20, the council members were asked to
decide the fate of the schema *De Fontibus*. But, in an action found
strange by several observers, the board of presidents did not ask
the members to give a judgment of *placet* or *non placet* on the
schema itself, as had been done a week before on the draft-text on
liturgical renewal. Instead, the motion was on procedure: does it
please the fathers to interrupt treatment of *De Fontibus Revelatio-*

Joint Commission (from the Doctrinal Commission and the Secretariat for Promoting Unity among Christians) to revise it.

28. *Acta Synodalia*, 1.3:166–68 (Gracias), 169–70 (Meyer), 178–79 (Henriquez
Jiminez), 184–86 (De Smedt), and 198–200 (Hurley). Archbishop Hurley mentioned as a
good example of pastorally positive expression the Unity Secretariat's schema *De Verbo Dei*
(The Word of God) approved in the June 1962 meeting of the Central Preparatory Commission. I give that text in English in "Scripture Reading Urged *vehementer* (DV no. 25)," 573–
77, reprinted in *Fifty Years On. Probing the Riches of Vatican II*, ed. Schultenhover, 383–87.

nis by setting the text aside? Thus, opponents of the schema had to vote *placet*, agreeing to interrupt debate, while its backers had to vote *non placet*, against the interruption. This was explained in Latin, French, Spanish, German, English, and Arabic. Despite some remaining confusion, those voting to interrupt debate and set the text aside were 1,368 council members, 62 percent of those voting. Those wanting to keep the schema on the agenda were 822. But the council's rules stipulated that passage of a procedural vote required a two-thirds majority. So, the November 20 motion to interrupt did not carry, and the council seemed destined to discuss chapter by chapter a text which a majority had wanted removed from the immediate agenda.

But the vote was still of enormous importance, as it showed that the speakers of the previous days who spoke against the schema, although making up fewer than half of those heard from (thirty-two of eighty-two), had swayed a majority of the council members, 62 percent, by their arguments, especially by their appeals to Pope John XXIII's goals, which the document was said not to promote. The pope was buoyed up by this evidence of his goals taking hold and so he intervened. The next day's assembly, on November 21, began with a notice that the pope was removing the text *De Fontibus Revelationis* from the immediate agenda and setting up a new Joint Commission, with members from the Doctrinal Commission and the Unity Secretariat, to rework the text, by emending, abbreviating, and improving it, so it could in time come back in a revised form and gain the full approval of the council fathers.[29]

Pope John's Directives to the Council

The intervention by the pope on November 21 was not the end, but instead the beginning, of his actions to steer Vatican II along paths on which he now knew many council members were ready

29. *Acta Synodalia*, 1.3:259.

to follow. On December 6, the council members heard read out a set of directives, coming from the pope, on the work to be done in the months following, before they would reconvene on September 8, 1963. The next day, December 7, the text of these directives was in their hands in a booklet.[30]

First, the council's commissions are mandated to once more examine the texts they have produced or are still working on. A new context has been set by the clarification of the council's goals, and so they must reevaluate the work done so far. Second, this examination has its guidelines, namely those given in Pope John's inaugural discourse of October 11, from which the text cited twenty-eight lines, to leave no doubt about the norms of work in this new phase. John gave *Gaudet Mater Ecclesia* an effective impact on what is to follow in Vatican II. This appears in six guidelines cited from or based on his opening discourse:

1. Study afresh all Catholic doctrine, with a view to its deeper penetration of souls

2. Reformulate Catholic teaching in ways that our times require

3. Truths of the deposit of faith are given; now find for them better formulations

4. Act as a Catholic Magisterium that is prevalently pastoral in nature

5. Raising the torch of truth, the church regards with maternal love its estranged children among other Christians

6. To suffering humankind, we say with Peter, "Silver and gold I have not, but what I have I give you, 'in the name of Jesus Christ, rise and walk'" (Acts 3:6)

This is how Pope John's words at the opening of Vatican II entered the council's work, in the form of directives for revising the texts that Vatican II would take up for treatment.[31]

---

30. *Acta Synodalia*, 1.1:96–98; partial English translation, *Council Daybook*, 114.

31. Pope John also cited the central passage of his October 11 inaugural, in Italian, on

Third, John mandated that the revised draft-texts be subject-
ed to a selection process in order to assure that the council would
move ahead only on topics pertaining to the universal church,
to all believers in Christ, or to the whole human family. Other
matters should pass to a commission for the revising the Code of
Canon Law or to post-conciliar commissions which will be set up
to deal with special issues.

Fourth, this work of selection and revision in the council
commissions will be supervised by a Coordinating Commission
of seven cardinals, which will soon be created. They will follow
closely this new phase of commission work, especially to ensure
that the revised schemas conform to the goals of the council—as
these have now been clarified. Fifth, the commissions should
expand their competency, by consulting others, especially those
experienced in the pastoral and apostolic works of the church.
Sixth, and finally, once the schemas are ready, they will go by
mail to the council members, who must examine them and send
in their feedback, so that the commissions may further emend
their texts before they come up for evaluation in the council hall.

This was how Pope John XXIII took charge of Vatican II. Some
early results emerged when the Coordinating Commission began
reviewing and formulating tasks for the commissions in early 1963, as Vatican II's "second preparation" began.[32] This work
was now clearly under directives and criteria given by Pope John.
His goals had "taken hold." Now the commissions had to translate
them into texts which the council will adopt with the aim of rejuvenating the church *ad intra* and speaking words *ad extra* of guidance, healing, and encouragement to the whole human family.

December 23, at his pre-Christmas gathering of the cardinals and officials of the Roman
Curia. *Acta Apostolicae Sedis* 55 (1963): 43–45, at 44–45.

32. Jan Grootaers gives an ample narrative in "The Drama Continues between the
Acts: the 'Second Preparation' and Its Opponents," in *History of Vatican II*, ed. Alberigo and
Komonchak, 2:359–495. Grootaers's reference to "opponents" indicates the existence of
pockets of resistance to the new directions, especially, it turned out, in council commissions in which some influential members held doggedly to the drafts already prepared.

Two Further Words of Pope John XXIII

A notable statement by Pope John went out in his Epiphany 1963 letter on the council addressed to each bishop of the Catholic church.[33] He insisted that during the recess the council's work continues, not only in the commissions but as well in the focused attention of all the bishops, who should keep in mind the council's topics. Even though the pope will in time officially promulgate documents expressing Vatican II's decisions, "it is nevertheless the duty of the council Fathers to put forward all such decrees, deliberate on them, decide on their final form, and eventually subscribe to them together with the Roman Pontiff." The council is having a worldwide impact. "Indeed, the energy and activity displayed by the church in recent months has exceeded all expectations. Such is the joyful and consoling news that reaches us daily from all quarters of the globe. It is indicative of the church's abundant vitality." He is very pleased with the presence of the delegated observers from the separated communities. This prompts his reflection that while the council must deal with realities which impact the lives of Catholics, it cannot confine itself to these; otherwise, it would be inadequate to Christ, who gave himself for the sins of the whole world (1 Jn 2:2). Thus, the council members must be ready to receive draft-texts which will look *ad extra* and speak to points of urgency for the well-being of all peoples.

Finally, for interpreting the "first movement" of Vatican II in 1962, we have another statement by Pope John, recorded by Fr. Roberto Tucci, director of *La Civiltà cattolica*, after a long audience with the pope on February 9, 1963. Tucci had asked how the pope saw the council's work so far.

He said that he was fully satisfied. The council entered fully into its work only during the final weeks, when it began to grasp the implications of his message of September and his inaugural address of October 11....

33. Latin text, entitled "Mirabilis ille," in *Acta Apostolicae Sedis* 55 (1963): 149–59, in English in *The Encyclicals and Other Messages of John XXIII*, ed. John F. Cronin, Francis X. Murphy, and Ferrer Smith (Washington: TPS Press, 1964), 444–58.

During the first session, he preferred not to intervene in the debates, so as to leave to the Fathers their freedom of discussion and the chance to find on their own the right way.... The bishops had to learn on their own, and they had done so.[34]

A Glance Ahead to Vatican II's Documentary Outcome

The "second preparation," set in motion and guided by Pope John XXIII, led directly into the further unfolding of Vatican II during the council's three further periods and in the sixteen Vatican II documents approved and then promulgated by Pope Paul VI. The documents are the lasting fruit, which Catholics and the world now have, of what Pope John initiated.

Ad intra Vatican II gives us *Dei Verbum*, on God's saving revelation and inspired scripture. Vatican II gives us *Lumen Gentium*, on the mystery of the church and the universal call to holiness. And Vatican II gives us *Sacrosanctum Concilium*, on the worship by those associated with Christ the high priest in glorifying God and sanctifying souls. These are three notable texts that can still promote what John XXIII longed for, that is, the church's ongoing rejuvenation.

Ad extra Vatican II gives us and gives the world *Gaudium et Spes*, on human dignity and on human tasks in the face of critical issues of modern life (family, culture, economic activity, war and peace). Vatican II gives us and the world *Nostra Aetate,* on respect for the world religions and especially on the Jews as our elder brothers in covenant with God. Vatican II gives us and the world *Dignitatis Humanae*, on the basic human right of immunity from any coercion regarding religion. These are three notable words to humankind, loving words of solidarity and wise guidance, well aligned with the intentions of Pope John XXIII toward a better life for humanity in our world.

---

34. From *Giovanni XIII*, ed. Sale, 159–60, translated from Italian by Jared Wicks.

7

Vatican II in 1963

Renewing Ecclesiology and Turning to
Ecumenical Engagement

This chapter on Vatican II's second period in 1963 will move
through five topics, walking at a deliberate pace for some and
moving more briskly for others. First comes a visit to the council
during a normal meeting, or "congregation." Second, the chapter
offers a global scheme of the council's dynamics and dramas. In
the third place comes an appreciative introduction to Vatican II's
new leader in 1963, Pope Paul VI. Fourth, there is a brief review
of the topics of the chapter title, ecclesiology and ecumenism.
Finally, I will take note of the council's advance in 1963 to completing the Liturgy Constitution, but with a fateful coincidence of
date with another event far from Rome.[1]

This chapter was originally published as "Vatican II's Turn in 1963: Toward Renewing
Catholic Ecclesiology and Validating Catholic Ecumenical Engagement," *Josephinum Journal
of Theology* 19 (2012 [published 2014]): 194–206. It was given as a lecture at the Pontifical
College Josephinum, Columbus, Ohio, on October 16, 2013.

1. Surveys of Vatican II's second period are Ratzinger, *Theological Highlights of Vatican II*,
55–123, and O'Malley, *What Happened at Vatican II*, 160–98.

A Day's Work at Vatican Council II

On October 16, 1963, the 2,200 members of the Second Vatican Council assembled in St. Peter's Basilica at 9 a.m. This was the forty-ninth general meeting of the council and the thirteenth assembly for work in 1963. The bishops first looked on as a bishop of the Coptic Catholic church of Egypt celebrated Mass with melodic Coptic chants that few understood. After the hour-long Mass, a deacon, accompanied by two acolytes, came to the altar to place there, on a small throne, a fifteenth-century manuscript volume of the four Gospels. That Gospel book lay open, in view of all, during every assembly of the council to express Christ's transcendent presidency over the Second Vatican Council.[2]

Then, during this October 16 meeting, nine speakers gave their evaluations of the draft-text of *De Ecclesia*, which had been sent to the members three months before. On that day they were on chapter II, concerning the church's hierarchical structure, mostly pertaining to the episcopate, but with a paragraph on priests and deacons.[3] A year later, in November 1964, a revised form of the whole text was chapter III of the Dogmatic Constitution on the Church, which begins, "*Lumen gentium cum sit Christus*" (Because Christ is the light of the nations).

Addresses by the council fathers on this chapter had begun on October 4, and 109 council members had already spoken on it. On the day before our meeting, October 15, the general secretary of the council asked the fathers to vote on ending interventions on the

2. During Vatican II's third period, the council members received a volume, in different languages, on the history, going back to the Council of Ephesus (431 A.D.), and the significance of daily "enthroning" the open Gospel book. It intends to express that Christ is presiding at the council. Romeo De Maio, *Le livre des évangiles dans les conciles œcuméniques* (Vatican City: Biblioteca Apostolica Vaticana, 1963). Henri de Lubac read De Maio's volume and once noted that the French Catholic newspaper, *La Croix*, amid its ample reporting on the council, never mentioned the enthroned Gospels. De Lubac, *Vatican Council Notebooks*, 2:279 and 363–64.

3. *Acta Synodalia*, 2.1:215–81, giving the 1963 draft of *De Ecclesia*, with what was then chap. II on 231–55, treating priests and deacons in no. 15 on 234–35.

chapter so they could move on to the next chapter, on the people of God, especially the laity, in the church. Those in favor of closing discussion were asked to stand up. The seminarian-assistants for each section of the banks of seats had begun counting those standing. But this ended quickly, as a large majority clearly favored ending discussion on the chapter.[4]

But as the session began on October 16, the general secretary announced that among those cut off from speaking by yesterday's vote, nine bishops were the designated spokesmen for groups of bishops. These included a speaker for a group of Polish bishops, one for the Melkite bishops of Lebanon, and another for the episcopal conference of Venezuela. The rules prescribed that such members should speak, even after a vote to close discussion. These nine got to speak on October 16, which added complexity to the discussion of the chapter. Regarding the passage on the diaconate, two of the nine spoke for restoring the permanent diaconate, but the Polish bishops were contrary, as the atheistic government of 1960s Poland would try to plant "moles" in this new part of the clergy.[5] The Melkite spokesman found the draft chapter on the episcopate excessively concerned to repeat statements on papal primacy as Vatican I had defined this in 1870. The present text should affirm the primacy quite strongly, but just once, and then calmly treat the foundation of the episcopate, the bishops' collegial unity, and their ministries of teaching, sanctifying, and governing. The Venezuelan bishops wanted another part of the text to say very clearly that it is by episcopal sacramental ordination that a bishop has the episcopal powers, while for exercising the powers in a diocese one needs a mission from the pope. This is important, the Venezuelans argued, to show that the fundamental structure of the church is sacramental and not ju-

---

4. *Acta Synodalia*, 2.1:597.

5. *Acta Synodalia*, 2.1:608–9 (bishops of Thailand and Laos for the diaconate), 623–24 (also the episcopal conference of Ecuador), and 624–26 (Polish bishops contrary).

ridical by its ordering of authorities established by God's will and specified by law.[6]

After the nine bishops spoke, the October 16 debate moved on to the draft chapter III, treating the people of God, especially the laity, with interventions that day by four cardinals. But the published record of this part of Vatican II gives, after the speeches on chapter II, no less than 150 written comments on that chapter by bishops and episcopal conferences who did not ask to speak, but handed in written comments on the chapter.[7] Their comments went together with the texts of the 115 speakers to make up a sizeable package of 887 pages, all on chapter II of *De Ecclesia*, principally on the episcopate. The council's Doctrinal Commission had these pages duplicated by mimeograph and then set up three teams of its member-bishops to review all the proposals on chapter II given by council members. The teams also included designated *periti* of the Commission. For example, both Rahner and Ratzinger were among the twenty-seven *periti* assigned to help on revising chapter II. Examination of all the interventions brought convergences to light, many of which confirmed the draft just discussed, while other comments voiced criticisms. The study identified some new enlightening amendments to this text and the other chapters. The revision process lasted into 1964, when the Doctrinal Commission produced a further draft of *De Ecclesia*, which was mailed to the council members, so they could prepare to vote on it during the Vatican II's third period in 1964.[8]

For the evening of October 16, 1963, Congar recorded in his council diary that he went with Rahner and other *periti* to a meet-

---

6. *Acta Synodalia*, 2.1:615–17 (the Melkite intervention) and 610–13 (Venezuelan bishops).

7. *Acta Synodalia*, 2.1:643–913.

8. Pope Paul VI approved the revised schema for sending to the fathers on July 3, 1964. It is published in *Acta Synodalia*, 3.1:158–373. The paragraphs of the new text were printed beside those of the prior text of 1963. An accompanying commentary (*Relatio*) gave reasons for every change in the text, usually by indicating an oral or written intervention by a council father who called for the modification which has entered the revised text.

ing with some Spanish bishops and their *periti* to discuss the next chapter on the people of God. A Spanish theologian proposed basing the chapter in definitions of a "rational sociology," but this made no impression. Instead, "Rahner, as always, monopolized the dialogue. He is marvelous, but he does not realize that when he is there, no room left for anything else." The Spaniards hoped to move out of their isolation, for example, by circulating a statement with a history-of-salvation framework, but the visitors could not help on this, as they were fully occupied in helping their own bishops and the council commissions.[9]

This sketch of a single day of work at Vatican II suggests what a huge ecclesial event the council was and introduces several parts of the complicated itinerary along which the council's draft-texts travelled before they became the sixteen final Vatican II documents.[10] Great care was taken to hear what the bishops of the church brought to the event. The commission work was taxing, both for the episcopal members and the *periti*. Great effort went into the renewal of Catholic teaching and the rejuvenation of Catholic life that Pope John XXIII had envisioned when he convened Vatican II.

A Global View and Interpretation of Vatican Council II

To know "what really happened at Vatican II," one naturally must take note of the number and kinds of documents the council issued, as the next chapter will review. But to go deeper, two Vatican II dramas are especially important. The first drama was surprising for many council participants, but it proved quite decisive. Early in the council, decisions were made to set aside most, but

9. Congar, *My Journal of the Council*, 379–80.
10. See the appendix of this chapter, below (185–86), giving a sketch of the full itinerary of a completed Vatican II document.

not all, of the texts produced by the commissions that had worked before Vatican II formally opened. This first drama focuses on the first period (1962) of the council. It unfolded through the gradual awakening of the bishops to dissatisfaction with many of the prepared schemas as not being right in tone and emphasis for the council's work. The preceding chapter introduced this development of 1962, with attention to Pope John XXIII's several statements of his council aims and objectives. His aims gradually took hold in the minds and hearts of most of the members to become guidelines for what the council should be doing. John XXIII gave criteria for revising, or even leaving behind, schemas not advancing these aims. As the first period ended in December 1962, Pope John issued directives on thoroughgoing revisions of the existing texts to make them conform more closely with his and the fathers' goals of church-wide spiritual and doctrinal renewal, along with turning in a welcoming way to other Christians and to the modern world.

This first drama had a long third act, which was Vatican II's "second preparation" during 1963, by the council's commissions, to revise some prepared texts, set others aside, and to assemble some new schemas.[11] The council majority then welcomed most of the new texts and put its own stamp on them by amendments before approving them as the Vatican II documents to be promulgated by Pope Paul VI.

Why were the revised texts of the second preparation welcomed as promoting the council's aims? One reason lies in the presence in the revised texts of a great harvest of twentieth-century, pre-conciliar, renewal movements in theology. The revised schemas made use of work by the Catholic pioneers—of 1930 to 1960—of biblical, liturgical, patristic, and ecumenical thought. These movements proved to constitute the effective theological

---

11. Jan Grootaers relates the first phase of implementing Pope John XXIII's goals between Vatican II's first and second periods, "The Drama Continues between the Acts," in *History of Vatican II*, ed. Alberigo and Komonchak, 2:359–495.

preparation for Vatican II, which, however, many of the appointed preparatory commissions of 1960–62 had neglected.[12] But these movements left many marks on the new and revised texts of the second preparation.

However, a satisfactory global account of Vatican II must also include the second major drama, about which Joseph Komonchak has written.[13] This broke out in 1964, during the third period of the council, when several divisions emerged amid groups of the council majority about what to feature in the revised schemas then moving toward approval. This second drama will be a topic of the following chapters of this volume, on Vatican II's third and fourth periods, to show how the divisions within the majority left their marks on council documents and especially how the divisions had their post-conciliar continuations. But what follows about the second period (1963) deals with the constructive results of the first great drama of the council.

The New Vatican II Leadership of Pope Paul VI

Pope Saint John XXIII died on June 3, 1963, and on June 21 the archbishop of Milan, Cardinal Giovanni Battista Montini, was elected as pope, taking the name Paul VI. People have said it was not easy for Paul VI to become pope while a general council was un-

12. The Louvain church historian Roger Aubert described the ferments of these pre-Vatican II renewal movements in *La théologie catholique au milieu du XXe siècle* (Paris: Casterman, 1954). O'Malley tells of the movements in *What Happened at Vatican II*, 71–80 (liturgical and patristic movements; new currents in philosophy) and 84–86 (Pius XII's biblical and liturgical encyclicals).

13. See "Recapturing the Great Tradition. In Memoriam Henri de Lubac," *Commonweal* (January 31, 1992): 14–17, and "Le valutazioni sulla *Gaudium et spes*: Chenu, Dosseti, Ratzinger," in *Volti di fine concilio. Studi di storia e teologia sulla conclusione del Vaticano II*, ed. Joseph Dore and Alberto Melloni (Bologna: Il Mulino, 2000), 115–53. The latter article is condensed as "Augustine, Aquinas or the Gospel *sine glossa*? Divisions over *Gaudium et spes*," in *Unfinished Journey: The Church 40 Years after Vatican II*, ed. Austen Ivereigh (London: Continuum, 2003), 102–18. Also, Jan Grootaers, "Diversité des tendencies à l'intérieur de la majorité conciliare: Gérard Philips et Giuseppe Dossetti," in *The Belgian Contribution to the Second Vatican Council*, 529–62.

derway—something like climbing into the engine as engineer of an already fast-moving train. But the image is wrong. Cardinal Montini was very much "on the train" from the beginning and he had his ideas about the journey and the destination. Paul VI knew the inner workings of Vatican II, because he served in 1961–62 on the Central Preparatory Commission and during the first period on the council's Secretariat for Extraordinary Matters.

In weekly meetings of the Secretariat during the first period of Vatican II, the eight cardinal-members had taken up numerous issues concerning the council's procedures, beginning with a far-reaching proposal by Cardinal Bea, president of the Secretariat for Promoting Christian Unity, on the aims of Vatican II. A Secretariat member, Cardinal Suenens, expounded to them his plan for organizing the council topics. Shortly after the council opened, Montini—the future Paul VI—submitted to the Secretariat a three-stage plan of movement through the council topics of (1) the mystery of the church itself; (2) the activities of the church *ad intra* in teaching, worship, and pastoral care; and (3) the relation of the church to the world around it, whether near (other Christians) or further away (culture, economics, other religions, enemies of the church).[14]

Cardinal Montini also gave a programmatic address in the closing days of the first period, on December 5, 1962, highlighting the task of issuing a comprehensive portrayal of the church itself. This would show how the church is rooted in Jesus Christ, from whom she receives all her being and her calling as the instrument by which he, the Lord, actively works to teach and sanctify. The episcopate needs treatment to complement what Vatican I, ninety years before, taught on papal primacy. But today the episcopate's sacramental foundation must stand out. In preparing a new sche-

---

14. Bea's proposal is in *Acta Synodalia*, 6.1:200–204, with Montini's following on 206–8. Suenens's plan given to the Secretariat is not in *Acta Synodalia*, but Lamberigts and Declerck treat it in "The Role of Cardinal Léon Joseph Suenens at Vatican II," in *The Belgian Contribution*, 61–217, at 75–78.

ma on the church, the Doctrinal Commission should collaborate with the Secretariat for Promoting the Unity of Christians.[15] Thus, when Paul VI began leading the council, he was well-informed and deeply engaged in Vatican II.

Furthermore, Paul VI undertook consultations on the future course of the council. One consultation began just nine days after his election, when Paul VI asked Cardinal Döpfner, a member of both the Secretariat for Extraordinary Affairs and of the council's Coordinating Commission, to suggest ways of making good progress in the council. Döpfner's suggestions came out in a recently published letter to Pope Paul.[16] Döpfner proposed, first, that the existing schemas be examined with a view to setting aside texts giving little promise of fostering the council's main goals. The central goal is the church's pastoral renewal, while grounding this theologically. An ecumenical concern must mark every document. Work toward the pastoral goal unfolds within a universal horizon in which topics are taken up which have significance for all peoples. For the second period in autumn 1963, ecclesiology should unify the work, by treating five draft-texts, namely, those on the church, the Virgin Mary, ecumenism, the ministry of bishops, and the lay apostolate.[17] Döpfner addressed Paul VI frankly about some schemas being problematic. Few impulses for church renewal appear in the existing drafts on priests, seminaries, reli-

---

15. Cardinal Montini, address of December 5, 1962. *Acta Synodalia*, 1.4:291–94.

16. Julius Kardinal Döpfner, *Konzilstagebücher, Briefe und Notizen zum Zweiten Vatikanischen Konzil*, ed. Guido Treffler (Regensburg: Schnell und Steiner, 2006), 476–87, letter to Pope Paul VI of July 19, 1973. In another letter in this edition, Cardinal Döpfner thanked Fr. Johannes Hirschmann, SJ, of the St. Georgen School of Theology in Frankfurt, for contributions which went into the memorandum that he, Döpfner, sent to the pope (487).

17. These five draft-texts were in fact discussed during the second period. But soon after Döpfner sent his recommendations to Pope Paul, Cardinal Bea submitted to the council's Coordinating Commission two annexes to the ecumenism schema, treating the Jews and religious liberty, which became new topics and in time distinct schemas which unleashed heated discussion at the council. See Döpfner, *Konzilstagebücher, Briefe und Notizen*, 500–501 and 518–19, giving letters by Bea, of August 30 and October 9, proposing these added texts for Döpfner's backing in the Coordinating Commission.

gious life, and schools, while the texts on sacraments, except one on mixed marriages, should be relegated to the future revision of the Code of Canon Law. Döpfner's passion was to give Vatican II a sharp focus. But, most importantly, his letter documents Paul VI's early gathering of expert opinion as he prepared for Vatican II's second period, which opened on September 29, 1963.

On that day, Pope Paul VI delivered an hour-long discourse, which was the second inaugural discourse of Vatican II and deserves attentive study.[18] The address contains the new pope's striking declaration of faith in Christ the Lord, which must be cited here.

The starting point and the goal [of the council] is that here and at this very hour we should proclaim Christ to ourselves and to the world around us: Christ our beginning, Christ our life and our guide, Christ our hope and our end.

O let this council have the full awareness of this relationship between ourselves and the blessed Jesus—a relationship which is at once multiple and unique, fixed and stimulating, mysterious and crystal clear, binding and beatifying—between this holy church which we constitute and Christ from whom we come, by whom we live, and toward whom we strive.

Let no other light be shed on this council, but Christ the light of the world! Let no other truth be of interest to our minds, but the words of our Lord, our only master! Let no other aspiration guide us, but the desire to be absolutely faithful to Him! Let no other hope sustain us, but the one that, through the mediation of His word, strengthens our pitiful weakness: "And behold I am with you all days, even to the consummation of the world" (Mt. 28:20)....

This council should have as its starting point this vision, or mystical celebration, which acknowledges Him, our Lord Jesus Christ, to be the Incarnate Word, the Son of God and the Son of Man, the Redeemer of the world, the Hope of humanity and its Supreme Master, the Good Shep-

18. The Latin original is in *Acta Synodalia*, 2.1:183–200, and *Acta Apostolicae Sedis* 55 (1963): 841–59. The text was printed in a booklet given to the Vatican II participants on October 11, 1963. In English: *Council Daybook*, 143–50. A partially digested version can be found in the second appendix of my *Doing Theology*, 154–62.

herd, the Bread of Life, the High Priest and our Victim, the sole Mediator between God and men, the Savior of the world, the eternal King of ages; and which declares that we are His chosen ones, His disciples, His apostles, His witnesses, His ministers, His representatives, and His living members together with the whole company of the faithful.

From this profound confession, Pope Paul passed on to explain four objectives of the council's work. It intends (1) to enunciate a fairly precise definition of the church itself; (2) to give guidelines for renewal of the church by pruning and correcting herself in conformity with the model given in Christ; (3) to promote unity among all Christians, by repentance, which occasioned Paul VI's word of regret and forgiveness addressed to other Christians, as he turned to the non-Catholic council observers at this point; and (4) to enter dialogue with the world, solicitous for the poor and afflicted, while showing respect for promoters of culture, learning, science, and art, along with leaders of nations.[19]

A very practical change, introduced as the second period opened, was Paul VI's appointment of four cardinal "moderators," who rotated in presiding over the assemblies and with whom the pope had regular contact and through them carefully oversaw council developments. They were Cardinals Gregorio Agagianian (Prefect of the Congregation for the Propagation of the Faith), Julius Döpfner (archbishop of Munich, Germany), Giacomo Lercaro (archbishop of Bologna, Italy), and Léon Joseph Suenens (archbishop of Malines, Belgium).

---

19. The Vatican II Constitution on the Sacred Liturgy began with a parallel statement of the council's objectives in its no. 1: "The sacred Council has several aims in view: it desires to impart an ever-increasing vigor to the Christian life of the faithful; to adapt more suitably to the needs of our own times those institutions which are subject to change; to foster whatever can promote union of all who believe in Christ; to strengthen whatever can help to call the whole of humanity into the household of the Church." *The Documents of Vatican II: Vatican Translation* (Strathfield: St. Paul's Publications, 2009), 91.

The Council's Second Period Work on Ecclesiology, Bishops, and Ecumenism

This chapter indicated above how the first major deliberation in 1963 concerned the draft of a Dogmatic Constitution on the Church, aiming to fulfill Paul VI's first council objective. Historically, this doctrinal self-presentation of the church was needed. It was, first, taking up unfinished business left from the First Vatican Council of 1869–70. There a complete draft of *De Ecclesia* had been prepared, but when France and Prussia began moving toward war, only a part of the draft, on the primacy and infallibility of the pope, was discussed, emended, and promulgated before Vatican I suspended its work. Second, what Vatican I defined on the papacy left a one-sided account of the Catholic hierarchy. When the bishops of the world were canvassed in 1959–60 on topics needing treatment at Vatican II, many said the new council should complement Vatican I by teaching on the episcopate and the episcopal college. Third, in the decades before the convocation of Vatican II, ecclesiology was a topic of intensive theological reflection, which had already affected the encyclical of Pope Pius XII, *The Mystical Body of Christ* (1943).[20]

An early Vatican II draft on the nature of the church had met heavy criticism during the final days of the first period, in 1962.[21] The Doctrinal Commission set out to thoroughly revise it under the scrutiny of the Commission on Coordinating the Council's Work established by Pope John XXIII.[22] For the council fathers, even be-

20. Examples of this reflection are the works of Romano Guardini, Émile Mersch, Henri de Lubac, Otto Semmelroth, and Lucien Cerfaux, in books published from 1922 to 1959, as listed above on 128n8.

21. This draft-text is given in the original Latin in *Acta Synodalia*, 1.4:12–91. Joseph Komonchak's English translation of this important Vatican II starting-point is available online at his blog, in the section *The Council That Might Have Been*, at https://jakomonchak .wordpress.com/2013/07/27/draft-of-a-dogmatic-constitution-on-the-church.

22. The Coordinating Commission sent quite exigent specifications for revising *De Ecclesia* to the Doctrinal Commission in late January 1963. The text is given in *Acta Synodalia*, 5.1:185–88.

fore they returned to Rome for the second period, it was clear that the council's commissions had been working. The bishops had received fourteen schemas, among which was a new four-chapter *De Ecclesia*, discussed first in the 1963 period.

After Pope Paul VI's opening discourse, the fathers spent two days giving their general evaluations of the 1963 revised *De Ecclesia*.[23] Most spoke positively about the depth and biblical freshness of the text. It shows the church deriving from the plan of God the Father, from the mission and saving action of the Son, and from the sanctifying work of the Holy Spirit. It features historical process, with the church being on pilgrimage, not yet at its destination. Catholics belong fully to the church by the threefold bond of faith, the sacraments, and union with the rightful pastors. But baptized Christians of other churches and confessions pertain fundamentally to the church, not so much by their sincerity and good will, as by objective realities, called *elementa sanctificationis* (elements, or means, of sanctification) constituting the church, which are their baptism, the proclaimed and biblical word of God, their creedal confession of Christ, and sharing in the life-giving Spirit. The commentary given the fathers on this passage says that these "elements" are in fact the "theological principle of ecumenism," which indicates that those who are related by sharing in saving realities are now dedicating themselves to overcome their separation and estrangement by dialogue and cooperation.[24]

De Ecclesia's chapter on the episcopate clarified the "collegial" relationship between pope and bishops—of which the council was a notable expression. It also moved toward a doctrinal clarification of the roles of the episcopal conferences, in which the bishops were gathering during and between the periods of the council. Chapter II on the people of God, especially the laity, pleased

23. *Acta Synodalia*, 2.1:343–87 (addresses of September 30 and October 1, 1963).
24. *Acta Synodalia*, 2.1:231; Gil Hellín, *Synopsis*, 124.

the bishops by sketching a doctrine not yet treated officially in the Catholic church. Chapter IV was on the call to holiness in the church, both of all and of consecrated persons in religious life. On the second day of discussing the new schema, the fathers voted to adopt the schema as their basis of further work, with 2,301 favorable and only 43 against moving ahead with the draft.[25]

But when the fathers began their detailed examination of the schema's chapter II on the hierarchy, especially the episcopate, the initial unity seemed to fragment as difficulties were raised, especially about the coherence of the new text on the episcopate with the settled doctrine from Vatican I on the unique and supreme powers of the pope governing the universal church. Controversy was just beneath the surface in the interventions of October 16 recalled in the first section above. Central in the schema is the point that bishops exercise a proper power. They are shepherds, ordained for pasturing—teaching, sanctifying, governing—the faithful, which they do as true pastors and not as delegates of the pope.

During 115 addresses over nine days, with the stack of further written comments growing as well, it was difficult to perceive the "mind of the assembly" on the episcopate. To obtain clarity, the moderators introduced an orientation vote on five topics. The votes would, they hoped, give clear directives to Doctrinal Commission, which would have to revise the text in the light of all that had been said. The vote took place on October 30, 1963—a crucial event in the council. In the outcome, large majorities of the council members upheld the innovations of the draft schema.[26]

---

25. *Acta Synodalia*, 2.1:391, on the vote taken toward the end of the meeting of October 1, 1963.

26. The topics and results were as follows. (1) Episcopal consecration is the highest grade of the sacrament of holy orders: 2,123 *placet* (98.4 percent). (2) Bishops in the Catholic communion are members of a body, or college, of bishops: 2,049 *placet* (95 percent). (3) This college succeeds the college of the apostles and, in communion with the pope, has supreme power over the universal church: 1,808 *placet* (84.2 percent). (4) This power of the college comes from God [not by papal delegation]: 1,588 (80.3 percent). (5) It is opportune to consider making the diaconate a permanent grade of ordained ministry: 2,120 *placet*

The reality of collegiality in the episcopal college would now become Catholic doctrine in a Dogmatic Constitution. But just how to formulate this teaching still gave rise to much discussion. Beginning in these days, an opposing minority fused together and began working against innovations. After all, on two of the October 30 questions about the powers of the episcopal college, the *non placet* (not approved) votes came from over 15 percent and over 19 percent of the council members, which had to be considerably reduced to give the needed moral unanimity when the council would enunciate Catholic doctrine.

In October 1963, before the votes on the five topics, the fathers took up chapter III, on the people of God, especially the laity. But a restructuring of the schema had been proposed and decided, namely, to move passages treating the whole people of God, with their charisms and share in Christ's priestly role, to a position before the chapter on the hierarchy—which was done and remains in the Dogmatic Constitution *Lumen Gentium*.[27]

Just before the October 30 vote, speakers evaluated chapter IV of the schema, on holiness in the church. One paragraph of the chapter spoke of a "universal call to holiness" in the church, before treating the consecrated life of vowed religious. Again, a restructuring found favor, to develop what became the inspiring chapter V of the Constitution on the Church, "The Universal Call to Holiness." Chapter V typifies Vatican II's way of addressing people in idealistic terms which complement our dignity and potential, while calling us to raise our standards of life and service,

---

(75 percent). The questions are given at *Acta Synodalia*, 2.3:573–75, with the results of the voting on 670.

27. The first public request for this came on September 30, at the end of the first day of discussion of the new ecclesiology schema. The bishop of Bolzano, Italy, Joseph Gargitter proposed it, with reasons for it, in his address given in *Acta Synodalia*, 2.1:359–62, at 360. On October 9, a booklet was distributed giving proposed emendations mailed in by the fathers on chaps. III and IV. At the beginning, the booklet gave an account of the reordering of the chapters proposed by Cardinal Suenens, which the Coordinating Commission had accepted. *Acta Synodalia*, 2.1:324–29.

much in the way of the late Pauline letters to the Ephesians and Colossians. This is the much discussed "style of Vatican II," in texts which, in teaching doctrine and depicting of roles of service, present ideals attractively and offer encouragement. In this the council gives a valuable model for preaching that uplifts and spreads delight in the Christian vocation.[28]

The time needed to give a full hearing to the council members' comments on *De Ecclesia* led to curtailing the agenda. Concerning a prepared schema on Mary, the second period saw only one question treated, namely, whether Vatican II should present a distinct doctrinal text on the Virgin Mary or should such a text become the final, crowning chapter of the Constitution on the Church. On October 29, a slight majority opted for incorporation into *De Ecclesia,* by only a forty-vote margin, but with the result that we have Vatican II's Marian doctrine in chapter VIII of *Lumen Gentium.*[29]

In November 1963, the bishops treated critically a schema on the Bishops' Pastoral Governance of Dioceses, especially because it omitted the theme of collegiality expressed in *De Ecclesia* and accepted in the votes of October 30. A cardinal from India and the auxiliary bishop of Barcelona both faulted the schema for giving no clear definition of a diocese as the context of a bishop's ministry. Others complained about the schema's neglect of episcopal conferences. Bishop Correa Léon (Colombia), a member of the Commission on Bishops, revealed that the members of the responsible commission had not been called together to discuss the draft and approve its text for presentation to the assembly. The Commission president, Cardinal Paolo Marella, had convoked a small group based in Rome to revise an earlier draft

28. These lines adopt the insightful analysis of O'Malley, *What Happened at Vatican II*, 43–52.

29. Before the vote, on October 24, Cardinal Santos of Manila gave reasons in favor of a distinct Constitution (*Acta Synodalia*, 2.3:338–42) and Cardinal König of Vienna laid out reasons for incorporation into the Constitution on the Church (*Acta Synodalia*, 2.3:342–45).

and slanted the text of 1963 toward the authority over bishops exercised by officials of the Roman Curia. Naturally, this text went back to the Commission with a sizeable packet of observations to serve in creating a thoroughly revised schema—in a notable extension of the "second preparation" into 1964.

In the final days of the 1963 council period, the assembly gave a warm welcome to a draft in three chapters on Catholic principles to guide ecumenical relations with other Christians and their churches and communities and on fields and norms of ecumenical collaboration. On November 21, 96 percent of the fathers voted to make the three chapters the basis of a council decree, with amendments and voting to come in the next council period.

But the text on ecumenism also had two added chapters over which controversy broke out, with the result that no votes took place on them during the second period. These were, first, a short text on Christian relations with the Jews, aiming to exorcize anti-Semitism from Catholic life. Pope John had added this to the council agenda and on it Cardinal Bea gave an impassioned introduction on November 18, 1963—one of the major addresses of Vatican II. The second added chapter expounded the civil right of religious liberty, which the Secretariat took up as a required presupposition to ecumenical engagement with the major confessional families of Western Christianity. These will be central parts of the further drama which will grow in intensity and difficulty of resolution in 1964–65.

Completing the Liturgy Constitution, with a Fateful Coincidence

During their meetings of 1963, the fathers of Vatican II had to practice multitasking, because while they discussed ecclesiology, bishops, and ecumenism, they also continued what they had begun in late 1962, namely, refining the text of the draft Constitution on the Sacred Liturgy to make it ready for approval and promulgation.

A year before, they had discussed each part of the schema, but in the first period they completed a definitive text of only the introduction and chapter I, on the general principles to guide the renewal and fostering of Catholic liturgical worship (in nos. 1–46). This completed part was rich in doctrine on Christ's redemptive work and his ongoing presence when the church gathers for worship, when Christ associates his body with himself in glorifying the Father (no. 7). Here a central component of ecclesiology was already proposed and accepted. Worship is "the high point towards which ecclesial activity is directed; it is, at the same time, the source from which all the church's power flows out" (no. 10). General principles are then given for the "general reform" (*instauratio*) of the church's liturgy, so that all may easily understand the liturgical texts and actions and so share in them in a celebration "which is full, active, and the community's own" (no. 21).

In the 1963 period, the fathers worked through the liturgy schema's chapters II to VII, which were applications of the principles of reform stated in chapter I, that is, on eucharistic celebration, other sacraments, the liturgy of the hours, the liturgical year, sacred music, and sacred art and furnishings. On October 4, just six days into the second period, the fathers received a booklet explaining the reasons for Liturgy Commission's revision of chapter II on eucharistic celebration. The revised portions depended on the oral and written comments that the fathers had made on this chapter a year before. On October 8, 1963, while speakers were treating *De Ecclesia* on the episcopate, the fathers began also voting *placet* or *non placet*, on each revised paragraph on the eucharistic liturgy (chap. II), resulting in large majorities favorable to all revised formulations.[30]

---

30. For example, that the order of the Mass should be reformed (SC 50): 2,249 *placet* and 31 *non placet*; that the vernacular should be introduced at Mass where pastorally helpful (SC 54): 2,139 *placet* and 67 *non placet*.

However, in their summary vote on the whole chapter, the council members could also vote *placet juxta modum*, that is, approving, but with a reservation on one or more points for which the member offered an amendment.[31] This brought complications, as many submitted precise amendments on points they felt could be better formulated. Thus, the Commission had more work, to review the amendments submitted and accept as many of them which improved the chapter, but without going against matters already approved by large majorities. This also happened on chapter III, on the other sacraments, on which many very specific amendments came in.[32] Large majorities voted simply *placet* on the further chapters, and the Commission brought back chapters II and III, with some changes in view of the amendments offered, which proved satisfactory to a large majority.

Thus, a final vote, approving the whole amended draft Constitution was taken on November 22, with the outcome of 2,158 *placet* votes and only 19 votes of *non placet*, which gave the council members a deeply felt sense of satisfaction over completing what they saw as a major text for the life of the church. At the period's concluding public session on December 4, 1963, after a ceremonial final vote and Pope Paul VI's solemn approval, the pope acted *una cum patribus* ("one with the council Fathers") to promulgate *Sacrosanctum Concilium* on a wide-ranging reform of Catholic worship.

But the fathers' first vote on the whole text had been on Friday, November 22, 1963. Later that day, Lee Harvey Oswald assassinated President John F. Kennedy. The shots in Dallas ushered in the raucous social turmoil of the mid-to-late 1960s. This pow-

---

31. Votes of simply *placet* totaled 1,417, which did not quite reach the two-thirds (1,495) needed for the chapter to gain approval. The votes *placet iuxta modum*, with amendments, were 781 in number.

32. Votes *placet iuxta modum* (approved with reservation) on chap. III totaled 1,045, which was significantly more than one-third of those voting. By the rules, the Commission was obliged to make revisions for the council to accept before the chapter was declared accepted for eventual promulgation by the pope.

erful and upsetting wave came to include other assassinations, inner-city race riots, and huge outbursts of student protests directed against existing authorities in academia, police departments, and government at all levels. Social turmoil, strife, and conflict abounded and this had a disturbing impact on the church life of Catholics, which was to be the very place where the elegant and idealistic final documents of Vatican II were destined to enter, to be received, and to be lived. It belongs to the complete history of Vatican II that this reception of the council's results did not occur in placid and peaceful times, but in a cultural and ecclesial ambience fraught with difficulties. Consequently, beyond the unfolding of Vatican II's dramatic developments, there will be another history of conciliar reception, which will occur amid turmoil and controversy extending into the lives of those who read these pages.

Appendix: The Itinerary of a Vatican II Document

A Vatican II document began with initial drafting by a Preparatory (1960–62) or a Conciliar Commission (1963–64), followed by approval, both by a Central Commission and by the pope, for the text's distribution to all council members. The central commissions for evaluating drafts produced by individual commissions were, first, the Central Preparatory Commission (1961–62) and, after the council began, the Commission for Coordinating the Council's Labors. After distribution of the text to the council members, the draft came on the council agenda for discussion during which the members evaluated its content and formulations both orally during General Congregations in the council hall (St. Peter's Basilica) or in written comments submitted to the responsible commission. After sufficient discussion, a vote was taken on accepting the draft as the basis of further work, which needed a two-thirds majority of those voting. If this majority was not attained, the draft returned to its commission for thorough revision. But if the draft was basically accepted, the commission would revise it with the aim of incorporating as many as possible of council members' criticisms and constructive proposals of revision. The revised draft then came back to the members for voting, section by section, whether for approval (*placet*), rejection (*non placet*), or approval with reservation (*placet iuxta modum*), accompanied by a reformulation offered as an amendment. The responsible commission then processed the offered amendments with the aim of incorporating changes to bring greater clarity, stronger documentation, or fine-tuning to the teaching or directives. Then, the text came back once more to the assembly for approval, by votes, both on the handling of amendments and on the completed text. The final action then occurred during a Public Session, namely, the formal approval by Pope Paul VI and the council fathers, leading to the pope's promulgation of the text as a Constitution, Decree, or Declaration of Vatican Council II.

8

Vatican II in 1964

Doctrinal Advances Paired with Tensions over
Facing the Modern World

This chapter takes up key developments of 1964, moving beyond the midpoint of the epoch-making ecclesial event which was the Second Vatican Council.[1] The council of 1962 to 1965 opened the era of church history in which we are still living. Vatican II was a turning point—a decisive shift in which the Catholic heritage of teaching and practice showed its dynamic character by reformulations, new configurations, and a new style, offering a new impetus for faith and witness, which, if one is rightly positioned to receive it, can to this day enhance the Christian lives of individuals, families, and communities.

However, in many places Catholics received Vatican II's elegant teaching and uplifting norms of practice very imperfectly, as indicated in this book's opening pages. Consequently, it is urgent to open doors to encountering Vatican II for a "re-reception" of its

This chapter was first given as a lecture at the Pontifical College Josephinum, Columbus, Ohio, on November 19, 2014.

1. Surveys of Vatican II's third period are Ratzinger, *Theological Highlights of Vatican II*, 55–123, and O'Malley, *What Happened at Vatican II*, 199–246.

doctrinal and spiritual riches. About these riches, the Australian Jesuit, Gerald O'Collins, says that after his fifty years of study of the Vatican II documents, rereading them these days often leaves him astonished over their "golden bits" of teaching and guidance.[2] Here, by concentrating on what Vatican II gave us in late November 1964, ways will open to find intellectual and spiritual bits of gold in the council. It can lift up minds and hearts, by the council's grand configuration of elegant texts on being the church of Christ and on living out vocations to service in the world amid the people of God.

The Sixteen Vatican II Documents, Chronologically and Hierarchically

In autumn 1964 the council held the third of its four working periods of daily meetings in St. Peter's Basilica. The third period's last meeting, on November 21, 1964, marked the second time the council completed documents and Pope Paul VI gave his assent and promulgated them as norms of teaching and service in the church for the salvation of the world.

To give the event at the end of the 1964 period its proper context, the following list indicates the sixteen documents issued by the council in their chronological order, from 1963 to 1965, according to the dates of their completion and promulgation by Pope Paul VI at the five Public Sessions, which were Vatican II meetings of notable solemnity.

The Vatican II Documents (Chronological Order)

Second Period

Constitution on the Sacred Liturgy, *Sacrosanctum Concilium* (SC), December 4, 1963

Decree on the Mass Media, *Inter Mirifica* (IM), December 4, 1963

---

2. *Second Vatican Council: Message and Meaning*, ix.

Third Period

Dogmatic Constitution on the Church, *Lumen Gentium* (LG),
November 21, 1964

Decree on Ecumenism, *Unitatis Redintegratio* (UR), November 21,
1964

Decree on the Catholic Eastern Churches, *Orientalium
Ecclesiarum* (OE), November 21, 1964

Fourth Period

Decree on the Pastoral Office of Bishops, *Christus Dominus* (CD),
October 28, 1965

Decree on the Training of Priests, *Optatam Totius* (OT), October
28, 1965

Decree on Up-to-date Renewal of Religious Life, *Perfectae
Caritatis* (PC), October 28, 1965

Declaration on the Church's Relation to Non-Christian
Religions, *Nostra Aetate* (NA), October 28, 1965

Declaration on Christian Education, *Gravissimum Educationis*
(GE), October 28, 1965

Dogmatic Constitution on Divine Revelation, *Dei Verbum* (DV),
November 18, 1965

Decree on the Lay Apostolate, *Apostolicam Actuositatem* (AA),
November 18, 1965

Pastoral Constitution on the Church in the Modern World,
Gaudium et Spes (GS), December 7, 1965

Decree on the Ministry and Life of Priests, *Presbyterorum
Ordinis* (PO), December 7, 1965

Decree on the Church's Missionary Activity, *Ad Gentes* (AG),
December 7, 1965

Declaration on Religious Liberty, *Dignitatis Humanae* (DH),
December 7, 1965

This list indicates the final event of the third council period of
1964 in the second cluster of three documents, promulgated on

November 21, 1964: on the church, ecumenism, and the Catholic Eastern churches. Three more solemn sessions followed during the final period in 1965, when the council brought in its harvest from extensive labors that extended from preparations begun in 1960 through the four working periods. But the same sixteen documents of the council can also be listed in a "hierarchical" order according to their level of solemnity and the kind of content issued to the church and the world in each of them.

The Vatican II Documents ("Hierarchical" Order)

Constitutions

Lumen Gentium

Dei Verbum

Sacrosanctum Concilium

Gaudium et Spes

Decrees

Christus Dominus

Optatam Totius

Presbyterorum Ordinis

Apostolicam Actuositatem

Ad Gentes

Perfectae Caritatis

Orientalium Ecclesiarum

Inter Mirifica

Unitatis Redintegratio

Declarations

Gravissimum Educationis

Nostra Aetate

Dignitatis Humanae

The hierarchical ordering of the Vatican II documents distinguishes constitutions (four), decrees (nine), and then declarations (three). One text promulgated in 1964 stands at the head of this list—deservedly so, as we shall see.

The four constitutions begin with the dogmatic text *Lumen Gentium*, which states amply the church's self-understanding as the people of God become the body of Christ and now on pilgrimage in history. The widely-used designation given by the opening words, *Lumen Gentium* ("light of the nations") concerns the radiant light of the risen Christ reflected from the church to benefit the human family. Never forget: the church is a moon, not the sun. The second constitution concerns the Word of God, *Dei Verbum*, received in the saving message of the Gospel and in scripture—promulgated in 1965. Chapter 3 in this volume, along with chapters 9 and 10, to follow, show *Dei Verbum*'s truly foundational place in the set of documents issued to us by Vatican II. Among the constitutions, the third treats the church's liturgical worship, in listening to, adoring, and giving God all honor and glory through, with, and in Christ. The fourth and final constitution gives the principles, in a pastoral key, of human graced existence and action in the world of today. More will be said about *Gaudium et Spes* below, as the council discussed a draft of it in fifteen meetings spread over three weeks during the third period of the council in 1964. These four constitutions are the primary and fundamental statements of Vatican II's teaching and guidance for faithful life and action on the part of all believers.

Moving down the hierarchical list, one comes to the council's nine decrees, which aim to guide practice and action in roles of service in and by the church. The decrees address bishops, priests, lay apostles, missionaries, persons consecrated for life and service in religious communities, Catholics of the Eastern traditions, communicators via the media, and the whole church in its ecumenical engagement with separated Christians, so "that they may be one," as our Lord prayed to the Father on the eve of his saving death. The fact that Vatican II issued *nine* decrees is often forgotten in discussions of the council's continuity with what went before it in the Catholic church. By its decrees, Vatican II mandated *change* in ways of action of the whole church and in performance in their roles by church members. In its nine decrees, as also in parts of other Vatican II documents, the council was clearly in its intent and purpose a council of reform.[3]

The hierarchical ordering of the Vatican II documents ends with declarations in which Vatican II speaks mainly *ad extra* to the world in the Declarations on Non-Christian Religions and on Religious Liberty, that is, the human right of immunity from coercion in living one's personal religious convictions. As declarations, these might seem less important than the documents above them, but this can deceive. The texts on world religions and religious liberty fit together closely with the Pastoral Constitution on the Church in the Modern World. We have to ask whether here, in this cluster of three momentous and innovative orientations *ad extra*, the council was not in fact realizing one of its main goals. These documents on personal and social life in the world correspond to central points of the council's aims and purposes as given by Popes John XXIII and Paul VI. Did a "final cause" give to Vatican II a central dynamic, under the surface, driving toward the identity of a servant church, formed by Christ's own *pro-existence*? The Pastoral Constitution looks to a church deeply committed to benefitting the whole human family with its "joys and hopes, grief and anguish" (*gaudium et spes, luctus et angor*), as that document says in its opening passage. This question will be central in the next chapter, on the texts that Vatican II promulgated during its final act in 1965.

---

3. The Liturgy Constitution, finalized in December 1963, sets forth doctrine in chap. I, nos. 5–13, but then it turns to encouraging and prescribing reform of liturgical *practice*, both in nos. 14–46 on general aspects of renewal and all through chaps. II–VII, which mandate revisions in eucharistic worship, sacraments, sacramentals, the liturgy of the hours, the liturgical year and calendar, liturgical music, and sacred art and furnishings. In a similar way, *Dei Verbum* expounds doctrine in its chaps. I–V, but turns to *reforming practice* in chap. VI, on the roles that scripture should have in the church's life. Chapter 10 of this volume will bring out key aspects of the renewed practice mandated in *Dei Verbum*, chap. VI.

A first conclusion can arise from this review of just the titles and types of the Vatican II documents. The subject matters indicated by their titles stirs amazement over the broad range of topics on which Vatican II spoke through its documents. The council was no small undertaking. A person who is informed about all the significant topics on which Vatican II taught, decreed, and made declarations will become uncomfortable with popular formulas about the council, such as saying it "opened the church's windows to the world" or it was "catching up with the times." People speaking in this way reduce simplistically and unbearably Vatican II's huge labors and wide span of vision evident in the topics it addressed. But the breadth and range of topics make a further question arise inevitably. *How* should one put the sixteen documents together into coherent sets or clusters, to escape fragmentation or a sense of overload by so many teachings and directives?

Vatican II's Coherent Unfolding of Ecclesiology into Decrees on Roles and Practice

One way to find coherence among these documents is take inspiration from the Council of Trent, held from 1545 to 1563 but with two suspensions of its meetings. Trent had to give doctrinal clarifications on the teachings espoused by the Lutheran and Calvinist Reformations. Doing this, Trent issued doctrinal decrees on original sin, on God's grace to convert and justify persons in interaction with human freedom, and then on each of the seven sacraments. But Trent was also a reform council of notable reach in its practical orientations, concretely in several reform decrees on the clergy, parishes, and whole dioceses. The young Fr. Angelo Giuseppe Roncalli, who was to become Pope Saint John XXIII, studied the archival records of Trent's reforming impact on his own Diocese of Bergamo. Then he oversaw publication, in five volumes, of these records of how parishes and clergy of Bergamo were set aright and given new vitality when reformed in 1575, twelve years after Trent concluded its work.[4]

In Trent's reforming impact on early modern Catholic life, historians customarily identify five "pillars" put in place by mandates of Trent: (1) that bishops *reside* continuously in their dioceses; (2) that the bishops carry out regular *visitations* of diocesan parishes; (3) that regular *diocesan or provincial synods* be held to codify norms of pastoral responsibility; (4) that *seminaries* be opened for developing in future priests an elevated spirituality and pastoral competence; and (5) that Catholic instruction follow a new *catechism* of essential teaching.

Trent pursued twin goals, namely, to define and clarify doctrine and to reform pastoral practice. The connection with Vatican II is that a large block of its production mirrors the same duality of doctrine and reformed practice. But where Trent's decrees came out in accidental juxtaposition of doctrine and practice, the Vatican II documents show a coherence and interdependence in their content. First in the hierarchical list is the major doctrinal text of the Dogmatic Constitution on the Church. It is rightly first, because the Vatican II decrees then unfold pastorally and practically several topics of the ecclesial doctrine set forth in *Lumen Gentium*. This coherence deserves closer attention.

The following outline shows how Vatican II's ecclesiology in *Lumen Gentium* not only enunciated doctrine but also, in the same Constitution, laid the basis for emphasizing the Christian practice treated in the council's decrees. Furthermore, the conciliar constitution and decrees began trajectories along which Catholic teaching oriented to practice moved during the years after the Second Vatican Council.

---

4. See the account of this in chapter 1, above.

**Lumen Gentium, the Council's Implementing Decrees
and Declarations, and Later Texts**

Chapter I: The mystery of the church (nos. 1–8)

Chapter II: The people of God (nos. 9–17)

    Diversity among the particular churches (no. 13)

        Orientalium Ecclesiarum

        [John Paul II, Apostolic Letter, *Orientale Lumen*
          (1995)]

    Catholics share with non-Catholic Christians in realities
      of truth and sanctification which the others receive in
      their churches and ecclesial communities (no. 15)

        Unitatis Redintegratio

        [John Paul II, Encyclical Letter, *Ut Unum Sint*
          (1995)]

    Non-Christians (Jews, Muslims, and others), all of whom
      God's grace seeks to lead to good living and salvation,
      but evil threatens them (no. 16)

        Nostra Aetate

        [Congregation of Doctrine of the Faith, *Dominus
         Iesus* (2000)]

    The church's missionary effort to bring Christ's salvation
      to the whole world (no. 17)

        Ad Gentes

        [Paul VI, Post-Synodal Exhortation, *Evangelii
         Nuntiandi* (1975)]

        [John Paul II, Encyclical Letter, *Redemptoris
         Missio* (1990)]

Chapter III: The church's hierarchical constitution (nos. 18–29)

    Bishops and the episcopal college (nos. 18–27)

        Christus Dominus

        [John Paul II, Post-Synodal Exhortation,
         Pastores Gregis (2003)]

Priests (no. 28)

 Optatam Totius

 Presbyterorum Ordinis

 [Synod of Bishops, *The Ministerial Priesthood*
  (1971)]

 [John Paul II, Post-Synodal Exhortation,
  Pastores Dabo Vobis (1992)]

Chapter IV: The laity in the church (nos. 30–38)

 Apostolicam Actuositatem

 Inter Mirifica

 [John Paul II, Post-Synodal Exhortation,
  Christifideles Laici (1988)]

Chapter V: The universal call to holiness (nos. 39–42)

Chapter VI: The consecrated life of the evangelical councils
 (nos. 43–47)

 Perfectae Caritatis

 [Paul VI, Apostolic Exhortation, *Evangelica
  Testificatio* (1971)]

 [John Paul II, Post-Synodal Exhortation,
  Vita Consecrata (1996)]

Chapter VII: The church's eschatological character and union
 with the heavenly church (nos. 48–51)

Chapter VIII: Mary in the mystery of Christ and of the church
 (nos. 52–69)

 [Paul VI, Apostolic Exhortation, *Marialis
  Cultus* (1974)]

 [John Paul II, Encyclical Letter, *Redemptoris
  Mater* (1987)]

This is, first, an outline of *Lumen Gentium*'s eight chapters. The outline adds for chapters II and III some of the numbered paragraphs. The chart also lists Vatican II's nine decrees, placing each in relation to a passage of the Constitution on the Church. The Vatican II commissions responsible for drafting and revising the nine decrees took orientations on roles and practice from what *Lumen Gentium* said doctrinally. Practice has its grounds in doctrine, not just in the will and mandate of an authority.

During the third period of Vatican II, the council leadership insisted on intensive work to complete *Lumen Gentium* by the end of the 1964 period, because only with that constitution in its final form could work proceed to complete the remaining pastoral and practical decrees. The decrees are not simply expressions of the will of the council majority, but are consequences from stated doctrines of the Dogmatic Constitution on the Church.

The derived character of Vatican II's decrees already suggests the rich contribution of the Dogmatic Constitution on the Church in the overall strategy of the council. But *Lumen Gentium* itself deserves careful attention, as it is a singular expression of the church's understanding of itself. The constitution treats in its first and last chapters the "mystery of the church" and Mary "in the mystery of Christ and the church." These were the topics presented in the first and final chapters of Henri de Lubac's book, dense with ideas from the Church Fathers, published in 1953 and translated as *The Splendor of the Church* in 1956.

Lumen Gentium's chapter I treats the church as proceeding from the triune God and then as seen through several biblical designations and images. This first chapter entered the text as a replacement chapter in 1963, when the fathers agreed to set aside much of the content of the earlier draft of chapter I, "on the church militant." Chapter II, on the people of God, came from remnants of that discarded chapter combined with matter which had earlier introduced the chapter on the laity. The great survey of the "people of God" in chapter II (nos. 9–17), stands in the promulgated text *before* chapter III, on the ordained hierarchy, and chapter IV, on the laity. These following chapters then explain the ordained hierarchy and the laity, each in their own dignity and roles as subjects of ecclesial action. But the two, hierarchy and laity, come back together again in chapter V as addressed by the call to holiness, which God directs to all who are incorporated into the church—to all without exception. Chapter VII, on the union of the earthly and heavenly church, came into *Lumen Gentium* after promulgation of the Constitution on Renewing the Liturgy at the end of the second period in 1963, because it is in worship that the church is most fully herself, especially in its eucharistic prayer, acting in communion and concert with the angels and saints who give God all honor and glory in heaven.[5] While the length of *Lumen Gentium* may make it daunting to take up to read, the sketch just given suggests the grandeur of its contents and the promise of enrichment for the reflective Catholic reader.

Selectively, we can note how three of the Vatican II decrees, oriented to action and pastoral practice, follow from the doctrine of the Dogmatic Constitution on the Church. First, no. 15 of *Lumen Gentium*, on the Christian elements that non-Catholics receive and cherish in their own communities, gives to the Decree on Ecumenism its doctrinal foundation. That Decree makes a high claim in its opening words, "The restoration of unity [*Unitatis redintegratio*] among Christians is one of the principal concerns of the Second Vatican Council." That claim was not an invention of Cardinal Bea's Secretariat for Promoting Christian Unity, but comes from two official statements of the council's goals and aims, namely, Pope Paul VI's opening discourse of the second period (1963) and the first lines of the council's Constitution on the Liturgy. Ecumenism arises from Vatican II's ecclesiology, as shown by the promulgation of the Decree on Ecumenism on the same day that the Dogmatic Constitution on the Church was promulgated.[6]

Second, *Lumen Gentium*'s third chapter, nos. 18–27, on bishops

---

5. Christopher Ruddy brings this out in "'In the end is my beginning': *Lumen gentium* and the Priority of Doxology," *Irish Theological Quarterly* 79 (2014): 144–64.

6. On the grounding of ecumenical action, chapter 5, above, identifies certain developments during the genesis of *Lumen Gentium* that led to laying foundations for the dialogues that have followed the council.

and the episcopal college, grounds the dependent Decree on the Pastoral Office of Bishops. This is broadly valuable, even to us who are not bishops, because of its account of what is a "local church," which is a diocese, as a portion of God's people, entrusted to the bishop with his clergy, for being formed in the Holy Spirit through the Gospel and the eucharist. In such a church, also called a "particular" church, the church of Christ—one, holy, catholic, and apostolic—is truly present and active (no. 11). That is a concise but precious specification of "local church" in the Catholic sense.

Also, in no. 17 the Constitution states the missionary dedication of the church to bring Christ to the world, as it concludes the chapter on the people of God. During the fourth period, the Decree on the Church's Missionary Activity reached completion and was promulgated on December 7, 1965. Along with its mandate of missionary action, *Ad Gentes* in fact offers a concise Catholic ecclesiology which developed in a calm atmosphere, untroubled by the tense arguments that had accompanied the redaction of chapter III of the Constitution on the Church, on bishops and their collegiality. On can and should still read *Ad Gentes* for its precious seams of gold, both theological and spiritual.

The outline just given also shows that *Lumen Gentium* has further powers to unify documents and make them cohere. Note the references on the page, in brackets, to thirteen official Catholic documents issued after the council. In these, the council's teaching prolonged itself into fresh formulations. The council's mandated roles and actions were updated for the vitality of the church. For example, *Lumen Gentium*, no. 15, along with the Decree on Ecumenism, received a notable updating in Pope Saint John Paul II's encyclical letter of 1995, *Ut Unum Sint*, on the irrevocable Catholic commitment to moving along the ecumenical way. Also, the council's Decree on the Training of Priests, arising from *Lumen Gentium* (chap. III, no. 28), was further actualized in John Paul II's Apostolic Exhortation on priestly formation,

Pastores Dabo Vobis (1992), the papal text that harvested what the Synod of Bishops had produced on priestly formation in 1990.

These further developments in continuity with Vatican II clarify an important aspect of the council's nine decrees of 1963–65. They were first implementations, set forth in the era of the mid-1960s. As documents on action and practice in history, the decrees in time needed further updating and nuancing, as given by more recent interventions of the Magisterium. Thirteen of these are named in brackets, as documents which recalled, refreshed, and further plotted the realization of Vatican II in Catholic life. The post-conciliar documents reveal the dynamic trajectory of Vatican II into further applications down to today.

A final point in this vein is to note how chapter V of *Lumen Gentium*, on God's universal call to holiness, has no implementing decree of the council and no further application in a post-conciliar document. Why this omission? One acute observer who saw this outline made the point that God's call of all to holiness does not look to documents, but to persons and communities. The implementation must be lived and it is being done so, with special concreteness in the post-Vatican II ecclesial movements and new communities—all fostering holiness of life, especially in lay Christians—such as the Focolari, Emmanuel, Sant'Egidio, Cum Christo, and Communion and Liberation.[7]

Light and Shadows over Vatican II's Third Period (1964)

Light

In 1964 Vatican II completed a very demanding agenda of work.[8] The third period began on September 14, 1964, in an opening ses-

---

7. I am grateful to Rev. Timothy Hayes, pastor of St. Timothy parish in Columbus, for this observation.

8. A comprehensive account can be found in *History of Vatican II*, ed. Alberigo and Komonchak, 4:1–452 (on LG chaps. I–VII) and 617–40 (on LG chap. VIII).

sion that included the first public concelebration of the eucharist, with Pope Paul VI presiding and twenty-four council members from nineteen nations joining him around the expanded high altar of St. Peter's and using thin missals of a rite of concelebration created *ad hoc* by Monsignor Annibale Bugnini.

The third period was remarkable in the way the work moved rapidly and efficiently on fourteen documents, which were then in different stages of their development. The three texts promulgated at the end of the period, on November 21, on the church, ecumenism, and the Catholic Eastern churches, were well along as the period began, but their amended paragraphs had to gain approval one by one, with initial votes possibly being to approve *iuxta modum*, that is, with a requested amendment. The responsible commission then had to assess each amendment for its coherence with the text's established main directions, after which the accepted amendments were put a further vote by all the members.

The remaining decrees and declarations were treated expeditiously during the 1964 period, sometimes with only two days of discussion on a single text, but the council members regularly offered shared comments on texts in interventions prepared in meetings of episcopal conferences before the period began. Among these draft decrees, those on the life and ministry of priests and on the missions drew sharp criticism for not yet being in accord with the pastoral priorities of the council, followed by votes to send them back to the responsible commissions, for another redrafting and later review and possible acceptance.

Two of the constitutions destined to be promulgated in 1965 came before the council during the third period. The amended text on revelation, tradition, and scripture met a mostly cordial welcome in five days of discussion, which was a decisive step toward the Dogmatic Constitution *Dei Verbum*, which will have its own set of practical decrees for action regarding scripture in chapter VI.[9]

9. Hanjo Sauer relates the 1964 advance toward the Dogmatic Constitution on Revelation in *History of Vatican II,* ed. Alberigo and Komonchak, 4:196–231. I related how this

The longest stretch of work on one document during the 1964 period was in the fourteen meetings in which the fathers commented on draft chapters of what became a year later the Pastoral Constitution on the Church in the Modern World. The 171 speakers made it clear that much redrafting lay ahead on this momentous document. It had no conciliar precedents, although the papal social encyclicals since Leo XIII had enunciated norms for action in the social fields. Still, it was a shift in Vatican II's work, after it dealt with liturgical worship, divine revelation and scripture, ecclesiology, and relations with other Christians. The draft on the Church in the Modern World addressed concrete contemporary issues and problems, such as world peace and a just socio-economic order. It was a new-style council text: as John O'Malley nicely put it, "it projected an image of the church as a helpmate to all persons of good will, whether Catholic or not, whether Christian or not, with the church as a beacon of hope for a better world."[10]

Shadows

Every detailed historical account of Vatican II tells about the choppy waters through which the good ship Vatican II sailed during the final week of the third period in 1964. Three dramatic incidents occurred, with each involving the relation between Pope Paul VI and the council majority. In his one-volume history of the council, O'Malley adds to the title of the chapter on the 1964 period a subtitle, "Triumphs and Tribulations." I have mentioned several "triumphs." The "tribulations" came in the final week.

(1) The last week of the 1964 period opened on Monday, November 16. The general secretary, Monsignor Pericle Felici, re-

---

advance was prepared in "*De revelatione* under Revision (March–April 1964)," in *The Belgian Contribution to the Second Vatican Council*, 461–94.

10. O'Malley, *What Happened at Vatican II*, 233. Norman Tanner treats the 1964 debate on this text in *History of Vatican II*, ed. Alberigo and Komonchak, 4:270–331, in sections on the human vocation, Christian responsibilities, marriage and the family, promotion of culture, economic life, and international issues of war and peace.

minded the fathers of the coming votes on the next two days on the revised texts of chapters III to VIII of the schema *De Ecclesia*, to be followed on Thursday by a vote on the entire text. The previous Saturday, the council members had received these revised chapters in booklets which gave as well the Doctrinal Commission's account of its reasons for accepting or rejecting each of the amendments submitted during the voting in late September and early October on the previous texts of these chapters. Since the start of the period, a behind-the-scenes battle had raged over the third chapter, on the episcopate and its collegial unity and authority, on which a minority of council members had insistently urged Pope Paul VI to intervene to obstruct passage of a magisterial teaching on episcopal collegiality, as the objectors construed the chapter as undermining Vatican I's dogmatic definition in 1870 of the papal primacy of authority.[11]

The minority's agitation was strong enough to sow serious concerns in the minds of Paul VI and of the leaders of the Doctrinal Commission. Would the opposition to episcopal collegiality lead to a final vote on *De Ecclesia* in which the number of *non placet* votes would be large enough to deny to this central Vatican II text the morally unanimous conciliar approval needed for a major action of magisterial teaching? To avert this threat by winning over many or all of the minority objectors, the pope and his close advisers decided to prepare an additional "note" on the Doctrinal Commission's final revisions of chapter III, which would both explain why amendments proposed by the minority did not enter the text and would show that the text presented for final voting did not in any way undermine the pope's authority.[12]

11. See the concise account given by Luis Antonio G. Tagle, in *History of Vatican II*, ed. Alberigo and Komonchak, 4:417–32. The same author treated the same matter more amply in *Episcopal Collegiality and Vatican II: The Influence of Paul VI* (Manila: Loyola School of Theology, 2004), 201–36.

12. Tagle relates the genesis and contents of the "Note" in *History of Vatican II*, ed. Alberigo and Komonchak, 4:432–37, while treating the contents more fully in *Episcopal Collegiality and Vatican II*, 236–60.

Consequently on Monday, November 16, Felici announced that regarding chapter III of *De Ecclesia*, a "Preparatory Explanatory Note" had been prepared in the Doctrinal Commission, and now by mandate of "higher authority," namely the pope, it was to become an official part of the council's records, to interpret that chapter in its newly amended form.[13] Felici then read the "Explanatory Note," while promising that a printed copy of it would be distributed the next day, before the vote on the amended text of chapter III. The text clarified both the term "college" applied to the episcopate and explained that one becomes a member of the college not only by sacramental ordination to the episcopate but as well by communion with the head of the college, the pope. It set in relief the pope's singular role, by his office as vicar of Christ and pastor of the universal church—by which he "may exercise his power at any time, as he sees fit." This explanation of select contents of *De Ecclesia*, chapter III, led to the revised chapter, explained in key parts by the "Explanatory Note," being approved on November 17 by a vote of 2,099 (*placet*) to 46 (*non placet*). The opponents of episcopal collegiality were moving toward assenting to the constitution. When the complete text of the amended schema came to a vote on Thursday, November 19, the outcome was a practically unanimous approval: 2,134 (*placet*) to 10 (*non placet*).

But while this strong papal intervention gained adherents to the Constitution on the Church, it also caused consternation among some members of the majority, to the point that an influential Vatican II historian, from the circle of Cardinal Giacomo

13. *Acta Synodalia*, 3.8:11–13, gives the note in Latin, while English translations place it at the end of *Lumen Gentium*. See, e.g., the Austin Flannery translation (93–95), or *Decrees*, ed. Tanner, 2:899–900. Monsignor Gerard Philips of Louvain, the reporter on *De Ecclesia* for the Doctrinal Commission, composed a first draft of the note on November 2, 1964, which the Commission amended and accepted on November 10 and Paul VI approved on November 13. See Jan Grootaers, *Primauté et collégialité. Le dossier de Gérard Philips sur la Nota Explicativa Praevia* (Leuven: Peeters, 1986), 98–99 (first draft) and 116–18 (formulation approved by Paul VI).

Lercaro of Bologna, criticized the "Note," because it "appeared to be a mosaic composed of propositions, taken, often word for word, from interventions made at the council by leaders of the minority," and it needlessly repeated what chapter III of the schema already affirmed.[14] For others, the "Nota" revealed Paul VI's affinity with some curial members of the minority, based on his years of work with them in the papal Secretariat of State. But these criticisms fall by the way when one appreciates Paul VI's role as head of the conciliar assembly with the duty to reconcile oppositions and judge the soundness of Vatican II teaching.[15]

(2) A tribulation suffered especially by the American cardinals and bishops at Vatican II concerned a vote to accept a revised text of a Declaration on Religious Liberty as the working basis for the council on this topic. The vote was scheduled for Thursday, November 19, but Bishop Luigi Carli of Segni, Italy, a leader of the organized minority group, the *Coetus internationalis Patrum*, protested to the Administrative Tribunal of the council that what had been distributed and scheduled for a vote was not simply a revision of the earlier text but practically a new document, on which a vote should be taken only after study and discussion in the council hall.[16] The Tribunal and Council of Presidents agreed with Bishop Carli's protest and Paul VI declined to overrule their decision. So, the announced vote on September 19 was not taken, but was postponed to the fourth period, nine months in the fu-

14. Giuseppe Alberigo, *A Brief History of Vatican II* (Maryknoll, N.Y.: Orbis Books, 2006), 274.

15. Tagle, *Episcopal Collegiality and Vatican II*, 260–63, gives the second criticism within his survey of different judgments on Paul VI's involvement in the "Nota," on which he brings out several positive aspects of the pope's intervention.

16. Yves Congar had read over the revised text on October 14, 1965, and foresaw the tribulation to come. He wrote in his diary: "Hardly anything is left of the previous text. In these circumstances a new discussion is needed. I find that there is a certain superficiality in this approach. The redactors . . . have no idea of the difficulties that their text will raise." Congar, *My Journal of the Council*, 626. Congar knew well what Smulders learned when revising the text on the diaconate, namely, that the commissions' *periti* had to offer revisions of prior texts which were documented by reference to the oral and written comments by council members. See above, 70–71.

ture. The American bishops were deeply upset and they gathered nearly 500 signatures on petitions to the pope to allow the vote—which he did not do.[17]

(3) Another tribulation, for many, also involved Pope Paul VI, this time regarding the text of the Decree on Ecumenism.[18] As a general practice, the pope had been seeing the results of evaluations of amendments by the Secretariat for Promoting Christian Unity before they were printed and distributed to the council members. But in the press of business during November 1964, this documentation had not come to the pope before the text was printed with its final amendments entered and other proposed amendments rejected.[19]

Before the final vote to accept or not the whole text as amended, petitions began arriving on the pope's desk appealing against the Secretariat's decisions regarding certain amendments not received into the text of the decree. The papal theologian, Fr. Luigi Ciappi, OP, along with Fr. Charles Boyer, SJ, of Gregorian University, drew up a list of forty such rejected contributions on which the pope might well request reconsiderations of the Secretariat's decisions on amendments. Paul VI studied these proposals and marked with a blue pencil twenty-one of them on which he would not call for a reconsideration. This left nineteen points, some of just one word, for forwarding to the Secretariat for their last-minute consideration before the vote to make the revised draft definitive. A small group of priests from the Secretariat—Jan Willebrands, Gustave Thils, Emanuel Lanne, and Pierre Duprey—worked through the night to rephrase the draft on ecumenism ac-

---

17. On this incident, see Tagle, in *History of Vatican II*, ed. Alberigo and Komonchak, 4:395–406.

18. Tagle recounts the disturbed arrival in port of the Decree on Ecumenism in ibid., 4:406–17.

19. On February 19, 1965, Willebrands told Congar of the Secretariat's omission of this crucial step. See Congar, *My Journal of the Council*, 729. See the detailed account by Pierre Duprey, "Paul VI et le decret sur l'ecumenisme," in *Paolo VI e i problemi ecclesiologici al concilio* (Brescia: Istituto Paolo VI, 1989), 225–48, at 238–47.

cording to most of the pope's suggestions of amendments at the last minute. A mimeographed page of the changes was given to the council members, so they would consider them parts belonging to the Decree on Ecumenism on which they would vote.

Each of these incidents of tribulation upset groups of council members and their expert theological advisers. But their importance diminishes notably when we take a broader, long-term perspective. The Constitution on the Church (with the explanatory note) and the Decree on Ecumenism (with the late amendments) both came through their final votes quite successfully at the end of the final week of the 1964 period.[20] By what Paul VI did (and did not do), a small group of reluctant cardinals and bishops were won over to accept the two texts. Most of all, for fifty years these two documents have contributed greatly to Catholic ecclesiology and to ecumenical dialogues. The "speed bumps" that they hit in November 1964 have played no appreciable role affecting their wider reception as major Catholic teachings and orientation to ecumenical practice. The promulgated texts on the church and ecumenism were celebrated on their fiftieth anniversary in 2014 around the world, for they have proven themselves as they were issued on November 21, 1964.

A Fissure Opens between the Majority's Experts

Another "tribulation" calls for examination, which was the beginning in 1964 of the first serious rift within the majority of council members and experts who had worked together, in the earlier Vatican II drama, to set aside many of the first drafts given

20. The completed Constitution on the Church was approved in the General Congregation of November 19, 1965, by 2,134 votes of *placet*, against only 10 of *non placet*, while at the Public Session of November 21 the votes were 2,151 *placet* and 5 *non placet*. The completed Decree on Ecumenism, when voted in the General Congregation of November 20 received 2,054 votes of *placet*, against 64 of *non placet*, but at the Public Session of November 21, it was 2,137 *placet* and 11 *non placet*.

to the council by the preparatory commissions. This new drama is well articulated in the diary notes of council expert Henri de Lubac, the esteemed proponent of renewal from the early Christian sources, as in *The Splendor of the Church*, already mentioned as seminal for the renewal of ecclesiology. De Lubac's diary notes of the second half of 1964 are filled with concern and alarm, because some theologians are interpreting the draft on the church in the modern world in a way portending serious danger.[21] De Lubac told people, in conversations and letters, to be careful, even wary, that this text not become such a Catholic "opening to the world" that it leads to an invasion of the church by the world and by its secular concerns. He sensed here an overshadowing of "the eternal and divine vocation of human beings." For de Lubac, it is only in the light of our true human destiny that the text should encourage action aiming to foster culture, economic and political well-being, and world peace. In France, before going to Rome for Vatican II's third period, de Lubac heard popular slogans about the church in council "opening herself to the world," but listening carefully, he noted a drive to make common cause with unbelievers for secular progress in a manner marginalizing Christian dogma, prayer, and intimacy with God.[22]

During the third period, de Lubac thought journalists were not perceiving a central point, namely that the council's reforms—updating worship, ecumenical outreach, and affirming religious freedom—arose from a purified and deepened Christian spirit.

21. De Lubac, *Vatican Council Notebooks*, 2:100–101 (September 10, 1964), 124 (September 24), 127–28 (September 25), 195 (October 16), and 197–98 (October 17). I presented de Lubac's diary, working from the French original of 2007, in "Further Light on Vatican Council II," 546–62. This article documents (556–62) de Lubac's many critical observations of 1964–65, while also referring to his and others' published laments over post-Vatican II developments. On this later phase, see Christopher J. Walsh, "De Lubac's Critique of the Post-Conciliar Church," *Communio* 19 (1992): 404–32.

22. De Lubac, *Vatican Council Notebooks*, 2:127–28, including a strong letter to Henri Denis of September 25, 1964, on the danger of a dialogue with the world which marginalizes the church's hopes founded in Jesus Christ and the high dignity given in Christ to humans.

About this, popular reports were falling silent. The schema on the church in the modern world was exerting a magnetic attraction to problems of the temporal order, without a countervailing insistence on the human "eternal vocation," which de Lubac had treated in his works on nature and grace.[23]

A troubling notion lay just under the surface of the "church and world" themes, namely, the idea that the world where humans strive for justice is already substantially Christian beneath its surface in personal ethical dedication and drive, but independently of evangelical revelation. In this notion, the proclaimed Gospel and faith effect only a passage from the implicit to the explicit. In Rome, de Lubac read the Flemish Dominican Edward Schillebeeckx's lecture on "church and world" shortly before the council treated the schema.[24] De Lubac thought he heard an analysis of the world as implicitly Christian by God's subtle influence amid human existence and action to develop the world and society. The church only discloses explicitly God's nearness and influence, which already reached individuals when they apply themselves to develop the well-being of family, the economy, and their city and nation. Christianity would be thus a *disclosure*, but not a *mediation*, of grace and spirit to bring forth constructive action. De Lubac missed the basis of an evangelical dedication to service in the world. In contrast, he noted, how deep, how reflective, and how Christian is the thought on the same issue of Pierre Teilhard de Chardin!

A rift was opening, which after Vatican II led to the founding of two Catholic journals: *Concilium*, organized by Schillebeeckx (with Hans Küng, Karl Rahner, and Johann Baptist Metz) and

23. De Lubac summed up his concerns about emerging risks of misinterpreting the council in a letter to Cardinal Léger on October 17, 1964. *Vatican Council Notebooks*, 2:199. See the text in de Lubac's *At the Service of the Church* (San Francisco: Ignatius Press, 1993), 340–41.

24. For the text, see "Church and World," in E. Schillebeeckx, *World and Church* (New York: Sheed and Ward, 1971), 97–114, on which see de Lubac's *Vatican Council Notebooks*, 2:198. De Lubac published his critical response in appendix B of his *Brief Catechesis on Nature and Grace* (San Francisco: Ignatius Press, 1984), 191–234.

Communio, inspired by de Lubac (with Hans Urs von Balthasar, Joseph Ratzinger, and Walter Kasper). But the rift emerged into the light earlier, in the fourth period (1965) of Vatican II, as the following chapter 9 will relate. A crucial step toward the final text of the Pastoral Constitution on the Church in the Modern World will be the offensive mounted in 1965, especially by German theologians and bishops who agreed with the diagnosis of de Lubac. They received valuable input from a counter-schema from Poland presented by Archbishop Karol Wojtyla. *Gaudium et Spes*, consequently, gained greatly by late revisions to give it a striking Christocentrism, about which the following chapter will report.

Thus, at the end of Vatican II's third period, major advances had occurred, especially by the completion and promulgation of major documents on the nature of the church, *Lumen Gentium*, and on the Catholic commitment to enter the ecumenical movement, *Unitatis Redintegratio*. Eleven other documents, including future constitutions, decrees, and declarations, were moving along in their development toward the form in which the council will approve them during the fourth period of 1965. But this further movement will also bring with itself dramatic clashes that the council will labor to settle satisfactorily in the months before its conclusion on December 8, 1965. This labor and its results call for well-focused attention, as they will give to the Second Vatican Council major traits essential to its doctrinal identity and church-historical significance.

9

Vatican II in 1965

Renewed Doctrine and Directives of Service

This chapter on "bringing in the harvest" of Vatican II attends to the documents of the council's fourth working period, from September 14 to December 8, 1965. The completing and promulgating of the Vatican II constitutions, decrees, and declarations had begun at the end of the second period (December 4, 1963), with the Constitution on the Sacred Liturgy and the Decree on the Mass Media. Harvesting continued at the end of the third period (November 21, 1964), with the Dogmatic Constitution on the Church, the Decree on Ecumenism, and the Decree on the Catholic Eastern Churches. To these five completed texts, Vatican II added in its fourth period of 1965 no fewer than eleven further documents, completed laboriously and under considerable time pressure. Council work in 1965 included three public sessions at which the council members formally approved the final texts

This chapter was first published as "Vatican II in 1965: Bringing in an Ample Harvest of Renewed Doctrine and Directives of Service," *Josephinum Journal of Theology* 22 (2015): 4–22. It was first given as a public lecture at the Pontifical College Josephinum, Columbus, Ohio, on October 8, 2015.

of eleven documents by large majorities of votes, after which in each session Pope Paul VI promulgated the texts.[1]

Public Session VII, October 28, 1965

Decree on the Pastoral Office of Bishops in the Church
(*Christus Dominus*)

Decree on the Training of Priests (*Optatam Totius*)

Decree on the Up-to-Date Renewal of Religious Life
(*Perfectae Caritatis*)

Declaration on the Relation of the Church to Non-Christian
Religions (*Nostra Aetate*)

Declaration on Christian Education (*Gravissimum Educationis*)

Public Session VIII, November 18, 1965

Decree on the Apostolate of Lay People (*Apostolicam Actuositatem*)

Dogmatic Constitution on Divine Revelation (*Dei Verbum*)

Public Session IX, December 7, 1965

Declaration on Religious Liberty (*Dignitatis Humanae*)

Decree on the Missionary Activity of the Church (*Ad Gentes*)

Decree on the Ministry and Life of Priests (*Presbyterorum Ordinis*)

Pastoral Constitution on the Church in the Modern World
(*Gaudium et Spes*)

The decrees of the council look to action in roles of service in the life of the church by bishops, priests, lay apostles, and missionaries. The previous chapter showed how the nine Vatican II decrees have doctrinal bases in sections and passages of the Dogmatic Constitution on the Church.[2] Taking account of such connections brings out a systematic unity which organizes a large block of the sixteen documents of Vatican Council II.

1. See the appendix of chapter 8, on the itinerary of the documents through the conciliar process.

2. See 195–96, above.

In what follows, attention will fall selectively on three developments during the council's fourth period: (1) on how the Pastoral Constitution on the Church in the Modern World came to have a remarkable *Christological grounding* for its dialogue with the modern world; (2) on how the Constitution on Divine Revelation, *Dei Verbum*, gives what should be taken as *the theological starting point* of all Vatican II teaching and reform measures; (3) on an understanding of *Gaudium et Spes*, along with the Declarations on Non-Christian Religions and on Religious Liberty, as forming Vatican II's *counter-syllabus* by which the church set aside a critical hostility to aspects of modernity which had marked Catholic thinking for over a century. On the third development, we will note how an energetic minority of Vatican II members opposed this fundamental change of ecclesial attitudes in envisioning modern history and the world that emerged during this history.[3]

Christological Convictions to Ground Dialogue with the Modern World

On October 8, 1965, the council held the last meeting, or General Congregation, at which the members spoke on the draft of the eventual Pastoral Constitution, completing a discussion begun on September 21. Three speakers treated issues of its final chapter on war/peace and the international community of nations. But other speakers were critical of the text as a whole and insisted on needed revisions. Their main desire was to transform the schema's social and historical account of human problems into a discourse arising from central Christian convictions about Jesus Christ.

Bishop William Philbin (Down and Connor, Ireland), noted how the schema abounded in duties people should carry out in sectors of life in the modern world. But Bishop Philbin wanted

3. Surveys of Vatican II's fourth period include Ratzinger, *Theological Highlights of Vatican II*, 199–266, and O'Malley, *What Happened at Vatican II*, 247–89.

this explicitly connected with Christ, the one hope of the world. Christ should not be only the teacher of natural law and social duties, but even more the source of the needed grace for fulfilling the duties. As it addresses the modern world, this text must proclaim with confidence the only remedy for our time and every time: "Jesus Christ, the same yesterday, today, and forever!" (Heb 13:8). Bishop Philbin insisted that the text be revised so as make Christ's role and grace a central theme.[4]

Another speaker was Archbishop Gabriel-Marie Garrone (Toulouse, France) who gave his report to the council fathers as president of the commission responsible for revising the schema before the fathers would vote on it. Archbishop Garrone assured the assembly that the commission had been attending carefully to their comments on the schema, both in speeches in St. Peter's (numbering 160) and in written evaluations and suggested revisions (already over 400 pages) they were handing in on the schema. Garrone assured them that the commission was going to revise the text to make it conform to their often-insistent recommendations. One point stood out as a topic for revision. Many of the fathers, he said, had found the text too philosophical in treating modern problems and in proposing ethical solutions. It was also too optimistic about good in the world of today, lacking a realistic sense of the Christian life as being a combat (*colluctatio*) against sin and the malign enemy of the human good.[5] In the revision, already begun, the mystery of Christ will be foundational, by a strong profession at the beginning of Christ's light and grace, so this might radiate into the treatments of the human vocation and today's major problems of human and social life.[6] Archbishop Garrone hoped

---

4. *Acta Synodalia*, 4.3:729–32. Philbin's cited text of Hebrews entered *Gaudium et Spes* (no. 10), to be cited below, and is echoed in no. 45.

5. Archbishop Garrone noted that some recommendations wanted the text to give a profound account of the human drama, "since human life in the world is a combat with Christ against sin and the Evil One" (*Acta Synodalia*, 4.3:737). The need for this point at an important place in the Pastoral Constitution goes back to Karl Rahner's suggestions to the German bishops. See 216n11, below.

6. In the promulgated Pastoral Constitution, no. 10 will make this profession of Christ.

that a prophetic flame would come to permeate the revised version on which he and his fellow commission members were setting to work.[7]

The commission responsible for presenting and amending the text on the church in the modern world, headed by Archbishop Garrone, was a mixed commission joining members and *periti* from the doctrinal and lay apostolate commissions of the council. They had already met on September 23, 1965, to prepare for revising the draft in the light of the members' interventions during the fourth period. Ten sub-commissions were set up, corresponding to the draft chapters, with each sub-commission including four to six council fathers and a group of six to ten *periti*.[8]

This discussion of late September and early October 1965 was on a draft that had the same structure as the eventual *Gaudium et Spes*. After a short preface (nos. 1–3), an "Introductory Exposition" in six sections sets forth the condition of human beings amid the ever-changing historical features of the modern world (nos. 4–9). Then Part I, in four chapters, treats human dignity, the person in society, and human creative work, adding an account of the church's role in the world. Part II then sets forth doctrine to meet the urgent challenges of social life in five sectors of life in the modern world, namely, marriage and the family, cultural development and access to culture, economic life, duties in the political community, and the fostering of peace through action in the community of peoples.[9]

At the time, the schema's chapters of Part I on the human vocation already concluded with Christological passages, now found in *Gaudium et Spes*, nos. 22, 32, 38, and 45. But Garrone had become convinced that Christology was so basic that later readers should encounter it earlier in the Constitution and thus not take nos. 22, 32, 38, and 45 as being theological afterthoughts to a historical and social-psychological analysis.

7. Archbishop Garrone's report is given in *Acta Synodalia*, 4.3:735–39.

8. Giovanni Turbanti lists the members of the sub-commissions in *Un concilio per il mondo moderno. La redazione della costituzione pastorale "Gaudium et spes" del Vaticano II* (Bologna: Il Mulino, 2000), 632–34.

9. The full text of the draft discussed early in the fourth period is in *Acta Synodalia*, 4.1:435–516.

What lay behind the imperative voiced by Archbishop Garrone on October 8, 1965, namely, to revise the schema on the church in the modern world to make it more insistent on Christ and his grace? The call for a Christological basis, as a starting point, had been heard from the first day of the council's discussion of the mid-1965 draft, when Cardinal Archbishop Juan Landázzuri Ricketts (Lima, Peru) had urged that the section proclaim Christ's Gospel forthrightly and show the meaning of human life from our Lord's death and resurrection.[10] On the next day, Cardinal Döpfner, speaking for ninety-one fathers, insisted that the church speak to the world out of its faith convictions to show that it has deeper insights into the human situation than do secular disciplines of historical and social analysis.[11] The Coadjutor-Bishop Simon Lourdisamy (Bangalore, India) spoke for sixty-two Indian bishops to insist that the text show from the start the central position of Christ, in whom creation reaches its fulfillment.[12] On September 24, Bishop Hermann Volk (Mainz, Germany) called for revisions to make the text a properly theological account, that is, one in which the church says about the world what the world cannot on its own know and say about itself. The point is that Christ is the head and foundation of the universe and that human beings overcome sin and reach their supernatural end only through him, who offers light and life for all.[13]

10. *Acta Synodalia*, 4.1:561–64, esp. 562–63.

11. *Acta Synodalia*, 4.2:28–33, esp. 31. Döpfner's text included points made by Karl Rahner when he spoke to the German and Scandinavian bishops before the council's fourth period. Rahner criticized the schema for disregarding the situation of the world in the light of the incarnation, death, and resurrection of Christ. A Christian theology of history must take account of the fact that after God's saving intervention in Christ, the antagonism between the devil and Christ's disciples has not lessened but become more bitter. See the account of Rahner's criticism given by Joseph Komonchak, "Le valutazioni sulla *Gaudium et spes*," in *Volti di fine concilio*, 118–19; in English, briefly, in *Unfinished Journey*, 104–5, and completely at https://jakomonchak.wordpress.com/category/Vatican-II.

12. *Acta Synodalia*, 4.2:380–83. See esp. 382 on Christ.

13. *Acta Synodalia*, 4.2:406–10. Volk offered a dense account of Christ in creation and human history at 407–8, which should not only appear in the final paragraphs of the chapters of Part I as done now in the draft but should be declared forthrightly near the beginning,

Thus, when Archbishop Garrone presented the agenda of the revisers of the schema, his emphatic words on the role of Christ in the coming text were taking up a recurrent theme urged by the Vatican II membership. Nine days later, on October 17, *peritus* Joseph Ratzinger delivered a formulated text to the redactors of the revision which started a development toward a key addition to the schema of the Pastoral Constitution, namely, its Christ-centered point of departure for treating the human calling.[14] Part of Ratzinger's suggestion included the following:

The church places its hope in the kingdom of the man who is at the same time true God and in whom the kingdom of God and the human kingdom coincide. In him, as well, she learns the true expanse of the human calling, which extends to participating in God himself.... Human beings, with a calling infinitely transcending their own essence, can find no equilibrium in themselves, because their desires are always greater than finite realities and are never fulfilled by them. In the face of Jesus Christ crucified, moreover, the church knows that humans are ... wounded by that divine love that embraces them and makes their hearts restless.... Thus, the church believes that the definitive answers to the pressing questions of the human race are found in Christ, true God and true man. Therefore, she intends to respond to these questions of today in the light that God makes resplendent in the face of Christ (2 Cor 4:6).

In time, the Pastoral Constitution (no. 10) evolved further from Ratzinger's text by the suggestions of others to become a "Christological Credo," in three articles, affirmed as the council turned to treat in its main parts the human vocation and principal areas of human and social problems.[15] This is one of Vatican II's

---

to bring out Christ's essential role in creation and in the redemption of human beings from sin. Bishop Volk had been professor of dogmatic theology at the University of Münster prior to his appointment as bishop of Mainz in 1962. To succeed him, the Münster theology faculty called Joseph Ratzinger to its dogmatic theology chair in 1963.

14. See Wicks, "Six Texts by Prof. Joseph Ratzinger as *Peritus*," 246–49 (introduction), 291–93 (text in English), and 309–11 (the Latin original of the proposed amendment).

15. Thomas Gertler called *Gaudium et Spes*, no. 10, a "Christological Credo" in his study

great texts on Jesus Christ, from a document which has often been "misremembered" by not taking these lines into account:

The church firmly believes [*firmiter credit*] that Christ, who died and was raised for the sake of all (cf. 2 Corinthians 5:15), can through His Spirit offer human beings the light and the strength to measure up to their supreme destiny. Nor has any other name under heaven been given by which they can be saved (cf. Acts 4:12). She likewise believes [*similiter credit*] that in her most kindly Lord and Master is to be found the key, the center, and the goal of human beings and of all human history. The church also maintains [*affirmat insuper*] that beneath all changes there are many realities which do not change and which have their ultimate foundation in Christ, "the same yesterday, today, and forever" (Hebrews 13:8). Hence under the light of Christ, the image of the unseen God, the firstborn of every creature (Colossians 1:15), the council proposes to address all people in order to shed light on the mystery of human life and to cooperate in finding the solution to the outstanding problems of our time.[16]

For appropriating the vision of Vatican II, one can do well to meditate on this precious formulation. The paragraph added during the fourth period expresses just how the Catholic church turns to the world as its dialogue partner. It is with an explicit and firm conviction about the Christological basis of what it offers to the conversation on the human calling (*Gaudium et Spes*, Part I, chaps. I–IV) and on the areas of human life in which problems need solving (*Gaudium et Spes*, Part II, chaps. I–V).

---

of the text in *Jesus Christus Antwort der Kirche auf die Frage nach dem Menschen* (Leipzig: St. Benno Verlag, 1986), 107–14.

16. *Gaudium et Spes*, no. 10. Pope John Paul II recognized the importance of this passage when he cited it in full in the conclusion of his Apostolic Letter of November 10, 1994, on the coming of the new millennium, *Novo Millennio Adveniente*, par. 59. The urgency of correcting the misremembering of key Vatican II texts on Jesus Christ has been set forth by Robert Imbelli in *Rekindling the Christic Imagination: Theological Meditations for the New Evangelization* (Collegeville, Minn.: Liturgical Press, 2014).

Dei Verbum: Christ the Savior as God's Central Revelation of Himself to Us

On November 18, 1965, at the fourth period's second Public Session, Vatican II completed and promulgated its Dogmatic Constitution on Divine Revelation (*Dei Verbum*). This came three full years after the council had treated critically an earlier text on God's word, The Sources of Revelation (*De Fontibus Revelationis*) in November 1962.[17] Thus the Constitution on the word of God evolved in a process which was nearly coterminous with the historical life of the council itself. Because of this, the history of *Dei Verbum* offers precious insights for understanding Vatican II in a manner going beyond popular formulas or slogans about the council.

Dei Verbum is also valuable for helping us understand the place of Vatican II in the modern history of Catholic teaching. The Constitution says explicitly in its prologue that its teaching follows in the footsteps of the Council of Trent (1545–63) and Vatican Council I (1869–70). *Dei Verbum* relates to Trent and advances along its path in chapter II, on "the transmission of divine revelation," by the Gospel in apostolic preaching and teaching, by the church's living tradition, by the scriptures, and by the church's teaching office or Magisterium (nos. 7–10).[18] *Dei Verbum*'s chapters III–VI, on scripture, have bases in both Trent and Vatican I, but they are as well a coherent updating of teachings given in the encyclicals on scripture issued by Popes Leo XIII, Benedict XV, and Pius XII.[19]

17. On the 1962 debate and its outcome, that is, Pope John XXIII's removal of the schema on the "sources" from the immediate council agenda, see chapter 6, above. This crucial development had an initial stimulus from the theological criticisms formulated "behind the scenes," which chapter 3, above, presents.

18. See the texts of Trent's Session IV (April 8, 1546), (1) on the "Canonical Books and Apostolic Traditions" and (2) on the "Latin Vulgate and Rules of Interpreting Scripture," in *Decrees*, ed. Tanner, 2:663–66, and in *The Scripture Documents: An Anthology of Official Catholic Teachings*, ed. Dean P. Béchard (Collegeville, Minn.: Liturgical Press, 2002), 3–6.

19. See, especially, the passage of Vatican I (1870) on biblical inspiration and interpretation in *Decrees*, ed. Tanner, 2:806, and in *The Scripture Documents*, ed. Béchard, 16–17. Pope Leo XIII, *Providentissimus Deus*, Encyclical Letter, November 18, 1893; Pope Benedict XV,

Dei Verbum's first chapter, on revelation itself and on faith, is a notable revision of Vatican I's Dogmatic Constitution on the Catholic Faith (*Dei Filius*). That earlier document influenced deeply the notion of God's revelation and of faith's response as these were taught and held by generations of Catholic theology teachers and their students from 1870 to 1965. On God's revelation, *Dei Filius*, in chapters II and III, gives a quite terse account of *what* God reveals to the human race, namely, "Himself and the eternal decrees of His will" (*se ipsum ac aeterna voluntatis suae decreta humano generi revelare*). Vatican I illustrates this revelation by a single scriptural text, the opening verse of Hebrews: "In times past, God spoke in partial and various ways to our ancestors through the prophets; in these last days, he spoke to us through a Son" (Heb 1:1–2, from the Latin Vulgate with the verbal forms denoting speaking, *loquens . . . locutus est*, to indicate God's revelatory action).

But closer study of Vatican I on revelation shows that that council was mainly concerned to clarify aspects that qualify and surround the content of God's revelation, as was called for and made urgent by directions taken in nineteenth-century theology. God revealed himself and the decrees of his will (1) in a *supernatural manner*, requiring an elevating grace of apprehension and conveying some truths ("mysteries") lying beyond the reach of human reason and research—all of which, however, fits with our supernatural calling to the vision of God. The divine locution in revelation has been (2) *accompanied by outward signs*, especially the miracles of Jesus and the fulfillment of prophecies, to show even to reason the *credibility* of God's word. Further, in Vatican I's account, the revealed content, even though involving supernatural mysteries, is nonetheless, once it is received in faith, (3) *open* to believers' rational inquiry for gaining beneficial and religious-

---

Spiritus Paraclitus, Encyclical Letter, September 15, 1920; and Pope Pius XII, *Divino Afflante Spiritu*, Encyclical Letter, September 30, 1943. The texts are in *The Scripture Documents*, ed. Béchard, 17–59, 81–110, and 115–36.

ly fruitful insights into its meaning, that is, in theology. Thus, in the 1870 Dogmatic Constitution, *what* God revealed of himself and his decrees has a supernatural character, is credible to reason, and is penetrable by intellectual investigation of its meaning in theology. On revealed content—the message and account given of God—Vatican I stated a bare minimum, while expanding on three qualities that needed emphasis in 1870 and which mark God's revelation and affect our reception of it in faith.

Dei Verbum's chapter I, on revelation, fills out amply the revealed *content* God gives us, a content that is salvific and has a redemptive or soteriological focus, that is, the revelation of God-with-us in Christ both to liberate us human beings from sin and death and to lead us into communion with himself. This begins in *Dei Verbum's* prologue, which evokes the beginning of 1 John on the apostolic message gathering hearers into communion both with the apostles and with the Father and the Son. In its unfolding across history, God's revelation culminates in Jesus Christ, who mediates divine revelation and sums it up (no. 2), even recapitulating all that God reveals (no. 7). The Christ-event shows God to our human family, by our Lord's presence and epiphany, by his words and deeds, by his signs and miracles, and especially by his death, resurrection, and sending of the Spirit—all of which fuse together to reveal God as Emmanuel, who is with us to free us from the shadowy realm of sin and death and raise us to eternal life (no. 4). This then is the ample account of God's saving address in deed and word to humankind.

Faith, then, is what Vatican I stated as "the full submission of intellect and will to God who reveals," to which Vatican II characteristically adds the personalist expression that in faith "one freely commits oneself entirely to God." Faith is also, for *Dei Verbum*, open to deepening, toward which the Holy Spirit's gifts gently lead not only individual believers but indeed the whole community of faith (no. 5).

Vatican II states revelation's evangelical content in five paragraphs, citing or referencing thirty-two biblical passages, including Hebrews 1:1–2 (no. 4). It gives us a text which, if remembered rightly and appropriated, can contribute much to the personal and community *rejuvenation* in faith and life about which Pope Saint John XXIII spoke more often than he spoke about *aggiornamento*.[20] *Dei Verbum*'s chapter I lays a fine basis for preaching, which should never pass over Christ the savior in silence. From him, the center of God's word to us, the listening people can come to truly know "the joy of the Gospel."

Furthermore, in the inner logic of the sixteen Vatican II documents, *Dei Verbum*'s account of divine revelation stands in the first place.[21] This account formulates for our time, simply speaking, *the Gospel*. Regarding the rest of Vatican II's teaching and reform decrees, *Dei Verbum* gives the proclamation by which the church comes to be assembled as the *congregatio fidelium* and the priestly people for worship, as the Constitutions on the Church and on Divine Worship set forth. This revealed Gospel is the message that all church ministries and apostolates, treated in the council's nine reform decrees, serve and promote. The same Gospel creates the horizon of understanding within which Catholic Christians view the world and its structures for promoting the coherent unfolding of the human vocation, as set forth in *Gaudium et Spes* (no. 10). Consequently, the Vatican II Doctrinal Commission said at one point that the Constitution on Divine Revelation is in a certain

---

20. See chapter 1, above.

21. See chapter 3, above. Richard Gaillardetz agrees on the priority of *Dei Verbum*, because it opens with the church in the posture of humble listening. "Vatican II and the Humility of the Church," in *The Legacy of Vatican II*, ed. Faggioli and Vicini, 99–100. This is opposed to the view that takes the Constitution on the Liturgy as the key to the council texts, as argued by Faggioli in "*Sacrosanctum Concilium* and the Meaning of Vatican II." This latter position has been contested on good grounds by Christian D. Washburn in "The Theological Priority of 'Lumen gentium' and 'Dei verbum' for the Interpretation of the Second Vatican Council," *The Thomist* 78 (2014): 1–29; and "The Second Vatican Council and the Theological Authority of 'Sacrosanctum Concilium' as a Constitution," *Nova et Vetera* 13 (2015): 1093–1124.

way (*quodammodo*) the first of all the council's documents.[22] Many
editions of the documents place *Lumen Gentium* at the "head of
the book." But a few interpreters have seen more deeply and hold
that we contextualize the ecclesiology of Vatican II better when we
place the Dogmatic Constitution on the Church *after Dei Verbum*,
to give the whole corpus of documents, including its ecclesiology, the starting point of the opening reference to the church in the
Constitution on Divine Revelation, that is, the indication that it
is "hearing the word of God reverently and proclaiming it confidently" (*Dei verbum religiose audiens et fidenter proclamans*).[23]

But how has *Dei Verbum* been received? One astute American observer, Robert Imbelli, traces the post-Vatican II Catholic
fragmentation and polarizations to the eclipse of just what *Dei
Verbum* gives us, namely "the enlivening and unifying center of
the faith. That center is Jesus Christ himself . . . . Absent this concrete and vivifying center, fragmentation and division ensue."
Neglect of *Dei Verbum* shows itself in theologies of plural ways of
salvation, popular in recent decades. Neglect of this center motivated Pope Benedict XVI to write his volumes, *Jesus of Nazareth*.
The way ahead, Imbelli argues, is a comprehensive re-reception
of the council that moves in the Christocentric direction that *Dei
Verbum* has affirmed.[24]

And, I add, *Dei verbum*'s account of God's revelation summed
up in Christ is the doctrinal basis of the most striking passages in

22. The Commission said this in its explanatory *Relatio* accompanying the late 1964
revision of *De Revelatione*. The point was a defense of the ample intention stated at the end
of no. 1, i.e., that by this updated teaching the message of salvation may be heard in the
whole world, be believed, and so lead to hope and love. This can stand here, so the Commission argued, because from one viewpoint the passage was introducing the whole body
of Vatican II's main documents. *Acta Synodalia*, 4.1:341. The formulation of the intended
worldwide result came from St. Augustine, *De catechizandis rudibus*, chap. IV, no. 8.

23. Recently Robert Imbelli maintained that among the four constitutions of Vatican II,
"*Dei Verbum* deserves to be considered a 'first among equals.' The reason is simple. Unless
God revealed himself fully through Jesus Christ in the Holy Spirit, then the church is without
foundation and the liturgy a merely human construct." *Rekindling the Christic Imagination*, xv.

24. Ibid., xvi–xvii.

Pope Francis's exhortation, *The Joy of the Gospel* (2013). For example, "All revealed truths derive from the same divine source.... In this basic core, what shines forth is the beauty of the saving love of God made manifest in Jesus Christ who died and rose from the dead" (no. 36). Further, bearers of the Christian message should be "always keeping in mind the fundamental message: the personal love of God who became man, who gave himself up for us, who is loving and who offers us his salvation and friendship" (no. 128). Vatican II's *Dei Verbum* taught on God's revelation of himself in Christ as God-with-us to rescue and save, which Francis has actualized in *The Joy of the Gospel*. On June 22, 2015, the pope visited the principal Waldensian church of Turin, where he spoke of the fraternal bond linking Protestants and Catholics. "This bond is not based on simply human criteria, but on the radical sharing of the foundational experience of Christian life: the encounter with the love of God that is revealed to us in Jesus Christ and the transforming action of the Holy Spirit who assists us in the journey of life."[25]

The Dissenting Minority of Vatican II

During the General Congregation of October 8, 1965, from which this chapter began, an incident took place that is worth recalling. The council's general secretary took the microphone at one point to sharply admonish some of the council fathers who were passing out pamphlets and pages of texts to their fellow council members. The general secretary said this was bothering many who are listening to speeches on the church in the modern world. This private activity is greatly annoying to the fathers who are attending to the council's main work on its constitutions and decrees.[26]

This intervention by general secretary Pericle Felici calls attention to an aspect of Vatican II which many council participants

---

25. Given in the Zenit daily bulletin of June 23, 2015, at http://www.zenit.org/en.
26. *Acta Synodalia*, 4.3:735.

recall vividly, but is rarely noted by historians. This is the activity of individuals and groups who circulated during Vatican II a huge number of pamphlets and declarations, exerting themselves in this way to get their texts into the hands of as many of the council fathers as they could reach. One group engaged in this activity was the "International Group of Council Fathers," the *Coetus internationalis Patrum*.[27]

The group's activity began slowly during the second period of Vatican II by organizing Tuesday afternoon conferences by speakers who offered the fathers in attendance critical reviews of the schemas coming up on the council agenda. The group gained for the third period in 1964 a working space, the secretarial help of two Claretian priests, and a mimeograph machine, all furnished by the Claretian curial Cardinal Arcadio Larraona. The *Coetus* also opened a small office near St. Peter's where council fathers could pick up the group's ever more frequent circulars and especially the amendments (*modi*) prepared by the group's *periti* for attaching to a vote of approval with a reservation (*placet iuxta modum*) on the texts then being completed on the church and ecumenism. Leading the *Coetus* was an organizing and planning committee headed by Archbishop Marcel Lefebvre. Other leaders were Bishop Luigi Carli (Segni, Italy), Bishop Antonio de Castro Mayer (Campos, Brazil), Archbishop Geraldo de Proença Sigaud, SVD (Diamantina, Brazil), and Abbot Jean Prou, OSB (Solesmes, France).[28]

---

27. The *Coetus* appears regularly in Ralph Wiltgen, SVD, *The Rhine Flows into the Tiber* (Rockford, Ill.: TAN Books, 1985; original, 1967), 148–50, 178–80, 247–51, and 278. See also Luc Perrin, "Le *Coetus Internationalis Patrum* et la minoranza conciliare," in *L'evento e le decisioni: Studi sulle dinamiche del concilio Vaticano II*, ed. Maria Teresa Fattori and Alberto Melloni (Bologna: Il Mulino, 1997), 173–87, and Joseph Famerée, in *History of Vatican II*, ed. Alberigo and Komonchak, 3:170–75. A favorable account is spread throughout the second half of Roberto de Mattei, *The Second Vatican Council: An Unwritten Story* (Fitzwilliam, N.H.: Loreto, 2012; original Italian, 2010), beginning with the birth of the *Coetus* on 305–10. Very informative is Philippe Roy-Lysencourt, *Les membres du Coetus internationalis patrum au Concile Vatican II* (Leuven: Peeters, 2014), which I presented in "Yet More Light on Vatican Council II," 102–10.

28. See Roy-Lysencourt, *Les membres du Coetus Internationalis Patrum*, 21–76, for

Before the fourth period opened, the group's leadership had petitioned Pope Paul VI to give it status as an official entity of the council which could, at appropriate moments, give dissenting "minority reports" on schemas in addresses before the whole council at general congregations. In the name of Paul VI, Secretary of State Cardinal Amleto Cicognani responded with a sharply worded refusal, including a critique of the title, *Coetus internationalis Patrum*, as liable to inspire similar alliances, which would become factional pressure groups infringing on the freedom of the council fathers in dealing with Vatican II affairs.[29]

In early October 1965, when the deadline approached for handing in written comments on the draft-text on the church in the modern world, the *Coetus* circulated a statement to which 334 council members signed on in agreement. This called for adding a passage to the schema's statement on atheism by which the council would also repeat earlier papal condemnations of communism, thereby speaking against the form of atheism then exerting a wide, malevolent influence.[30] Two days later, on October 11, the same group distributed to as many fathers as they could reach an invitation to reject, by votes of *non placet*, the final emended schema

brief biographies of the five leaders and a list of references to the *Acta Synodalia* for the council interventions of each. The author goes on to treat the cardinals sympathizing with the group, the "fellow travelers" and occasional backers among council fathers, and the *periti* of the *Coetus*, particularly Fr. Victor-Alain Berto, Fr. Raymond Dulac, and Fr. Georges Frénaud, OSB.

29. See the texts in *Acta Synodalia*, 6.4:373–74 (petition of July 25, 1965, signed by Archbishop Lefebvre, Archbishop de Proença Sigaud, and Bishop Carli) and 410–11 (August 11, 1965, answer of Cardinal Cicognani). The cardinal's response is given in English in Roberto de Mattei, *The Second Vatican Council*, 431, with a critical observation based on the imagined existence of a "Rhine Alliance" of Vatican II progressives, as popularized by Wiltgen in *The Rhine Flows into the Tiber*.

30. Roberto de Mattei narrates the circumstances surrounding this intervention in *The Second Vatican Council: An Unwritten Story*, 469–81, giving the text of the proposed addition to the schema on 474–75. Such an insertion would have gone directly against Pope John XXIII's fundamental orientation of the council, stated in his inaugural address of October 11, 1962, to not continue further the well-established Catholic practice of authoritatively condemning errors but instead to attract people to what is true and good by confidently showing the validity and beauty of Catholic teaching.

of the Declaration on the Church's Relation to Non-Christian Religions, which spoke to the relation to Jews in its famous no. 4.[31] All during the fourth period, the *Coetus* also marshalled particularly vehement oppositions to the drafts that Vatican II eventually promulgated on its final day as the Declaration on Religious Liberty (*Dignitatis Humanae*) and the Pastoral Constitution on the Church in the Modern World (*Gaudium et Spes*).

Early in the fourth period, the *Coetus* circulated a mimeographed booklet of criticisms of the schema on religious liberty, a copy of which Bishop Carli submitted as an attachment to his own written comments on the emended text on religious liberty.[32] During the fourth period, Archbishop Lefebvre spoke in the council hall on September 20, 1965, against the schema on religious liberty, claiming that its doctrine came from Hobbes, Locke, Rousseau, and Voltaire, who had aimed to destroy the Catholic church. When nineteenth-century liberal Catholics took up the position of the schema, Leo XIII condemned them.[33] Several contrasting addresses in favor of the text on religious liberty then followed, for example, by Cardinal Giovanni Urbani of Venice of behalf of thirty-two Italian bishops and from Cardinal Archbishop Joseph Lefebvre (Bourges, France), who deftly refuted each of the objections of opponents like his fellow Frenchman and cousin Archbishop Marcel Lefebvre.[34]

---

31. De Mattei, *The Second Vatican Council*, 462.

32. *Acta Synodalia*, 4.1:683–92. Carli claims that the present-day system of religious liberty has its basis in laicism, religious indifferentism, and agnosticism, against which the council has to declare immutable, eternal principles drawn from the encyclicals of Leo XIII and Pius XII. Earlier, the two Brazilian leaders of the *Coetus*, Proença Sigaud and de Castro Mayer, had sent in a lengthy critique of the same schema when it was still chap. V of the schema on ecumenism (*Acta Synodalia*, 3.3:648–57).

33. *Acta Synodalia*, 4.1:792–94.

34. See O'Malley, *What Happened at Vatican II*, 254–57, on the speeches favoring the religious liberty text, along with the outcome of the vote taken shortly after, showing 1,997 fathers favorable and only 224 opposed to working ahead with the text on religious liberty recently revised by the Secretariat for Promoting Christian Unity, which shepherded the text through the conciliar process.

On September 22, 1965, Archbishop Proença Sigaud voiced opposition against the schema on the church's relation to the modern world. For him the schema adopts a phenomenological method which rejects objective truth and immutable metaphysical principles. The church already has a finely articulated body of teachings related to the world of today, which are at hand in the twenty volumes of discourses by Pope Pius XII (1939–58), from which the council ought to be drawing, instead of taking up the dangerous "Teilhardian" ideas of the schema.[35]

The counter arguments by the *Coetus* did have an influence, as shown in the numbers of *non placet* votes of disapproval by the fathers on the documents that the *Coetus* opposed most vigorously during the fourth period. These *non placet* votes occurred both in Vatican II regular meetings, the congregations, after the whole text was amended, and then in the public sessions just before Pope Paul VI's promulgation. There were about 2,000 voting members in the congregations, of which the number rose to 2,300 in the public sessions. On the Relation of the Church to Non-Christian Religions, especially the Jews, 250 council members voted *non placet* during the congregation, which fell to 88 in the public session of promulgation by the pope. On Religious Liberty, 249 members were opposed in the congregation, of whom 70 held to their *non placet* votes in the presence of Paul VI on the day of promulgation. Similarly, on the Pastoral Constitution on the Church in the Modern World, 251 members opposed it in the congregation, with 70 opposing it at the December 7, 1965, session of promulgation by Paul VI.[36] Thus when these final

35. *Acta Synodalia*, 4.2:47–50.

36. For the shifting numbers of *non placet* votes on *Nostra Aetate*, see *Acta Synodalia*, 4.4:824 (October 15, 1965, congregation) and 4.5:674 (October 28 promulgation). On *Dignitatis Humanae*, see *Acta Synodalia*, 4.6:780 (November 19 congregation) and 4.7:860 (December 7 promulgation). On *Gaudium et Spes*, see *Acta Synodalia*, 4.7:641 (December 6 congregation) and 4.7:860 (December 7 promulgation). For the contrasting case of *Christus Dominus*, see *Acta Synodalia*, 4.4:634 (October 6 congregation) and 4.5:673 (October 28 promulgation). On *Dei Verbum*, see *Acta Synodalia*, 4.4:753 (October 27 congregation) and

texts were completed and approved in a regular council meeting, just over 12 percent of the members rejected them, but when the pope stood ready to approve and promulgate them, a minority of only 3 percent still dissented from the documents' teachings. In contrast, on Vatican II's Decree on the Pastoral Office of Bishops, thirteen members voted *non placet* in the congregation, which fell to only two in the public session of October 28, 1965. On *Dei Verbum*, there were 27 *non placet* votes, out of 2,115 voting during the congregation of October 29 on the completed text, but only six of *non placet* in the public session of November 18. On the Church's Missionary Activity, eighteen voted *non placet* in the congregation, but only five held to this disapproval in the public session of December 7, 1965.

Vatican II thus ended with a minority in disagreement with three of its eleven fourth period documents, namely, those relating to other religions, to religious liberty in civil society, and to encountering the modern world in respectful dialogue. This minority, we know, became in time a serious wound of the post-Vatican II Catholic church: the schism begun by Archbishop Lefebvre and which today is given focus and ongoing life by the Sacerdotal Society of St. Pius X. One should note the substantial issues of the fourth period dissent by the *Coetus* on issues quite different from that of Latin in the liturgy and using only the Roman canon in eucharistic celebration.

To grasp more deeply the significance of the International Group of Council Fathers at Vatican II and of the documents they opposed during the fourth period, we can well consider Joseph Ratzinger's characterization of the three Vatican II documents against which the Group directed its dissent and redoubled its efforts to gain adherents to its rejection. Ratzinger said the following in an article of 1975 on *Gaudium et Spes*: "We might say

---

4.6:687 (November 18 promulgation). On *Ad Gentes*, see *Acta Synodalia*, 4.5:100 (November 3 congregation) and 4.7:860 (December 7 promulgation).

that (in conjunction with the texts on religious liberty and world religions) it a revision of the *Syllabus of Errors* issued by Pius IX [1864], a kind of counter-syllabus."[37] He continues: "The *Syllabus* established a line of demarcation against the determining forces of the nineteenth century: against the scientific and political world view of liberalism. In the struggle against modernism [1907 and after, under Pius X] this twofold delimitation was ratified and strengthened."[38]

Ratzinger added a remark about "the one-sidedness of the position adopted by the church under Pius IX and Pius X in response to the situation created by the new phase of history inaugurated by the French Revolution." But Vatican II set out to overcome this one-sided set of positions, based on a complicated network of causes which had come together to form the background of the Vatican II documents of the "counter-syllabus" on

37. At this point, Ratzinger inserted an explanatory footnote on Pius IX's *Syllabus of Errors*: "*Syllabus* was the designation given to the catalogue of eighty statements in which Pius IX took a critical stand with regard to the spiritual and political problems caused by secularization. The *Syllabus* was sent to the bishops in 1864 and led, especially in France, to sharp disagreements." The *Syllabus* collected censures already issued by Pius IX in twenty-four of his discourses and encyclicals from 1847 to 1861. See the entry "Syllabus Errorum," in *Oxford Dictionary of the Christian Church*, 3rd ed., ed. F. L. Cross and E. A. Livingston (Oxford: Oxford University Press, 1997), 1565–66. For the text of the Syllabus, see *Compendium of Creeds, Definitions, and Declarations on Matters of Faith and Morals*, compiled by Heinrich Denzinger, revised by Peter Hünermann, ed. Robert Fastiggi and Anne Englund Nash (San Francisco: Ignatius Press, 2012), nos. 2901–80 (590–98).

38. Ratzinger, "Church and World," 381. This essay appeared originally in *Internationale katholische Zeitschrift Communio* 4 (1975): 439–54. On "liberalism" in Ratzinger's usage, see the entry "Liberalismus," by E. Deuerlein in *Lexikon für Theologie und Kirche*, ed. Joseph Höfer and Karl Rahner (Freiburg: Herder, 1957–67), 6:1007–10. J. Hallowell's entry on "liberalism" in the *New Catholic Encyclopedia* (New York: McGraw-Hill, 1967), 8:701–6, is comprehensive and already notes a change, as found in John XXIII's *Pacem in Terris* (1963). But in the second edition of the *New Catholic Encyclopedia* (Detroit: Thompson-Gale, 2003), A. Simon's entry, "Religious Liberalism," highlights subjectivist tendencies and the condemnations of Pius IX and Pius X (8:540–42). The concise entry in *Oxford Dictionary of the Christian Church*, ed. Cross and Livingston, 977–78, refers on one hand to a liberalism of secular and anthropocentric humanism, which Newman rejected as opposed to dogmatic truth, but there was also the liberalism of nineteenth-century orthodox believers who favored political democracy and ecclesiastical reform. Therefore, attention to context is needed for grasping the intent of references to "liberalism."

religions, religious liberty, and the relation of church and world. On the Pastoral Constitution, Ratzinger added: "Let us be content to say here that the text serves as a counter-syllabus and, as such, represents on the part of the church, an attempt at an official reconciliation with the new era inaugurated in 1789."[39]

On the designation "counter-syllabus," adopted by Joseph Ratzinger, we note that it does not refer to a revocation of the condemnations issued by Popes Pius IX and Pius X. When Ratzinger wrote his essay for the German edition of *Communio* in 1975, his readers knew well the content of the three Vatican II documents under discussion, which do not revoke previous censures. The documents are, however, in sharp contrast to earlier papal ways of addressing the world, in being positive, respectful, and uplifting in their content. They contrast starkly with the *Syllabus* of 1864 and with the antimodernist catalogue issued by the Holy Office in 1907 with Pius X's approval, in the sixty-five censured positions of *Lamentabili,* to which the pope's encyclical *Pascendi* (also 1907) added a developed account of condemned modernist thinking. These papal documents dominated by censures of error were for many people, including many Catholics, prominent characteristics of the "face" of the Catholic church well into the twentieth century. In Vatican II, the Catholic church turned a quite different "face" to the world as it declined to issue censures but chose instead to speak to and about the world in respectful, hopeful, and encouraging ways.

The dissent fostered by the *Coetus,* which became persuasive to a shifting number of the council's members during the fourth period of 1965, contrasted with the council's majority and with Popes John XXIII and Paul VI. The Vatican II majority and the papal leadership were at one in charting a new direction that left behind the earlier condemnations of modernity originally framed

39. Ratzinger, "Church and World," 381–82.

by Pope Pius IX in 1864.[40] The vociferous minority was refusing to move on with the church's living tradition as guided by the Magisterium, as Paul VI set forth for Archbishop Lefebvre in 1976. The life of the church, and consequently also the Magisterium is—as we tend to forget—often *adaptive* to new situations and insights. It can adopt a different tone and change its rhetoric to express a developing new outlook. This characteristic was especially strong in the key documents of the fourth period of Vatican Council II and remains a characteristic essential to any global interpretation of the council.

Appendix: Pope Paul VI's Letter to Archbishop Lefebvre on the Church and Tradition (October 11, 1976)

In June 1974, Archbishop Marcel Lefebvre disobeyed Pope Paul VI's order not to ordain seminarians of the Econe Seminary to the priesthood. Nonetheless, the pope received the archbishop for a lengthy conversation at Castel Gandolfo on September 11, 1976. A month later, on the anniversary of the opening of Vatican II, Paul VI responded with a letter composed in Latin. After explaining that the archbishop is fomenting rebellion, the pope clarified the nature of tradition, based on *Dei Verbum*, chapter II, to correct the archbishop's thinking. He went on to defend the decrees of

40. On the origin of the stand by the *Coetus* on behalf of Catholic positions against strains of modern thought and politics, see Philippe J. Roy, "La préhistoire du *Coetus internationalis Patrum*. Une formation romaine, antilibéral et contre-révolutionaire," in *La théologie catholique entre intransigeance et renouveau*, ed. Routhier, Roy, and Schelkens, 321–54. Roy describes here the theological and formational directions received by the *Coetus* leadership and their *periti* in 1920–30, especially in the French Seminary in Rome and at the Gregorian and Lateran Universities. At the time, Roman theological and spiritual *formatores* propagated antimodernist convictions as they worked to prepare their students for militant efforts on behalf of an integrally Catholic society and against liberalizing currents in theology, politics, and culture. This became, at Vatican II, an important factor in the underlying motivation of the leaders and adherents of the *Coetus*.

Vatican II against charges of departing from the fundamental tradition of the church.[41]

Let us come now to the more precise requests which you formulated during the audience of September 11. You would like to see recognized the right to celebrate Mass in various places of worship according to the Tridentine rite. You wish also to continue to train candidates for the priesthood according to your criteria, "as before the council," in seminaries apart, as at Econe. But behind these questions and other similar ones, which we shall examine later on in detail, it is truly necessary to see the intricacy of the problem; and the problem is theological. For these questions have become concrete ways of expressing an ecclesiology that is warped in essential points [*ecclesiologiam, quae in capitibus praecipuis falsa esse cognoscitur*].

What is indeed at issue is the question—which must truly be called fundamental—of your clearly proclaimed refusal to recognize in its whole, the authority of the Second Vatican Council and that of the pope. This refusal is accompanied by an action oriented towards propagating and organizing what must indeed, unfortunately, be called a rebellion. This is the essential issue, and it is truly untenable....

You say that you are subject to the church and faithful to tradition by the sole fact that you obey certain norms of the past that were decreed by the predecessor of him to whom God has today conferred the powers given to Peter. That is to say, on this point also, the concept of "tradition" that you invoke is distorted [*traditionis notio, ad quam provocas, est vitiata*].

Tradition is not a rigid and dead notion, a fact of a certain static sort which at a given moment of history blocks the life of this active organism which is the church, that is, the mystical body of Christ [*Traditio enim non est quoddam quasi immotum et mortuum, vel factum quoddam staticum, ut appellant, quod certo ac definito tempore historico vitam instituti organici et actione praediti, quod est Ecclesia seu Corpus Christi mysticum, coerceat*]. It is up to the pope and to councils to exercise judgment in order to discern in the traditions of the church that which cannot be

41. The letter's full text is given in English translation in *Origins* 6 (December 16, 1976): 416–20, from which the following excerpt is taken (with very slight modifications).

renounced without infidelity to the Lord and to the Holy Spirit—the deposit of faith—and that which, on the contrary, can and must be adapted to facilitate the prayer and the mission of the church throughout a variety of times and places, in order better to translate the divine message into the language of today and better to communicate it, without an unwarranted surrender of principles.

Hence tradition is inseparable from the living Magisterium of the church, just as it is inseparable from sacred scripture. "Sacred tradition, sacred scripture and the magisterium of the church ... are so linked and joined together that one of these realities cannot exist without the others, and that all of them together, each in its own way, effectively contribute under the action of the Holy Spirit to the salvation of souls" [*Dei Verbum*, no. 10].

With the special assistance of the Holy Spirit, the popes and the ecumenical councils have acted in this common way. And it is precisely this that the Second Vatican Council did. Nothing that was decreed in this council, or in the reforms that we enacted in order to put the council into effect, is opposed to what the 2,000-year-old tradition of the church considers as fundamental and immutable. We are the guarantor of this, not in virtue of our personal qualities but in virtue of the charge which the Lord has conferred upon us as legitimate successor of Peter, and in virtue of the special assistance that He has promised to us as well as to Peter: "I have prayed for you that your faith may not fail" (Lk. 22:32). The universal episcopate is guarantor with us of this.

Again, you cannot appeal to the distinction between what is dogmatic and what is pastoral to accept certain texts of this council and to refuse others. Indeed, not everything in the council requires an assent of the same nature; only what is affirmed by definitive acts as an object of faith or as a truth related to faith requires an assent of faith. But the rest also forms part of the solemn Magisterium of the church to which each member of the faithful owes a confident acceptance and a sincere application.

You say moreover that you do not always see how to reconcile certain texts of the council, or certain dispositions which we have enacted in order to put the council into practice, with the wholesome tradition of the church and in particular with the Council of Trent and the affirmations of our predecessors. These are, for example: the responsibility of the college of bishops united with the sovereign pontiff, the new *Ordo Missae*, ecumenism, religious freedom, the attitude of dialogue, evangelization in the modern world.... It is not the place, in this letter, to deal with each of these problems. The precise tenor of the documents, with the totality of its nuances and its context, the authorized explanations, the detailed and objective commentaries which have been made, are of such a nature to enable you to overcome these personal difficulties. Absolutely secure counsellors, theologians, and spiritual directors would be able to help you even more, with God's enlightenment, and we are ready to facilitate this fraternal assistance for you.

But how can an interior personal difficulty—a spiritual drama which we respect—permit you to set yourself up publicly as a judge of what has been legitimately adopted, practically with unanimity, and knowingly to lead a portion of the faithful into your refusal? If justifications are useful in order to facilitate intellectual acceptance—and we hope that the troubled or reticent faithful will have the wisdom, honesty, and humanity to accept those justifications that are widely placed at their disposal—they are not in themselves necessary for the assent of obedience that is due to the Ecumenical Council and to the decisions of the pope. It is the ecclesial sense that is at issue.

In effect, you and those who are following you are endeavoring to come to a standstill at a given moment in the life of the church. By the same token, you refuse to accept the living church, which is the church that has always been: you break with the church's legitimate pastors and scorn the legitimate exercise of their charge.

10

Global Traits of Vatican II
in Chapter VI of *Dei Verbum*

Composed in late 2015, this chapter arose near the end of the fifty-year anniversaries of the Vatican II constitutions, decrees, and declarations. The anniversaries suggest the timeliness of a comprehensive examination of the council texts, together with their known itineraries through the council's process and even adding, where relevant, their documentary origins in 1960–62. Such an examination can reveal important global traits of Vatican II, which can free our interpretations from simplistic slogans attempting to formulate the council's characteristics as a major event in church history. Narrowing the field of study, I will compare here the final text of *Dei Verbum* with some parts of its predecessor, the schema *De Fontibus Revelationis*, with the hope of gaining from this study of contrasts both a heightened appreciation of *Dei Verbum* but also a source-based small set of traits belonging, with others, to a global interpretation of Vatican II.

A further motivation for the present approach comes from Karim Schelkens's book, *Catholic Theology of Revelation on the Eve of Vatican II: A Redaction History of the Schema* De fontibus revelationis *(1960–1962)*.[1] This Leuven dissertation of redaction history is also revisionist history, namely, "an attempt to revise somewhat" the negative view of the preparatory schema on the sources that dominates accounts of it in works on Vatican II. Schelkens says that the council majority that opposed the schema "had allowed itself to be influenced at the beginning of the council by theologically progressive lobby groups."[2] The book represents a challenge to my own view of the schema *De Fontibus*, on which I agree with the critical majority after study of the text and of the critical handling of it by theological *periti* whose council papers I have studied, namely, Joseph Ratzinger and Pieter Smulders, neither of whom belonged to "theologically progressive lobby groups."[3]

Identifying Global Traits of Vatican II from *Dei Verbum*

It is a commonplace about *Dei Verbum* that its genesis and Vatican II itinerary were nearly coterminous with the history of the council itself. The secretary of the Preparatory Theological Commission, Fr. Sebastian Tromp, composed on July 15, 1960, the first sketch of a draft on the sources of revelation.[4] The council's first period included the well-known conflicted discussion of *De*

1. Leiden: Brill, 2010. I reviewed it in *Zeitschrift der Kirchengeschichte* 123 (2012): 408–9.

2. Schelkens, *Catholic Theology of Revelation on the Eve of Vatican II*, 5.

3. See the critiques of *De Fontibus Revelationis* by Ratzinger and Smulders as related in chapter 3, above. From Ratzinger, a detailed and influential text is his conference on *De Fontibus* given to the German-speaking bishops on October 10, 1962, which I published in "Six Texts by Prof. Joseph Ratzinger as *peritus* Before and During Vatican Council II," 241–43 (introduction), 269–85 (English version), and 295–309 (German original). Smulders's concise case for rejecting *De Fontibus* circulated in roughly 1,500 mimeographed copies. I gave its Latin text in "Pieter Smulders and *Dei Verbum*: 2. On *De fontibus revelationis* during Vatican II's First Period, 1962," 590–93.

4. Schelkens, *Catholic Theology of Revelation on the Eve of Vatican II*, giving Tromp's July 1960 "Schema compendiosum" and its revisions in parallel columns on 76–80.

Fontibus in the third week of November 1962, in General Congregations 19 to 24. There followed discussion and three revisions of the text, under the new title *De Revelatione Divina*, which lasted into the fourth period, when *Dei Verbum* was promulgated on November 18, 1965, at Public Session VIII, held the day after the council's General Congregation 163.[5]

This long overlap of the histories of the constitution and the council suggests that study of the itinerary and successive revisions leading to *Dei Verbum* will yield some elements of importance for a global, source-based interpretation of Vatican II. The drafting and revision of texts on divine revelation, tradition, and scripture, leading to *Dei Verbum*, lasted over five years (July 1960 to November 1965). Along this timeline, excisions were made from earlier drafts on revelation and its sources and on scripture and its interpretation, to be replaced by important additions to the text, which came to have their places in the promulgated *Dei Verbum*. One can confidently assume that these changes along the way will give us some important keys to viewing and interpreting Vatican II globally.

Beyond the chronological setting of *Dei Verbum*, its fundamental contents concerning divine revelation, tradition, and scripture place it in manifold relationships with all the other topics taken up by Vatican II. This claim was made in the address of October 29, 1965, before voting on the last amendments to the text, by the reporter on chapters I and II, Cardinal Emenegildo Florit of Florence, who spoke for the conciliar Doctrinal Commission. He added that the text "places us at the heart of the mystery of the church and in the epicenter of the ecumenical problem."[6]

This hunt for characteristics of Vatican II as a whole will concentrate on *Dei Verbum*'s final chapter, "Scripture in the Life of

5. I related major moments in the itinerary from *De Fontibus* to *Dei Verbum* in a study paralleling this chapter, "Scripture Reading Urged *vehementer* (DV No. 25)," 557–70; reprinted in *50 Years On: Probing the Riches of Vatican II*, ed. Schultenhover, 367–82.

6. *Acta Synodalia*, 4.5:741.

the Church," which lays down that "like the Christian religion itself, all preaching of the church must be nourished and ruled by Sacred Scripture" (no. 21). In chapter VI, a further narrowed focus will be on *Dei Verbum*'s concluding directives on how scripture ought to become formative in Catholic theology and spirituality.

This approach takes the constitution's chapter VI as akin in nature and purpose to the nine Vatican II decrees on practice and service. Each of those decrees has a doctrinal basis in parts of *Lumen Gentium*, from which they make applications to persons and their practice of service in different areas.[7] Similarly, chapter VI of *Dei Verbum* has its doctrinal basis in the preceding five chapters on God's revelation, on tradition and the Magisterium in witnessing to revelation, and on scripture as inspired, requiring correct interpretation, and comprising the Old and New Testaments. In its own work of application to practice in the church, chapter VI also brings out several aspects of the inspired scriptures in their singular witness, in the church and in believers' lives, to God's revelation.

Finally, a synchronic reading of the Vatican II *corpus* shows that the topic of *Dei Verbum*'s penultimate paragraph on personal, meditative, and prayerful reading of scripture (no. 25) is significant for other Vatican II documents. Four of the council's decrees take up this theme, giving such biblical prayer a key role in the spiritual formation of seminarians (*Optatam Totius*, nos. 4 and 8), in the daily lives of priests (*Presbyterorum Ordinis*, no. 13), in the "assiduous cultivation" of prayer by members of all religious communities (*Perfectae Caritatis*, no. 6), and in the way lay apostles should seek to find God and his will in everything and everyone (*Apostolicam Actuositatam*, no. 4). Thus, the urging of *lectio divina* concludes the constitution on revelation, while also extending

---

7. See the chart showing the interrelation of passages of *Lumen Gentium* and the council's decrees on 195–96, above.

itself into key places in other texts of application, which are the Vatican II decrees on life, practice, and service in specific roles in the church.[8]

De Fontibus and *Dei Verbum*: Outline and Title

Chapter V of *De Fontibus Revelationis* had in 1962 the title "Scripture in the Church" and it comprised six paragraphs.[9] For these, the Preparatory Theological Commission gave to each an explanatory heading in brackets, which served to outline the chapter and introduce each paragraph, and thus to help the readers, especially the council members with voice and vote, to grasp the text. The paragraph headings were as follows (nos. 24–29):

> The Church's Actions [*De curis*] Regarding Holy Scripture
> The Vulgate Latin Translation
> Reading of Holy Scripture by Priests
> Reading of Holy Scripture by the Faithful
> Catholic Exegetes
> Theology's Relation to Holy Scripture

In *Dei Verbum*, this part became chapter VI due to actions before the end of the council's first period in 1962 carried out by the Mixed Commission, with members from the Doctrinal Commission and the Unity Secretariat. Pope John XXIII formed this group to revise *De Fontibus* and it prepared a new *Prooemium* or preface, which became in *Dei Verbum* the Constitution's chapter I, "Divine

---

8. The Decree on Ecumenism also highlights personal prayer nourished by scripture as a trait described admiringly in the devotional lives of separated Western Christians (*Unitatis Redintegratio*, nos. 21 and 23).

9. The Latin text of *De Fontibus* is in *Acta Synodalia*, 1.3:14–26, and in Francisco Gil Hellín, *Concilii Vaticani II Synopsis: Constitutio Dogmatica de Divina revelatione, Dei Verbum* (Vatican City: Liberia Editrice Vaticana, 1993), 181–90. An English translation by Joseph A. Komonchak is given in https://jakomonchak.wordpress.com/category/vatican-II, in the section *The Council That Might Have Been*, as "On the sources of revelation" (thirteen pages). On the redaction process of 1961 in the Preparatory Theological Commission that led to *De Fontibus*, see Schelkens, *Catholic Theology on the Eve of Vatican II*, 168–69, 207–17, and 232.

Revelation Itself" (nos. 2–6). By this step beyond *De Fontibus* into the doctrine of revelation itself, Vatican II showed higher ambitions than those envisaged by the Preparatory Theological Commission, whose schema was on "the sources," not directly revelation itself.[10] The expanded aim was to reformulate the mode and content of revelation itself, going beyond Vatican I's Constitution on the Catholic Faith, *Dei Filius*, chapter II. By following the developed first chapter on God's revelation, chapter VI of *Dei Verbum* could in time describe and prescribe a much more potent impact on believers' lives by scripture, that is, when the latter serves as an eminent witness to a theologically more potent account of revelation, as summed up in Christ (*Dei Verbum*, no. 2) and as soteriological at its center (no. 4), than it could have done without the Constitution's chapter I.

The sixth and final chapter of *Dei Verbum* has the title, "Sacred Scripture in the Life of the Church," on which the Doctrinal Commission explained that "life" referred both to the church's inner life *and* to the outreach of the apostolate and the missions, in which scripture also makes its contributions.[11]

In *Dei Verbum*, there are still six paragraphs, also with added titles to guide study of the revised drafts by the council members.

10. The Preparatory Commission treated revelation itself in another schema, "Guarding the Purity of the Deposit of Faith," chap. IV, published in the second place among the first seven schemas distributed to the council fathers in late summer 1962. The schema was a follow-up to Pius XII's encyclical *Humani Generis*, which had corrected deviant tendencies and positions circulating on several doctrines. Chap. IV of "De deposito" censures and corrects revived modernist ideas of revelation. See the Latin text in *Acta Synodalia*, 1.4:663–71, and in English translation in https://jakomonchak.wordpress.com/category/vatican-II, in the section *The Council That Might Have Been*, as "Defending Intact the Deposit of Faith," 9–15, giving chap. IV, "Public Revelation and Catholic Faith." I included that chapter in the article, "Christ the Fullness of Revelation in *Dei verbum*," 181–82.

11. From Gil Hellín, *Synopsis*, 144, one learns that the first revised title given to what was then chap. V, by the Mixed Commission was "The *Use* of Scripture in the Church." This was changed to the eventual title in 1964 because the Doctrinal Commission agreed with some council fathers' objections that the term "use" was demeaning regarding sacred texts. Also "life" regards as well the church's action regarding others, as in ecumenical and missionary outreach, in which scripture has a role, as the archbishop of Dalat, Viet-Nam, had proposed. See the *Relatio* on the changed title, also in Gil Hellín, *Synopsis*, 144.

The paragraph numbers are lower by three than in *De Fontibus*, because earlier paragraphs had been combined during the intervening work of revision. Chapter VI of *Dei Verbum* has these titles (nos. 21–26):

> The Church Venerates the Holy Scriptures (no. 21)
> A Recommendation of Accurate Translations (no. 22)
> The Apostolic Duty of Catholic Interpreters (no. 23)
> The Importance of Holy Scripture in Theology (no. 24)
> Recommendation of Reading of Holy Scripture (no. 25)
> Epilogue [of chapter VI] (no. 26)[12]

A comparison of the two sets of paragraph titles gives us an important first result of this study. The treatment of biblical reading by priests and people, in nos. 26 and 27, came in the middle of the chapter in *De Fontibus*. But by 1965 the two numbers were fused together and located in *Dei Verbum* at the end of the chapter (no. 25).[13] This makes the emphatic final point of *Dei Verbum* the constant and prayerful reading of scripture by all members of the church, with the recommendation to the faithful being made quite strongly (*vehementer*).[14] Placing the topic of biblical reading close to the end gives much greater importance to the spiritual benefits

---

12. Twice, the Doctrinal Commission specified that no. 26 concludes chap. VI on scripture in the life of the church, and not the whole Constitution. Other documents of the council do not have concluding resumes and no. 26 does not summarize this document, as it does not mention revelation, tradition, and the Magisterium, but speaks only of scripture. Gil Hellín, *Synopsis*, 174–75.

13. This transposition was done early, in the Mixed Commission's fifth sub-commission, which delivered its revision of the chapter to the whole Mixed Commission on December 5, 1962. Cardinals Paul-Émile Léger and Fernando Quiroga y Palacios presided over this sub-commission, whose members were Bishops Hermann Volk, James Griffiths, William Hart, and Master General Aniceto Fernandez, OP. See Tromp, *Konzilstagebuch*, 1:103, 105, 147.

14. Wicks, "Scripture Reading Urged *vehementer*, 555–80, at 568, and in *50 Years On*, ed. Schultenhover, 365–90, at 378. The changed order agrees with the Unity Secretariat's preparatory text, *De Verbo Dei*, in which the final two paragraphs treat biblical reading by priests and seminarians (no. 12) and by the faithful whom pastors should train in "frequent and devout Scripture reading" (no. 13). See the texts in English in my "Scripture Reading," 576–77, and in *50 Years On*, ed. Schultenhover, 386–87.

of biblical meditation and prayer than do the similar recommendations of *De Fontibus*, where they were present in the middle of the chapter. The 1962 draft had given, in its emphatic final place, guidelines for theologians to follow in their work in the church. Confirming this emphasis on scripture reading as a main intention of *Dei Verbum*, the brief epilogue of the chapter states the expectation that "a new impulse of the spiritual life may be expected from the increased veneration of the word of God" (no. 26), which the chapter promotes in different ways.

The "veneration" mentioned in the epilogue of *Dei Verbum*, chapter VI, echoes the remarkable content of no. 21, on scripture nourishing and ruling, with which the chapter begins. It also reminds one of the opening words of the whole Constitution, in which the council describes itself in a posture of veneration, that is, as "reverently hearing the Word of God" (*Dei Verbum religiose audiens*), which the council will confidently proclaim (*et fidenter proclamans*).

The change in the order of the paragraphs of chapter VI further suggests that Catholic exegesis (no. 23) and a biblical theology (no. 24) have in the Constitution of 1965 intermediate roles of communication between the biblical texts and the readers addressed in no. 25. This can be termed a "ministerial" placement of exegesis and theology, which becomes even more significant, when we consider the statements and notions that the Constitution *did not* take over from what *De Fontibus* said in 1962 on exegesis (no. 28) and on theology (no. 29). Each of these paragraphs deserves some attention, which will take us back to 1961–62. In each case, we will also look ahead to the quite notable changes made during the conciliar process of 1962–65 to give us corresponding sections of the promulgated *Dei Verbum*, nos. 23 and 24.

De Fontibus and *Dei Verbum*: Role and Service of Exegetes

The 1962 text of *De fontibus*, no. 28, on Catholic exegetes of scripture, began by restating an emphasis of Pope Pius XII's *Divino Afflante Spiritu* (1943), namely, that recent discoveries in the ancient Near East can and should serve in understanding the Bible's literal sense more deeply. *De Fontibus* also echoed briefly *Divino Afflante*'s specification of the literal sense as the main object of biblical exegesis. But *De Fontibus*, no. 28, then shifted, with an adversative *tamen*, to offer several cautionary reminders to scripture scholars working in the church and for the church. The rest of the paragraph arises from a worried concern that disproportionate efforts are being given to philology, history, and literary matters in work on scripture by Catholic scholars. Therefore, corrections follow, to make their labors spiritually fruitful in the church. (1) They must remember they always need the Holy Spirit's help in explaining the *holy* scriptures.[15] (2) They must aim to recover "the meaning Scripture has from the Holy Spirit, by whom it was composed" (*quo conscripta est*).[16] (3) God has not given the scriptures as a field where exegetes may display their ingenuity, for they ought to be setting forth spiritual teaching and in doing this combine their erudition with the elegance (*ea dicendi suavitas*) in which the Church Fathers excelled, who were solely motivated by love of the church and service of the salvation of souls. (4) Pius XII said in *Divino Afflante* that Catholic exegetes must attend especially (*quam maxime*) to the theological teaching of the sacred texts, which will enrich both themselves and theologians. Such doctrinal explanations will also help priests to explain Christian doctrine better to the people and will assist all the

15. A note refers to St. Jerome's commentary on Mi 1:1–15, as found in *Patrologia Latina*, ed. Migne, 25:1215 (hereafter "*PL*").

16. A note identifies the citation as coming from St. Jerome's commentary on Gal 5:19–21, as found in *PL* 26:445 (*quam sensus Spiritus Sanctus flagitat, quo conscripta est*).

faithful in leading holy lives.[17] (5) Generally, scholars will be able to serve all these purposes of exegesis by attending constantly (*iugiter*) to the analogy of faith, to the church's tradition, and to the norms given by the Apostolic See in these matters.

As Vatican II began in 1962, no. 28 of *De Fontibus* made an important statement on the aims and methods of biblical interpretation as an ecclesial service. Generalizing, one notes that while it echoes points from *Divino Afflante* on the primacy of the literal sense and the quest of doctrine in scripture, its greater concern was to set right, in a critical counter-action, the presumed neglect among Catholic exegetes of the religious character of scripture and the consequences of this for their interpretive work.[18] This reminds us that the redaction of *De Fontibus* took place between January and June 1961. These were the months of the first skirmishes of "battle of the Biblicum," during which the Pontifical Biblical Institute endured vehement attacks and accusations of neo-modernism and rationalism by individuals connected with the Pontifical Lateran University, such as Antonino Romeo, Francesco Spadafora, and, indirectly, Cardinal Ernesto Ruffini.[19]

But later in 1961, when Vatican II's Central Preparatory Commission examined *De Fontibus*, the completed draft-text came under a forceful attack by Cardinal Augustin Bea, who had been the Biblical Institute's rector for nearly twenty years. He showed the seventy-eight members of the Central Commission (cardinals, archbishops, religious fathers general) that the text was not

17. For this, a note indicates the source as Pius XII's *Divino Afflante*, in a passage given in *The Scripture Documents*, ed. Béchard, 125.

18. At least in part, the background of the concerns formulated in *De Fontibus*, no. 23, can be found in the preparatory Vatican II proposal, dated March 30, 1960, of the Sacred Congregation for Seminaries and Studies, in Part III, "De ratione docendi Sacram Scripturam praesertim in seminariis clericorum." *Acta et Documenta*, 1.3:328–33.

19. See Joseph A. Fitzmyer, "A Recent Roman Scriptural Controversy," reprinted in Fitzmyer's *The Interpretation of Scripture*, 17–36. See also Joseph A. Komonchak, "The Struggle for the Council During the Preparation of Vatican II (1960–1962)," in *History of Vatican II*, ed. Alberigo and Komonchak, 1:167–356, at 277–83. Schelkens, *Catholic Theology on the Eve of Vatican II*, 111–32, treats this in greater detail.

coherent with the main lines of papal biblical encyclicals and did not give Catholic exegetes the support they need in their taxing labors.[20]

In the contrasting conciliar text of *Dei Verbum*, no. 23, promulgated in 1965, the work of Catholic exegetes has its setting in the larger context of the church's efforts to grasp scripture more deeply so that it may "constantly pasture" (*indesinenter pascat*) its children with the divine words. This came into the text by adapting passages from the Unity Secretariat's draft of a pastoral decree, *De Verbo Dei*. That preparatory text stated that the teaching church not only defines dogmatic truths but also continually offers believers the spiritual nourishment of the inspired passages of both the Old and New Testaments (no. 8), doing this especially in preaching which offers spiritual food for eternal life (no. 11).[21] In *Dei Verbum*, no. 23, nourishing souls also motivates in the church an intent study of the Eastern and Western Church Fathers and of the liturgical texts of Christian worship, that is, the other areas of *ressourcement* for pastoral ends, among which biblical study has its place.

Dei Verbum, no. 23, envisages "many ministers of the divine word," as those to whom Catholic exegetes, linked with theologians, should supply the spiritual food of the scriptures (*Scripturarum pabulum*). Scripture nourishes the life of God's people by enlightening minds, strengthening wills, and drawing human hearts to love of God.[22] This points ahead to no. 25, soon to

20. Schelkens, *Catholic Theology on the Eve of Vatican II*, 241–44, drawing on the minutes of the Central Commission's meeting of November 10, 1961, in *Acta et Documenta*, 2.2:1. In addition to Bea's critical broadside, Cardinals König, Döpfner, and Alfrink took positions favoring a thorough revision of the text before circulating it to the future council members, to which Cardinal Frings added a vote of *non placet* on the late 1961 text of *De Fontibus*.

21. See the English version of *De Verbo Dei* in my "Scripture Reading Urged *vehementer*," 573–77; also in *Fifty Years On*, ed. Schultenhover, 383–87.

22. A note identifies sources of this theme of formative nourishment by scripture in the encyclical *Divino Afflante*, referenced from *Enchiridion Biblicum*, nos. 551, 553, and 576, from which similar passages entered the May 13, 1950, Biblical Commission instruction

come. Then no. 23 gives straightforward encouragement, based on *Divino Afflante*, to Catholic exegetes to continue in their work, in accord with the mind of the church, with renewed energy and dedication. In *Dei Verbum*, the battle of 1961 is over and the Constitution has set aside the admonitory reminders of *De Fontibus* while calmly depicting the direction of exegetical work in the church to supporting the ministries that serve to nourish the Christian life of the people of God.

De Fontibus and *Dei Verbum*: Scripture and Theology

Paragraph no. 29 concluded *De Fontibus* in 1962 by stating several ways in which theology should relate to scripture. (1) Leo XIII stated in *Providentissimus* that use of scripture was to be the "soul" of the whole teaching of theology.[23] *De Fontibus* sees "Sacred Scripture together *with Tradition*" as the soul animating the body of theology. By linking scripture and tradition, *De Fontibus* connects its final paragraph with its opening chapter on scripture and tradition as the dual sources of revelation, with tradition strongly asserted as necessary not only for interpreting scripture but as well for transmitting some revealed truths not found in scripture. (2) *De Fontibus*, no. 29, stated afresh the animating role of scripture by taking over what Pius XII said in *Humani Generis* about theology having always to return to the study of the biblical and traditional sources for the constant *rejuvenation* of sacred studies. It should be noted that this did not originate with the Preparatory Theological Commission, but was accepted by that Commission as a late addition in early 1962, as one among the many recom-

on the teaching of scripture in seminaries. For the latter text, see *Enchiridion Biblicum*, issued by the Pontifical Biblical Commission, 2nd ed. (Rome: Arnodo, 1954), nos. 582–610 (235–49).

23. See *Scripture Documents*, ed. Béchard, 50.

mended changes that Cardinal Bea had strongly urged during the November 10, 1961, meeting of the Central Preparatory Commission.[24] Because study of the sources gives youthful freshness to theology, theologians should hold in high esteem, for the progress of their discipline, the results attained by correct biblical interpretation. (3) Leo XIII's *Providentissimus* laid down a further point theologians should keep in mind, namely, that because God is the *auctor* of both the biblical books and the doctrine given to the church, it follows that when exegesis recovers a meaning of the text differing from this doctrine, then the claimed result cannot be the fruit of legitimate biblical work.[25] (4) The final sentence of the whole schema *De Fontibus* restates, albeit without a reference, a matter urged in Pius XII's *Humani Generis* by specifying the aim and purpose which theologians should pursue in all their work. Their scholarly efforts should lead to showing the "complete agreement" (*concordiam omnimodam*) between Catholic teaching as handed on through the ages to the present, and the sacred texts set in writing by the Holy Spirit's marvelous works and intent (*operibus et consilio*) for the church to serve the salvation of all people.[26]

Thus, the concluding paragraph on scripture in the church in the 1962 text distributed to the council fathers ends with two guidelines for theology. (1) On doctrines, any claim of having a bib-

24. *Humani Generis*, no. 21. See the text in *The Papal Encyclicals, 1939–58*, ed. Carlen, 178, or in *The Scripture Documents*, ed. Béchard, 140. Strangely, *De Fontibus* gave no reference to this statement on theological rejuvenation as coming from Pope Pius XII. On Bea's urging of this addition to *De Fontibus*, among his many critical remarks on its biblical chaps. II–V, see Schelkens, *Catholic Theology of Revelation on the Eve of Vatican II*, 254n98.

25. *De Fontibus* references *Providentissimus* as affirming this. See *The Scripture Documents*, ed. Béchard, 48.

26. *Humani Generis*, no. 21; *The Papal Encyclicals, 1939–58*, ed. Carlen, 178; or *The Scripture Documents*, ed. Béchard, 141. Pius XII's statement refers to its source in Pope Pius IX's post-Vatican I Apostolic Letter of October 28, 1870, on "theology's most noble office." Joseph Ratzinger's comment on *Dei Verbum*, no. 24, evokes this norm as common in the previous manuals, but as corrected both allusively in *Dei Verbum* and more explicitly in *Optatam Totius*, no. 16, which prescribes biblical themes as dogmatic theology's starting point, which is "a practical consequence of almost revolutionary importance." *Commentary on the Documents of Vatican II*, ed. Herbert Vorgrimler (London: Burns and Oates, 1967–69), 3:269.

lical warrant for a teaching that is discordant with Catholic magisterial teaching must be an unwarranted claim (from Leo XIII, *Providentissimus*, 1893). (2) More generally, the work of the Catholic theologian must aim at showing the doctrinal continuity between origins in scripture and present-day church teaching, as Pius XII had set down in his cautionary encyclical *Humani Generis* of 1950.

This makes clear a point not acknowledged by Karin Schelkens, namely that *De Fontibus Revelationis* was in several passages not a fresh treatment of its topic, but a confirmation of existing magisterial doctrines and guidelines. The parts of the schema we have examined do not show any considerations of new approaches suggested by the future members of Vatican II who were canvassed in 1959–60. Instead, it took its shape and form under guidance from above, that is (1) from the Holy Office, then the supreme congregation of the Roman Curia, and from (2) the Curia's Sacred Congregation for Seminaries and Studies, both of which featured guidelines from the antimodernist era of Pope Pius X and from Pope Pius XII's *Humani Generis* in their preparatory proposals of topics and positions to be taken up by Vatican II.

The preparatory proposal (*votum*) of the Holy Office (April 1960) laid down that the council must defend and confirm principles of Catholic teaching now being called into doubt by revived modernist positions. It must restate an accurate notion of objective revelation and faith as assent in submission to supernatural truth. The proposal treats scripture in its section on the Magisterium, to which, instead of individuals, the deposit of revelation is entrusted for its authoritative interpretation. The council should make clear that the Bible is not the source of revelation by itself without the Magisterium, but still the council should declare scripture's inspiration and inerrancy, while laying down from the biblical encyclicals, including *Humani Generis*, norms of valid biblical interpretation. The genuine Catholic notion of tradition needs emphasis, including the "plus" of tradition (*traditio addi-*

tiva) in conveying to theologians and the church some divinely revealed truths not given in scripture.[27]

Some major traits of the 1965 Constitution *Dei Verbum* emerge now more sharply when we turn to its no. 24 on theology, which differs notably from the *De Fontibus* treatment of how theology should relate to scripture. The Constitution positions theology differently, to give theology a mediatory role in bringing scripture to the people of the church as a many-sided enrichment. *Dei Verbum* has no aspiration to give theology its overall aim and purpose as occurred in the culminating lines of *De Fontibus*, no. 29, based on *Humani Generis*.[28]

(1) As *Dei Verbum*, no. 24, approaches the biblical contributions to theology, it does link the written word of God with sacred tradition, but this follows in the Constitution the innovative no. 8, on living tradition and it dynamic and spiritual character. Scripture, then, is the perennial foundation on which theological work builds, a solidification of exceptional stability for its positions, and the source of ongoing theological rejuvenation, as even *Humani Generis* stated.

(2) All this help comes from scripture into the theologian's labors when he or she is "searching out, in the light of faith, all the truth included in the mystery of Christ."[29] This elegant and

---

27. *Acta et Documenta*, 1.3:3–17, esp. 5 and 8–9. From the Seminaries' Congregation, material for *De Fontibus* came in Chapters I ("De sanitate et integritate doctrinae ... tradendae, pleno cum obsequio erga Ecclesiae Magisterium") and II ("De relatione scientiae theologicae cum Ecclesiae Magistero"), *Acta et Documenta*, 1.3:315–27. Several points of the last-named chapter appeared in an article by a consultor of the Seminaries Congregation, Monsignor Antonio Piolanti, in "Il magistero della Chiesa e la scienza teologica," *Divinitas* 5 (1961): 531–51.

28. Implicitly the aim and purpose of theology appears in Vatican II's *Optatam Totius*, no. 16, on theology's concern for tracing the development of Christian doctrine and on the role that the sources regularly have in raising new theological matters for theological work.

29. This phrasing (*omnem veritatem in mysterio Christi conditam sub lumine fidei perscrutando*) replaced, at the suggestion of Archbishop Lorenz Jaeger of Paderborn, a pale wording of the early revision by the Mixed Commission of 1962–63, on the theologian deriving *argumenta* from the word of God. See Gil Hellín, *Synopsis*, 162, which documents the source of the new formulation "B" in no. 24 (mid-1964 version) by reference to intervention no. E/2255 by Bishop Jaeger, given by Gil Hellín on 472.

striking account of theological work connects this paragraph of *Dei Verbum*'s chapter VI with the Constitution's no. 4, which sets forth as the culminating content of God's revelation of himself the immanent meaning of the whole Christ-event. This is the evangelical truth that God is with us to liberate us from sin and death and raise us to eternal life. From *that*, as found at the doctrinal center of scripture, theology is truly well grounded, given stability, and rejuvenated.

(3) To ground the traditional theme of scripture being "the soul of theology," *Dei Verbum* (no. 24) takes over a simple but momentous statement from the Unity Secretariat's pastoral schema, *De Verbo Dei*, "that the Holy Scriptures ... not only contain God's word but in an eminent sense are God's word." This follows from their inspiration and leads to the consequence, "therefore, study of the sacred page should be much like the very soul of sacred theology."

(4) Finally, the Constitution of 1965, in no. 24, widens its horizon, under influence of several council fathers' interventions, to extend the scope of scripture's nourishing and vitalizing effect to the ecclesial ministry of the word, to pastoral preaching, especially in homilies, and to all Christian instruction, in which the council hopes scripture will have an eminent place.

De Fontibus and *Dei Verbum*: Reading Scripture

The Preparatory Schema of 1962 devoted its paragraphs 26 and 27 to priests and the faithful as readers of scripture.[30] Priests will keep in mind the inspiration and broad pastoral impact of scripture attested by 2 Timothy 3:16–17. Then follow citations from Gregory the Great, Jerome, and Augustine on how preachers must be steeped in scripture if they are to preach well. Scripture

---

30. I treated these passages in "Scripture Reading Urged *vehementer*," 557–59, on their genesis and content, and gave them in English translation on 571–73; also in the reprint in *50 Years On*, ed. Schultenhover, 367–69 and 382–83.

can orient its readers toward salvation by faith, when they receive it from the church and when the reader approaches it with docility and the desire to learn what contributes to spiritual growth.

De Fontibus, no. 27, on the wider practice of scripture reading by lay people, is similar in its structure to no. 28, on Catholic exegetes, treated above. It first notes as praiseworthy that some Catholics are reading scripture in the original languages and that, for the good of all, translations from the original texts into current languages are now abundant. Love of the Gospels and apostolic writings is leading to their publication and reading by many. The latter is a sacred *lectio* which proves to be spiritually beneficial, even to inflaming hearts with love of God. But after this praise of wider scripture reading, well over half of the paragraph of 1962 then follows a sharp *attamen* ("however") introducing a series of warnings by the council on points which should not be forgotten. (1) The faithful must take care to approach the sacred texts attentively aware of Catholic teaching and in ready observance of norms inculcated by solid and suitable training. (2) This is especially relevant to reading the Old Testament, but also to the New Testament, in which "some things are hard to understand that the ignorant and unstable distort to their own destruction, as they do with the other scriptures" (2 Pt 3:16). (3) Translations used by Catholics must be approved by the bishops, who pass on the apostolic teaching.[31] (4) Translations must annotate the biblical text in a manner conformed to the mind of the church, whose living Magisterium is for the Catholic faithful "the proximate norm of belief."[32] (5) In fact the true meaning of the divine words is not for individuals, however learned, to ascertain authoritatively, for the Magisterium is to determine this, as it is the office to which the

---

31. A note references Irenaeus, *Adverses Haereses*, IV.32, on the bishops being bearers of apostolic doctrine.

32. Here the schema echoes Pius XII, who declared in 1950 that for theology the Magisterium is "the proximate and universal norm of truth." *Humani Generis*, no. 18, given in *The Papal Encyclicals 1939–58*, ed. Carlen, 177.

scriptures are entrusted for their interpretation.[33] (6) Finally, any program of making scripture more widely present and explained among the Christian people has to be submitted for authoritative approval by the bishops.

Again, a key passage of the 1962 draft-text, *De Fontibus*, arises from a worried concern about unruly practices needing correction. The council is here being prepared to set right a suspected neglect by church members of what Catholic practice calls for. But, once more, in *Dei Verbum* of 1965 worry and suspicion have faded away so as to leave no characteristic marks on the promulgated text on biblical reading in the church.

In contrast with chapter V of the 1962 schema, *Dei Verbum*'s chapter VI opens by indicating themes which prepare well for what will be its final extolling and urging of reading scripture. The divinely inspired "fixed form" of the biblical texts allows the Holy Spirit's voice to resound through what prophets and apostles have set down. In the texts "the Father who is in heaven comes lovingly to meet his children, and talks with them," as no. 8 of the Unity Secretariat's *De Verbo Dei* had said and now echoes in *Dei Verbum*, no. 21. Above, we reviewed the contributions of nourishment and vitality coming from scripture which *Dei Verbum* expects from the work of exegetes (no. 23) and theologians (no. 24).

In the Constitution's penultimate paragraph, no. 25, one-fourth of the text states the obligation of priests, deacons, and catechists to prepare for their instructional efforts by immersing themselves in scripture by constant reading and study.[34] This same paragraph then issues its remarkable and forceful recom-

33. This point comes from the continuation of the passage of *Humani Generis* just referenced in the previous note.

34. Earlier *De Fontibus* cited 2 Tm 3:16–17 in its exhortation to priests (no. 26), but *Dei Verbum* cites the text earlier, in no. 11 on biblical inspiration. Of the three patristic texts of the early text, only Augustine's warning remained against priests becoming "empty preachers" because they have not heard God's word interiorly.

mendation of scripture reading to all the faithful. Here the paragraph represents an abrupt turn away from the 1962 reservations of the Preparatory Theological Commission about recommending all of scripture to all the faithful. Pope Benedict XV had already gone ahead of *Dei Verbum* on this issue in his encyclical *Spiritus Paraclitus* of 1920.[35] One notices *Dei Verbum*'s uncommon and vigorous adverb modifying this recommendation and exhortation, *vehementer exhoratur*.[36] The places of this encounter with the biblical word are the liturgy, the quiet of personal and recollected reading, and the programs of biblical formation which were spreading at the time of the council. What Vatican II exhorts people to do is *lectio divina*, as the late addition makes especially clear: "Let them remember, however, that prayer should accompany the reading of Sacred Scripture, so that it becomes a dialogue between God and the human reader." This recalls the striking passage of no. 21 on God's loving approach through the sacred text to his children to converse with them. That grounds *Dei Verbum*'s forceful urging in no. 25 of frequent scripture reading done in the mode of prayer.

But we meet another matter in the final five lines of no. 25, namely, the recommendation that specially annotated biblical texts should be published for reading by non-Christians, which pastors and lay Catholics should prudently put into circulation. This reminds us that a global interpretation of Vatican II will feature several themes of *rapprochement* with other groups and peoples, which is a characteristic of the council, along with the *ressourcement* we are treating here.

---

35. In the concluding passage of his 1920 encyclical on the fifteenth centenary of St. Jerome, *Spiritus Paraclitus*, Benedict XV wrote, "Our one desire for all the church's children is that, being saturated with the Bible, they may arrive at the all-surpassing knowledge of Jesus Christ." *The Scripture Documents*, ed. Béchard, 110.

36. On the entry of this formulation into the 1964 emended text of the schema *De Revelatione*, see my "Scripture Reading," 567–68, especially on the calls for such a recommendation from council members, from both individual bishops and episcopal conferences; in the reprint *50 Years On*, ed. Schultenhover, 377–78.

Conclusion

What does this study give us for our global interpretation of the Second Vatican Council? First, there are the sharp contrasts between the promulgated *Dei Verbum* and its early predecessor text, *De Fontibus Revelationis* of 1962. The latter text proposed, as the council began, that Vatican II include further acts of the censorious and admonitory Magisterium of the antimodernist censures (1907) and the warnings by Pius XII in *Humani Generis* (1950). This occurred in *De Fontibus* on the role of theology, namely, to show Catholic doctrinal continuity with scripture. But, with this outlook set aside, the constitution says suggestively that theology scrutinizes in the light of faith the truth stored up in the mystery of Christ. Even sharper is the contrast between the admonitory insistence on safeguards and magisterial guidance of scripture reading in *De fontibus* and the council's warmth and vigor of recommending *lectio divina* to all the faithful. A first impression of such changes in content and tone might lead one to see Vatican II as breaking with or even rejecting previous church tradition and teaching.[37] But such a conclusion takes no account of how *De Fontibus* was prepared in isolation from, and even suspicious opposition to, important developments of Catholic theology in the years before Vatican II. *Dei Verbum* was clearly discontinuous with *De Fontibus*, proposed three years earlier, but the constitution of 1965 shows notable continuities with central and strong movements of biblical, theological, and pastoral renewal among Catholics before

37. On September 10, 1965, in a conversation with Henri de Lubac in the sacristy of the Church of St. Ignatius in Rome, Sebastian Tromp complained about the confusion the council has spread and about a decline of obedience in the church and the Jesuit Order. De Lubac agreed, but he added in his diary that one reason for the disorder was that in 1960–62 Tromp and his group had so adamantly opposed all the many renewal proposals. Their closure gave to the first actions taken by Vatican II in late 1962 a revolutionary allure which opened a way for the para-conciliar disorders that Tromp was lamenting; see de Lubac, *Vatican Council Notebooks*, 2:357. The schema *De Fontibus*, strongly influenced by Tromp in the Preparatory Theological Commission, exemplifies de Lubac's point quite well.

Vatican II.[38] There was rupture, but on the small scale of contrast between the council's official preparation and the directions taken from late 1962 onward. When the scale of consideration widens to view the broader historical development, *Dei Verbum* is in chapter VI a homogenous extension of earlier and recently developed themes.

Second, this study gives us good reason to stress how Vatican II, whatever else it achieved, did hold firmly to pursuing a council aim formulated as primary by the far-seeing Preparatory Liturgical Commission. For that body put first among council aims in their draft schema of 1962 that the council aimed "to intensify the daily growth of Catholics in Christian living" (*Concilium sibi proponat vitam Christianam inter fideles in dies augere*), a formulation which passed into the first sentence of the promulgated Constitution on the Sacred Liturgy.[39] This global trait of Vatican II needs emphasis when many are arguing on behalf of the ecclesiastical aims and traits of the council, especially concerning the decentralization of decision-making powers. Congar's diary entry of November 18, 1965, on the day of *Dei Verbum*'s promulgation, celebrated the constitution as "a great text which provides theology the means of becoming fully evangelical."[40] The same can be said regarding spirituality, because of the evangelical contribution of *Dei Verbum*, nos. 23–25, to Catholic growth in Gospel joy and dedication through nourishment and vitality gained by the *lectio divina* of scripture.

Third, the final paragraphs of *Dei Verbum* urge deeper im-

38. Ample evidence underlying this view comes, for example, from Aubert's classic survey, *La théologie catholique au milieu du XXe siècle*.

39. Translation from the early version in Abbot-Gallagher. Other translations: "to impart an ever-increasing vigor to the Christian lives of the faithful" (Flannery and the Vatican online version); "to improve the standard of daily Christian living among Catholics" (*Decrees*, ed. Tanner, 2:820); in Italian, "di far crescere sempre più la vita christiana tra i fedeli" (*Enchiridion Vaticanum*, 1:349); German: "das christliche Leben unter den Gläubigen mehr und mehr zu vertiefen" (Vatican online edition).

40. Entry of Thursday, November 18, 1965, in Congar, *My Journal of the Council*, 845.

mersion in scripture as a spiritually enriching source. This immersion, we can say, would be a "vertical" movement of Catholic thought and spirit downward from surface concerns into the believer's deep encounter with the Lord revealing himself, radiating his grace, and issuing his calls. The ideal is daily entry into the depths of God's saving and sanctifying work, to which scripture gives so many engaging witnesses.

Many interpreters of Vatican II feature the *outward* movements urged by the council to move Catholics toward *rapprochement* with others in ecumenical efforts, interreligious dialogue, and respectful exchanges over salient features of the contemporary world's culture, economics, politics, and struggle for world peace. But the concluding passages of *Dei Verbum* point Catholics toward another movement, that is, *inward and downward* toward personal *ressourcement* as one cultivates spiritual self-care by daily nourishment of heart and soul, along with direction and guidance, from *lectio divina* of scripture. This is a movement going deeply into one's life of faith, where God addresses Christian believers in words of personal grace and rescue, while imparting the very gifts that empower rejuvenated disciples for their reconciling service of God in the world.

Selected Bibliography

Acta et Documenta Concilio Oecumenico Vaticano Secondo Apparando.
  Series I (Antepraeparatoria). 4 volumes in 13 parts. Vatican City:
  Tipografia Poliglotta Vaticana, 1960–61.
Acta et Documenta Concilio Oecumenico Vaticano Secondo Apparando.
  Series II (Praeparatoria). 4 volumes in 11 parts. Vatican City: Tipografia
  Poliglotta Vaticana, 1965–95.
Acta Synodalia Sacrosancti Concilii Vaticani II. 6 volumes in 32 parts. Vatican
  City: Tipografia Poliglotta Vaticana, 1970–99.
Alberigo, Giuseppe. "Studi e problemi relativi all'applicazione del concilio
  di Trento in Italia (1945–1958)." *Rivista storica italiana* 70 (1958):
  239–98.
———. "Carlo Borromeo come modello di vescovo nella chiesa post-
  tridentina." *Rivista storica italiana* 79 (1967): 1031–52.
———. *A Brief History of Vatican II.* Maryknoll, N.Y.: Orbis, 2006.
Alberigo, Guiseppe, and Joseph A. Komonchak, eds. *History of Vatican II.*
  5 volumes. Maryknoll, N.Y.: Orbis, 1995–2006.
Alberigo, Giuseppe, et al., eds. *Conciliorum oecumenicorum Decreta.* Basel:
  Herder, 1972. Original texts with English translation in *Decrees,* edited
  by Tanner.
Anderson, Floyd, ed. *Council Daybook.* 3 volumes. Washington, D.C.:
  National Catholic Welfare Conference, 1965–66.
Aparicio, Carmen. "Contributo di Lukas Vischer alla *Gaudium et spes.*"
  In *Sapere teologico e unità della fede,* edited by Carmen Aparicio Valls,
  Carmelo Dotolo, and Gianluigi Pasquale, 3–19. Rome: Gregorian Uni-
  versity Press, 2004.

Aubert, Roger. *La théologie catholique au milieu du XXe siècle*. Paris: Casterman, 1954.

Béchard, Dean. *The Scripture Documents: An Anthology of Official Catholic Teachings*. Collegeville, Minn.: Liturgical Press, 2002.

Benedict XV, Pope. *Spiritus Paraclitus*. Encyclical Letter. September 15, 1920. In *The Scripture Documents*, edited by Dean Béchard, 81–110. Collegeville, Minn.: Liturgical Press, 2002.

Benedict XVI, Pope (Joseph Ratzinger). "Zur Theologie des Konzils." *Catholica* 15 (1961): 292–304.

———. "Bermerkungen zum Schema *De fontibus revelationis*" (1962). In *Zur Lehre des Zweiten Vatikanischen Konzils. Formulierung Vermittlung Deutung*, from Ratzinger's *Gesammelte Schriften* (Freiburg: Herder, 2008–), 7.1:183–209. Translated into English in "Six Texts by Prof. Joseph Ratzinger as *peritus* Before and During Vatican Council II" by Jared Wicks in *Gregorianum* 89 (2008): 269–85.

———. *Theological Highlights of Vatican II*. Mahwah, N.J.: Paulist Press, 2009 (originally 1966).

———. [Commentary on *Dei verbum*, chapters I, II, and VI.] In *Commentary on the Documents of Vatican II*, edited by Herbert Vorgrimler, 3:155–98 and 262–72. London: Burns and Oates, 1967–69.

———. "Der Weltdienst der Kirche: Auswirkungen von 'Gaudium et spes' im letzten Jahrzehnt." *Internationale Katholische Zeitschrift Communio* 4 (1975): 439–54. Translated as "Church and World: An Inquiry into the Reception of Vatican Council II." In his *Principles of Catholic Theology*, 378–93. San Francisco: Ignatius Press, 1987.

———. "Sources and Transmission of the Faith." *Communio* 10 (1983): 17–34.

———. *The Ratzinger Report: An Exclusive Interview on the State of the Church*. Edited by Vittorio Messori. San Francisco: Ignatius Press, 1985.

———. *Principles of Catholic Theology*. San Francisco: Ignatius Press, 1987.

———. *Milestones: Memoirs 1927–1977*. San Francisco: Ignatius Press, 1998.

———. "Interpreting Vatican II." Address to the Roman Curia, December 22, 2005. *Origins* 35, no. 32 (2006): 534–39.

———. *Offenbarungsverständnis und Geschichtstheologie Bonaventuras: Habilitationsschrift und Bonaventura-Studien*. In Joseph Ratzinger, *Gesammelte Schriften*, vol. 2. Freiburg: Herder, 2009.

Betti, Umberto. *La dottrina del concilio Vaticano II sulla trasmissione della rivelazione*. Rome: Pontifical Athenaeum Antonianum, 1985.

———. *Diario del Concilio, 11 ottobre 1962 Natale 1978*. Bologna: Edizioni Dehoniane, 2003.

Brouwers, Jan. "Vatican II, derniers préparatifs et première session. Activités conciliares en coulisses." In *Vatican II commence . . . Approaches francophones*, edited by Étienne Fouilloux, 353–78. Leuven: Bibliotheek van de Faculteit der Godgeleerdheid, 1993.

Brunner, Peter. "Die abendländischen Kirchentrennung und das kommende Konzil." In *Erwägungen zum kommenden Konzil*, edited by Karl Forster, 35–50. Würzburg: Echter, 1961.

Cahill, Brendan. *The Renewal of Revelation Theology*. Rome: Gregorian University Press, 1999.

Camara, Dom Helder. *Les conversions d'un évêque. Entretiens avec José de Brouker*. Paris: L'Harmattan, 2004.

———. *Lettres conciliaires (1962–1965)*. 2 volumes. Edited by José de Broucker. Paris: Éditions du Cerf, 2006.

Capovilla, Loris. *Giovanni XXIII: Quindici Letture*. Rome: Edizioni di storia e letteratura, 1970.

Cerfaux, Lucien. "Regale sacerdotium." In his *Recueil Lucien Cerfaux*, 2:283–315. Gembloux: Duculot, 1954.

———. *Christ in the Theology of St. Paul*. New York: Herder and Herder, 1959.

———. *The Church in the Theology of St. Paul*. New York: Herder and Herder, 1959.

Clifford, Catherine. "*Elementa ecclesiae*. A Basis for Vatican II's Recognition of the Ecclesial Character of Non-Catholic Christian Communities." In *La théologie catholique entre intransigeance et renouveau: La réception des mouvements préconciliaires à Vatican II*, edited by Gilles Routhier, Philippe J. Roy, and Karim Schelkens, 249–69. Leuven: Universiteitsbibliotheek, 2011.

Committee on Ecumenical and Interreligious Affairs of the United States Conference of Catholic Bishops and Evangelical Lutheran Church of America. *Declaration on the Way: Church, Ministry, and Eucharist*. Minneapolis, Minn.: Augsburg Fortress, 2016.

Compendium of Creeds, Definitions, and Declarations on Matters of Faith and Morals. Compiled by Heinrich Denzinger, revised by Peter Hünermann, and edited by Robert Fastiggi and Anne Englund Nash. San Francisco: Ignatius Press, 2012.

Congar, Yves. *Vraie et fausse réforme dans l'Église*. Revised edition. Paris: Éditions du Cerf, 1968 (originally 1950). Translated by Paul Philibert as *True and False Reform in the Church*. Collegeville, Minn.: Liturgical Press, 2011.

———. "Les conciles dans la vie de l'Église." *Informations catholiques internationales* 90 (February 15, 1959): 17–26.

———. "La primauté des quatre premiers conciles oecuméniques." In *Le Concile et les conciles*, edited by Bernard Botte, 75–109. Chevetogne: Abbaye de Chevetogne, 1960.

————. "Conclusion." In *Le Concile et les conciles*, edited by Bernard Botte, 285–334. Chevetogne: Abbaye de Chevetogne, 1960.

————. "Exposition for the sub-commission *De ecclesia* of the Vatican II Preparatory Theological Commission" (12 pages). April 2, 1961. Archive of Gérard Philips, no. 123. Leuven University Theological Faculty Vatican II Archive. Leuven, Belgium.

————. "*Credo conciliaris, 1962.*" In *Glaube im Prozess, Festschrift K. Rahner*, edited by Elmar Klinger and Klaus Wittstadt, 51–64. Freiburg: Herder, 1984.

————. *Journal d'un théologien (1946–1956)*. Edited by Étienne Fouilloux. Paris: Éditions du Cerf, 2001.

————. *Mon Journal du Concile.* 2 volumes. Edited by Eric Mahieu. Paris: Éditions du Cerf, 2002. Translated as *My Journal of the Council* by Mary John Ronayne, OP, and Mary Cecily Boulding, OP, and edited by Denis Minns, OP. Collegeville, Minn.: Liturgical Press, 2012.

de Lubac, Henri. *Catholicism: Christ and the Common Destiny of Man*. London: Burns and Oates, 1950.

————. *The Splendor of the Church*. New York: Sheed and Ward, 1956.

————. *At the Service of the Church*. San Francisco: Ignatius Press, 1993.

————. *Carnets du Concile.* 2 volumes. Edited by Loïc Figoureux. Paris: Éditions du Cerf, 2007. Translated as *Vatican Council Notebooks* by Andrew Steffanelli and Anne Englund Nash, edited by Loïc Figoureux. San Francisco: Ignatius Press, 2015.

De Maio, Romeo. *Le livre des évangiles dans les conciles œcuméniques*. Vatican City: Biblioteca Apostolica Vaticana, 1963.

De Mey, Peter. "Johannes Willebrands and the Catholic Conference for Ecumenical Questions (1952–1963)." In *The Ecumenical Legacy of Johannes Cardinal Willebrands*, edited by Adelbert Denaux and Peter De Mey, 49–77. Leuven: Peeters, 2012.

Donnelly, Doris, et al., eds. *The Belgian Contribution to the Second Vatican Council*. Leuven: Peeters, 2008.

Döpfner, Julius. *Julius Kardinal Döpfner: Konzilstagebücher, Briefe und Notizen zum Zweiten Vatikanischen Konzil.* Edited by Guido Treffler. Regensburg: Schnell und Steiner, 2006.

Duprey, Pierre. "Paul VI et le decret sur l'ecumenisme." In *Paolo VI e i problemi ecclesiologici al concile*, 225–48. Brescia: Istituto Paolo VI, 1989.

Elert, Werner. *Ecucharist and Church Fellowship in the Early Church*. St. Louis, Mo.: Concordia Publishing House, 1966.

Faggioli, Massimo. "*Sacrosanctum Concilium* and the Meaning of Vatican II." *Theological Studies* 71 (2010): 437–52.

Faith and Order Commission of the World Council of Churches. *The Church. Towards a Common Vision*. Faith and Order Paper No. 214. Geneva: World Council of Churches, 2013.

Famerée, Joseph. "The *Coetus Internationalis Patrum*." In *History of Vatican II*, edited by Alberigo and Komonchak, 3:170–75.

Fitzmyer, Joseph. "A Recent Roman Scriptural Controversy." *Theological Studies* 22 (1961): 426–44. Reprinted in his *The Interpretation of Scripture: In Defense of the "Historical-Critical Method,"* 17–36. Mahwah, N.J.: Paulist Press, 2008.

Flannery, Austin, ed. *Vatican Council II: Constitutions, Decrees, Declarations*. Northport, N.Y.: Costello Publications, 1996; reprinted, Collegeville, Minn.: Liturgical Press, 2016.

Fogarty, Gerald P. *American Catholic Biblical Scholarship: A History from the Early Republic to Vatican II*. San Francisco: Harper and Row, 1989.

Fouilloux, Étienne. "Comment devient-on expert à Vatican II? Le cas du Père Yves Congar." In *Le duxième Concile du Vatican 1959–1965*, 307–31. Rome: École Français, 1989.

———. "Théologiens romains et Vatican II (1959–1962)." *Cristianesimo nella storia* 15 (1994): 373–90.

———. "The Antepreparatory Phase: The Slow Emergence from Inertia (January, 1959–October, 1962)." In *History of Vatican II*, edited by Alberigo and Komonchak, 1:55–166.

Francis, Pope. *The Joy of the Gospel*. Apostolic Exhortation. November 24, 1983. Washington, D.C.: United States Conference of Catholic Bishops, 2013.

———. "Address on the 50th Anniversary of the Synod of Bishops, October 17, 2015." *Origins* 45, no. 22 (2015): 381–84.

Gaillardetz, Richard. "Vatican II and the Humility of the Church." In *The Legacy of Vatican II*, edited by Massimo Faggioli and Andrea Vicini, 87–108. Mahwah, N.J.: Paulist Press, 2015.

Gertler, Thomas. *Jesus Christus—Antwort der Kirche auf die Frage nach dem Menschen. Eine Untersuchung zu Funktion und Inhalt der Christologie im ersten Teil der Pastoralkonstititon "Gaudium et spes" des zweiten Vatikanischen Konzils*. Leipzig: St. Benno Verlag, 1986.

Gil Hellín, Francisco, ed. *Concilii Vaticani II Synopsis . . . Constitutio Dogmatica De divina revelatione Dei Verbum*. Vatican City: Liberia Editrice Vaticana, 1993.

———, ed. *Concilii Vaticani II Synopsis . . . Constitutio Dogmatica De ecclesia Lumen gentium*. Vatican City: Liberia Editrice Vaticana, 1995.

Grootaers, Jan. *Primauté et collégialité: Le dossier de Gérard Philips su la Nota Explicativa Praevia*. Leuven: Peeters, 1986.

———. "The Drama Continues between the Acts: the 'Second Preparation' and Its Opponents." In *History of Vatican II*, edited by Alberigo and Komonchak, 2:359–514.

———. "Diversité des tendencies à l'intérieur de la majorité conciliare: Gérard Philips et Giuseppe Dossetti." In *The Belgian Contribution to the*

Second Vatican Council, edited by Doris Donnelly et al., 529–62. Leuven: Peeters, 2008.

Growth in Agreement. Edited by Harding Meyer and Lukas Vischer. Geneva: World Council of Churches, 1984.

Growth in Agreement II. Edited by Jeffrey Gros, Harding Meyer, and William G. Rusch. Geneva: WCC Publications, 2000.

Growth in Agreement III. Edited by Jeffrey Gros, Thomas F. Best, and Lorelei F. Fuchs. Geneva: WCC Publications, 2007.

Guardini, Romano. *The Catholic and the Church*. London: Sheed and Ward, 1935.

Imbelli, Robert. *Rekindling the Christic Imagination: Theological Meditations for the New Evangelization*. Collegeville, Minn.: Liturgical Press, 2014.

Indelicato, Antonino. *Difendere la dottrina o annunciare l'evangelo: Il dibattito nella Commissione centrale preparatoria del Vaticano II*. Genoa: Il Mulino, 1992.

Jacobs, J. "Les *vota* des évêques néerlandais pour le concile." In *À la veille du Concile Vatican II*, edited by Mathijs Lamberigts and Claude Soetens, 99–110. Leuven: Leuven University Press, 1992.

Jedin, Hubert. *Kleine Konziliengeschichte*. Freiburg: Herder, 1959. Translated by Ernest Graf as *Ecumenical Councils of the Catholic Church: An Historical Outline*. New York: Herder and Herder, 1960.

———. "Das Bischofsideal der katholischen Reformation." In his *Kirche des Glaubens Kirche der Geschichte. Ausgewälte Aufsätze und Vorträge*, 2:75–117. Freiburg: Herder, 1966.

———. *Lebensbericht*. Edited by Konrad Repgen. Mainz: Grünewald, 1984.

John XXIII, Pope (Angelo Roncalli). "Il cardinale Cesare Baronio." *La scuola cattolica* 36 (1908): 3–29. Reprinted as a monograph with an introduction by Giuseppe de Luca. Rome: Edizioni di storia e letteratura, 1961.

———. *My Bishop. A Portrait of Mgr. Giacomo Maria Radini Tedeschi*. Translated by Dorothy White. New York: McGraw-Hill, 1969 (originally 1915).

———. *Gli atti della visita apostolica di S. Carlo Borromeo a Bergamo (1575)*. Edited by Angelo G. Roncalli. 2 volumes in 5 parts. Florence: Olschki, 1936–57.

———. "La Sacra Scrittura e san Lorenzo Giustiniani. Lettera pastorale per la Quaresima [1956]." In his *Scritti e discorsi*, 2:329–51. Rome: Edizioni Paoline, 1959.

———. "Homily at the Solemn Pontifical Mass of Coronation, November 4, 1958." In his *Discorsi, Messaggi, Colloqui del Santo Padre Giovanni XXIII*, vol. I, *Primo anno del Pontificato*, 10–14. Vatican City: Tipografia Polyglota Vaticana, 1960.

———. "Homily during the Canonization of St. Gregorio Barbarigo, May 26, 1960." In *Scritti, messaggi, colloqui del Santo Padre Giovanni XXIII*, vol. II,

Secondo anno del pontificato, 335–65. Vatican City: Tipografia Poliglotta Vaticana, 1961.

———. *Humanae Salutis* (Constitution of December 25, 1961). In *Acta Apostolicae Sedis* 54 (1962): 5–13. Translated in *Council Daybook*, edited by Anderson, 6–9.

———. "Radio Address of September 11, 1962." In *Acta Apostolicae Sedis* 54 (1962): 678–85. Translated in *Council Daybook*, edited by Anderson, 18–21.

———. "Gaudet Mater Ecclesia." Inaugural Address at Vatican Council II, October 11, 1962. *Acta Apostolicae Sedis* 54 (1962): 786–96. Translated in *Council Daybook*, edited by Anderson, 25–29. Corrected translation in Wicks, *Doing Theology*, 141–51. Mahwah, N.J.: Paulist, 2009.

———. "Mirabilis ille." Letter to the Fathers of Vatican Council II. January 6, 1963. In *Acta Apostolicae Sedis* 55 (1963): 149–59. Translated in *The Encyclicals and Other Messages of John XXIII*, edited by John F. Cronin, Francis X. Murphy, and Ferrer Smith, 444–58. Washington, D.C.: TPS Press, 1964.

———. *Giornale dell'Anima. Soliloqui, note e diari spirituali*. Critical and annotated edition by Alberto Melloni. *Edizione nazionale dei diari di Angelo Giuseppe Roncalli Giovanni XXIII*, vol. 1. Bologna: Istituto per le scienze religiose, 2003.

———. *Nelle mani di Dio a servizio dell'uomo. I diari di don Roncalli, 1905–1925*. Edited by Lucia Butturini. *Edizione nazionale dei diari di Angelo Giuseppe Roncalli Giovanni XXIII*, vol. 2. Bologna: Istituto per le scienze religiose, 2008.

———. *Tener da conto. Agendine di Bulgaria, 1925–1934*. Edited by Massimo Faggioli. *Edizione nazionale dei diari di Angelo Giuseppe Roncalli Giovanni XXIII*, vol. 3. Bologna: Istituto per le scienze religiose, 2008.

———. *La mia vita in Oriente. Agende de delegato apostolico, 1935–1944*. 2 volumes. Edited by Valeria Martano. *Edizione nazionale dei diari di Angelo Giuseppe Roncalli Giovanni XXIII*, vol. 4. Bologna: Istituto per le scienze religiose, 2006–8.

———. *Anni di Francia, Agende del nuncio, 1945–1953*. 2 volumes. Edited by Étienne Fouilloux. *Edizione nazionale dei diari di Angelo Giuseppe Roncalli Giovanni XXIII*, vol. 5. Bologna: Istituto di scienze religiose, 2004–6.

———. *Pace e Vangelo. Agende del patriarca, 1953–1958*. 2 volumes. Edited by Enrico Galavotti. *Edizione nazionale dei diari di Angelo Giuseppe Roncalli Giovanni XXIII*, vol. 6. Bologna: Istituto per le scienze religiose, 2008.

———. *Pater amabilis. Agende del pontifice, 1958–1963*. Edited by Mauro Velati. *Edizione nazionale dei diari di Angelo Giuseppe Roncalli Giovanni XXIII*, vol. 7. Bologna: Istituto per le scienze religiose, 2007.

———. Angelo G. Roncalli and Giovanni Battista Montini. *Lettere di fede e amicizia. Correspondenza inedita (1925–1963)*. Edited by Loris F. Capovilla and Marco Roncalli. Rome: Edizioni Studium, 2013.

John Paul II, Pope. *As the Third Millennium Draws Near*. Apostolic Letter. November 10, 1994. *Origins* 24, no. 24 (November 24, 1994): 401–16.

Klinger, Elmar, and Klaus Wittstadt, eds. *Glaube im Prozess: Christsein nach dem II. Vatikanischen Konzils: Festschrift Karl Rahner*. Freiburg: Herder, 1984.

Komonchak, Joseph A. "The Enlightenment and the Construction of Roman Catholicism." *Annual of the Catholic Commission on Intellectual and Cultural Affairs* 4 (1985): 31–59.

———. "Recapturing the Great Tradition. In Memoriam Henri de Lubac." *Commonweal* 119, no. 2 (January 31, 1992): 14–17.

———. "U.S. Bishops' Suggestions for Vatican II." *Cristianesimo nella storia* 15 (1994): 313–71.

———. "The Struggle for the Council during the Preparation of Vatican II (1960–1962)." In *History of Vatican II*, edited by Alberigo and Komonchak, 1:167–356.

———. "Modernity and the Construction of Roman Catholicism." *Cristianesimo nella storia* 18 (1997): 353–85.

———. "Le valutazioni sulla *Gaudium et spes*: Chenu, Dosseti, Ratzinger." In *Volti di fine concilio: Studi di storia e teologia sulla conclusione del Vaticano II*, edited by Joseph Dore and Alberto Melloni, 115–53. Bologna: Il Mulino, 2000. Condensed into English as "Augustine, Aquinas or the Gospel *sine glossa*? Divisions over *Gaudium et spes*" in *Unfinished Journey: The Church 40 Years after Vatican II*, edited by Austen Ivereigh, 102–18. London: Continuum, 2003.

———. "The Council of Trent at the Second Vatican Council." In *From Trent to Vatican II: Historical and Theological Investigations*, edited by Raymond F. Bulman and Frederick J. Parrella, 61–81. New York: Oxford University Press, 2006.

———. "Interpreting the Council and Its Consequences." In *After Vatican II: Trajectories and Hermeneutics*, edited by James L. Heft, 164–72. Grand Rapids, Mich.: Eerdmans, 2012.

———. "Pope John XXIII and the Idea of an Ecumenical Council." Available at https://jakomonchak.wordpress.com/category/vatican-II.

———. "The Preparatory Theological Commission." Available at https://jakomonchak.wordpress.com/category/vatican-II.

———. "On the Sources of Revelation." Available at https://jakomonchak.wordpress.com/ category/vatican-II.

———. "Defending Intact the Deposit of Faith." Available at https://jakomonchak.wordpress.com/category/vatican-II.

Küng, Hans. *Konzil und Wiedervereinigung: Erneuerung als Ruf in die Einheit.*

Freiburg: Herder, 1960. Translated by Cecily Hastings as *The Council, Reform, and Reunion*. New York: Sheed and Ward, 1961.

———. *Strukturen der Kirche*. Freiburg: Herder, 1962. Translated by Salvator Attanasio as *Structures of the Church*. London: Burns and Oates, 1965.

———. *My Struggle for Freedom*. Grand Rapids, Mich.: Eerdmans, 2004.

Lamberigts, Mathijs. "The Liturgy Debate." In *History of Vatican II*, edited by Alberigo and Komonchak, 2:107–66. Maryknoll, N.Y.: Orbis, 1997.

Lamberigts, Mathijs, and Leo Declerck. "The Role of Cardinal Léon-Joseph Suenens at Vatican II." In *The Belgian Contribution to the Second Vatican Council*, edited by Doris Donnelly et al., 61–217. Leuven: Peeters, 2008.

Lefebvre, Archbishop Marcel. "Lettre de Mgr Lefebvre au cardinal Ratzinger" (April 17, 1985). Quoted in Gilles Routhier, "The Hermeneutic of Reform," 229. *Irish Theological Quarterly* 77 (2012): 219–34.

Leo XIII, Pope. *Providentissimus Deus*. Encyclical Letter. November 18, 1893. In *The Scripture Documents*, edited by Dean Béchard, 17–59. Collegeville, Minn.: Liturgical Press, 2002.

Lutheran–Roman Catholic Commission on Unity. *From Conflict to Communion: Lutheran–Catholic Common Commemoration of the Reformation in 2017*. Paderborn: Bonifatius, 2013.

Mattei, Roberto de. *The Second Vatican Council: An Unwritten Story*. Fitzwilliam, N.H.: Loreto, 2012.

Melloni, Alberto. "History, Pastorate, and Theology: The Impact of Carlo Borromeo upon A. G. Roncalli / Pope John XXIII." In *San Carlo Borromeo: Catholic Reform and Ecclesiastical Politics in the Second Half of the Sixteenth Century*, edited by John M. Headley and John B. Tomaro, 277–99. Washington, D.C.: Folger Shakespeare Library, 1988.

———. *Papa Giovanni. Un Cristiano e il suo concilio*. Turin: Einaudi, 2009.

Mersch, Émile. *The Whole Christ*. Milwaukee, Wis.: Bruce, 1938.

———. *Theology of the Mystical Body*. St. Louis, Mo.: Herder, 1951.

Mörsdorf, Klaus. "Der Codex Iuris Canonici und die nicht-katholischen Christen." *Archiv für katholischen Kirchenrecht* 130 (1961): 31–58.

Montaldi, Gianluca. *In fide ipsa essentia revelationis completur. Il tema della fede nell'evolversi del Concilio Vaticano II: la genesi di DV 5–6 e i suoi reflessi su ulteriori ambiti conciliari*. Rome: Gregorian University Press, 2005.

O'Collins, Gerald. *The Second Vatican Council: Message and Meaning*. Collegeville, Minn.: Liturgical Press, 2014.

O'Connell, Gerard. "The Extraordinary Synod." *The Month* 19 (1986): 41–46, 77–82, 123–30, 170–75.

O'Malley, John W. *What Happened at Vatican II*. Cambridge, Mass.: Belknap Press of Harvard University Press, 2008.

———. "'The Hermeneutic of Reform': A Historical Analysis." *Theological Studies* 73 (2012): 517–46.

————. *Trent: What Happened at the Council*. Cambridge, Mass.: Belknap Press of Harvard University Press, 2012.

Paul VI, Pope. "Inaugural Discourse at Period II." Vatican Council II. September 29, 1963. In *Council Daybook*, edited by Anderson, 143–50. Original Latin text in *Acta Synodalia*, 2.1:183–200, and in *Acta Apostolicae Sedis* 55 (1963): 841–59.

————. "Letter to Archbishop Marcel Lefebvre." October 11, 1976. *Origins* 6 (December 16, 1976): 416–20.

Perrin, Luc. "Le *Coetus Internationalis Patrum* et la minoranza conciliare." In *L'evento e le decisioni. Studi sulle dinamiche del concilio Vaticano II*, edited by Maria Teresa Fattori and Alberto Melloni, 163–87. Bologna: Il Mulino, 1997.

Philips, Gérard. "Note on members of the Church for the sub-commission *De ecclesia* of the Vatican II Preparatory Theological Commission, 7 April 1961" (7 pages). Archive Gérard Philips, no. 119. Leuven University Theological Faculty Vatican II Archive. Leuven, Belgium.

————. "Concilium duce Spiritu Sancto: Alternative draft of a Vatican II Constitution *De ecclesia* (November 1962)." In *Concilii Vaticani II Synopsis . . . Constitutio Dogmatica de Ecclesia Lumen gentium*, edited by Francisco Gil Hellín, 707–15. Vatican City: Liberia Editrice Vaticana, 1995.

————. *Carnets conciliaires de Mgr. Gérard Philips, Secrétaire adjoint de la Commission doctrinale*. French translation and commentary by Karim Schelkens. Leuven: Peeters, 2006.

Piolanti, Antonio. "Il magistero della Chiesa e la scienza teologica." *Divinitas* 5 (1961): 531–51.

Pius IX, Pope. *Syllabus of Errors*. December 8, 1864. In *Compendium* (Denzinger), 590–98, nos. 2901–80.

Pius XII, Pope. *Mystici Corporis Christi*. Encyclical Letter. June 29, 1943. In *The Papal Encyclicals 1939–1958*, edited by Claudia Carlen, 37–63. Ann Arbor, Mich.: Pierian Press,1990.

————. *Divino Afflante Spiritu*. Encyclical Letter. September 30, 1943. In *The Scripture Documents*, edited by Dean Béchard, 115–36. Collegeville, Minn.: Liturgical Press, 2002.

————. *Humani Generis*. Encyclical Letter. August 12, 1950. In *The Papal Encyclicals 1939–1958*, edited by Claudia Carlen, 175–83. Ann Arbor, Mich.: Pierian Press, 1990.

Pizzuto, Pietro. *La teologia della rivelazione di Jean Daniélou. Influsso su Dei Verbum e valore attuale*. Rome: Gregorian University Press, 2003.

Pontifical Biblical Commission. *Enchiridion Biblicum*. Second edition. Naples: M. D'Auria, and Rome: Arnodo, 1954.

Quisinsky, Michael, and Peter Walter, eds. *Personenlexikon zum zweiten Vatikanischen Konzil*. Freiburg: Herder, 2013.

Rahner, Karl. *Diaconia in Christo: Über die Erneurung des Diakonats*. Freiburg: Herder, 1962.

———. *Sehnsucht nach dem geheimnisvollen Gott*. Edited by Herbert Vorgrimler. Freiburg: Herder, 1990.

———. "Konzilsgutachten für Kardinal König." In his *Sämtliche Werke*, vol. 21, *Zweite Vatikanum: Beiträge zum Konzil und seiner Interpretation*, edited by Günther Wassilowsky, 1:37–214. Freiburg: Herder, 2013.

Rahner, Karl, and Joseph Ratzinger. *De revelatione Dei et hominis in Jesu Christo facta*. In Karl Rahner, *Sämtliche Werke*, vol. 21, *Zweite Vatikanum: Beiträge zum Konzil und seiner Interpretation*, edited by Günther Wassilowsky, 1:217–36. Freiburg: Herder, 2013. Translated by Brendan Cahill in his *The Renewal of Revelation Theology*, 300–317. Rome: Gregorian University Press, 1999.

Rimoldi, Antonio. "La preparazione del Concilio." In *Giovanni Battista Montini Arcivescovo di Milano e il Concilio Ecumenico Vaticano II: Preparazione e primo periodo*, 202–41. Brescia: Istituto Paolo VI, 1985.

Roncalli, Marco. *Giovanni XXIII. Angelo Giuseppe Roncalli. Una vita nella storia*. Milan: Mondadori, 2006.

Routhier, Gilles. "The Hermeneutic of Reform as a Task for Theology." *Irish Theological Quarterly* 77 (2012): 219–34.

Roy, Philippe J. "La préhistoire du *Coetus internationalis Patrum*. Une formation romaine, antilibéral et contre-révolutionaire." In *La théologie catholique entre intransigeance et renouveau: La reception des mouvements préconciliaries à Vatican II*, edited by Gilles Routhier, Philippe J. Roy, and Karim Schelkens, 321–54. Leuven: Universiteitsbibliotheek, 2011.

———. *Bibliographie du Concile Vatican II*. Vatican City: Libreria Editrice Vaticana, 2012.

Roy-Lysencourt, Philippe. *Les membres du Coetus internationalis patrum au Concile Vatican II*. Leuven: Peeters, 2014.

Ruddy, Christopher. "'In the end is my beginning': *Lumen gentium* and the Priority of Doxology." *Irish Theological Quarterly* 79 (2014): 144–64.

Ruffini, Ernesto. "Il Santo Padre Giovanni XXIII nel primo anno di pontificato." *Divinitas* 4 (1960): 7–28.

Sauer, Hanjo. *Erfahrung und Glaube: Die Begründung des pastoralen Prinzips durch die Offenbarungskonstitution des II. Vatikanischen Konzils*. Frankfurt: Peter Lang, 1993.

———. "The Doctrinal and the Pastoral: The Text on Divine Revelation." In *History of Vatican II*, edited by Alberigo and Komonchak, 4:196–231. Maryknoll, N.Y.: Orbis, 2003.

Scatena, Silvia. *La fatica della libertà. L'elaborazione della dichiarazione "Dignitatis humanae" sulla libertà religiosa del Vaticano II*. Bologna: Il Mulino, 2003.

Schäuffele, Hermann. *Schema de Deo* (1962). Vatican Secret Archive, *Vatican Council II*, Box 124, *Animadversiones Patrum ante Concilii Initium*.

Schelkens, Karim. *Catholic Theology of Revelation on the Eve of Vatican II. A Redaction History of the Schema* De fontibus revelationis (1960–1962). Leiden: Brill, 2010.

[Schillebeeckx, Edward]. "Commentary on the "prima series" of "Schemata Constitutionum et Decretorum de quibus disceptabitur." In Sebastian Tromp, *Konzilstagebuch*, vol. II, *Commissio conciliaris* (1962–1963), edited by Alexandra von Teuffenbach, 2.2:948–91. Nordhausen: Verlag Traugott Bautz, 2011.

———. *The Council Notes of Edward Schillebeeckx 1962–1963*. Edited by Karim Schelkens. Leuven: Peeters, 2011.

Schmidt, Stjepan. *Augustin Bea, the Cardinal of Unity*. New Rochelle, N.Y.: New City, 1992.

Semmelroth, Otto. *Die Kirche als Ursakrament*. Frankfurt a.M.: Knecht, 1955.

———. "Konzilstagebuch" (1962–65). Archive of the Jesuit Province of Germany, Berchmans College, Munich, Germany.

Smith, Christian, Kyle Longest, Jonathan Hill, and Kari Christoffersen. *Young Catholic America: Emerging Adults in, out of, and Gone from the Church*. New York: Oxford University Press, 2014.

Smulders, Pieter. "Vatican II Papers and Letters from Rome to the Maastricht Jesuit Community." Archive Pieter Smulders. Katholiek Documentatie Centrum, Nijmegen, The Netherlands.

Spalding, John Lancaster. "Education and the Future of Religion." In his *Religion, Agnosticism, and Education*, 147–92. Chicago: McClurg, 1902.

Stakemeier, Eduard. "Leimotive der Kirchenkonstitution in einem Votum des Einheitssekretariats vom 20. April 1961." In *Martyria Leiturgia Diakonia. Festschrift für Hermann Volk*, edited by Otto Semmelroth, 386–98. Mainz: Grünewald, 1968.

Stransky, Thomas. "The Foundation of the Secretariat for Promoting Christian Unity." In *Vatican II Revisited by Those Who Were There*, edited by Alberic Stacpoole, 62–87. Minneapolis, Minn.: Winston, 1986.

———. "Paul VI and the Delegated Observers/Guests to Vatican Council II." In *Paolo VI e l'ecumenismo*, 118–58. Brescia: Istituto Paolo VI, 2001.

Suenens, Léon-Joseph. "A Plan for the Whole Council" (1962). In *Vatican II Revisited by Those Who Were There*, edited by Alberic Stacpoole, 88–105. Minneapolis, Minn.: Winston, 1986.

———. *Mémoires sur le Concile Vatican II*. Edited by Werner Van Laer. Leuven: Peeters, 2014.

Tagle, Luis Antonio G. "The *Nota explicative praevia*." In *History of Vatican II*, edited by Alberigo and Komonchak, 4:417–45. Maryknoll, N.Y.: Orbis, 2003.

———. *Episcopal Collegiality and Vatican II. The Influence of Paul VI*. Manila: Loyola School of Theology, 2004.

Tanner, Norman, ed. *Decrees of the Ecumenical Councils*. 2 volumes. Washington, D.C.: Georgetown University Press, 1990.

———. "The Church in the World (*Ecclesia ad Extra*)." In *History of Vatican II*, edited by Alberigo and Komonchak, 4:269–331. Maryknoll, N.Y.: Orbis, 2003.

Teuffenbach, Alexandra von. *Die Bedeutung des subsistit in (LG 8): Zum Selbstverständnis der katholischen Kirche*. Munich: Herbert Utz, 2002.

Thils, Gustave. *Histoire doctrinale du movement œcuménique*. Revised edition. Paris: Desclée, 1963.

Thurian, Max. "Baptism, Eucharist and Ministry (the 'Lima text')." In *Dictionary of the Ecumenical Movement*, edited by Nicholas Lossky et al., 90–93. Geneva: WCC Publications, 2002.

Trippen, Norbert. *Josef Kardinal Frings (1887–1978)*. 2 volumes. Paderborn: Schöningh, 2005.

Tromp, Sebastian. *Konzilstagebuch, mit Erläuterunten und Akten aus der Arbeit der Theologischen Kommission*, vol. 1, *Commissio praeparatoria theologica (1960–62)*. 2 volumes. Edited by Alexandra von Teuffenbach. Rome: Gregorian University Press, 2006.

———. *Konzilstagebuch, mit Erläuterungen und Akten aus der Arbeit der Theologischen Kommission*, vol. 2, *Commissio conciliaris (1962–63)*. 2 volumes. Edited by Alexandra von Teuffenbach. Nordhausen: Verlag Traugott Bautz, 2011.

Tucci, Robert. *Giovanni XXIII e la preparazione del concilio Vaticano II nei diari del direttore della "Civiltà cattolica."* Edited by Giovanni Sale. Milan: Jaca Book, 2012.

Turbanti, Giovanni. *Un concilio per il mondo moderno. La redazione della costituzione pastorale "Gaudium et spes" del Vaticano II*. Bologna: Il Mulino, 2000.

Vatican Council I. *Dei Filius*. In *Decrees*, edited by Tanner, 2:804–11.

Velati, Mauro. *Una difficile transizione. Il cattolicesimo tra unionismo ed ecumenismo (1950–1964)*. Bologna: Il Mulino, 1996.

———. *Dialogo e rinnovamento. Verbali e testi del segretariato per l'unità dei cristiani nella preparazione del concilio Vaticano II (1960–1962)*. Bologna: Il Mulino, 2011.

———. *Separati ma fratelli. Gli osservatori non cattolici al Vaticano II (1962–1965)*. Bologna: Il Mulino, 2014.

Vereb, Jerome-Michael, CP. *"Because He Was a German!" Cardinal Bea and the Origins of Roman Catholic Engagement in the Ecumenical Movement*. Grand Rapids, Mich.: Eerdmans, 2006.

Vodola, Max. "John XXIII, Vatican II, and the Genesis of *aggiornamento*:

A Contextual Analysis of Angelo Roncalli's Works on San Carlo Borromeo in Relation to Late Twentieth Century Church Reform." PhD diss., Monash University, 2010.

———. "I met Charles Borromeo . . . and he brought me to Vatican II." *Pacifica* 26 (2013): 171–83.

Volk, Hermann. "Wort Gottes: Gabe und Aufgabe." *Catholica* 16 (1962): 241–51. Reprinted in his *Gesammelte Schriften*, 2:89–100. Mainz: Grünewald, 1966.

———. *Zur Theologie des Wortes Gottes*. Münster: Verlag Regensburg, 1962. Reprinted in his *Gesammelte Schriften*, 3:19–35. Mainz: Grünewald, 1978.

Vorgrimler, Herbert, ed. *Commentary on the Documents of Vatican II*. 5 volumes. New York: Herder and Herder, 1967–69.

———. "Karl Rahner: The Theologian's Contribution." In *Vatican II Revisited by Those Who Were There*, edited by Alberic Stacpoole, 32–46. Minneapolis, Minn.: Winston, 1986.

Washburn, Christian D. "The Theological Priority of *Lumen gentium* and *Dei Verbum* for the Interpretation of the Second Vatican Council." *The Thomist* 78 (2014): 1–29.

———. "The Second Vatican Council, *Lumen gentium*, and *Subsistit in*." *Josephinum Journal of Theology* 22 (2015): 145–75.

———. "The Second Vatican Council and the Theological Authority of *Sacrosanctum Concilium* as a Constitution." *Nova et Vetera* 13 (2015): 1093–1124.

Walsh, Christopher J. "De Lubac's Critique of the Post-Conciliar Church." *Communio* 19 (1992): 404–32.

Wassilowsky, Günther. *Universales Heilssakrament Kirche. Karl Rahners Beitrag zur Ekklesiologie des II. Vatikanums*. Innsbruck: Tyrolia Verlag, 2001.

Wicks, Jared. "*Dei Verbum* Developing: Vatican II's Revelation Doctrine 1963–64." In *The Convergence of Theology, Festschrift Gerald O'Collins, SJ*, edited by Daniel Kendall and Stephen T. Davis, 109–25. Mahwah, N.J.: Paulist Press, 2001.

———. "Pieter Smulders and *Dei Verbum*: 1. A Consultation on the Eve of Vatican II." *Gregorianum* 81 (2001): 241–97.

———. "Pieter Smulders and *Dei Verbum*: 2. On *De fontibus revelationis* during Vatican II's First Period, 1962." *Gregorianum* 81 (2001): 559–93.

———. "The Significance of the 'Ecclesial Communities' of the Reformation." *Ecumenical Trends* 30 (December 2001): 170–73. Translated into French in *Irénikon* 74 (2001): 57–66.

———. "Pieter Smulders and *Dei Verbum*: 3. Developing the Understanding of Revelation to Israel, 1962–63." *Gregorianum* 82 (2002): 225–67.

———. "Pieter Smulders and *Dei Verbum*: 4. Assessing the Mixed Com-

mission's 1962 Work on Scripture/Tradition and Biblical Inspiration."
Gregorianum 85 (2004): 242–77.

———. "I teologi al Vaticano II. Momenti e modalità del loro contributo
al concilio." *Humanitas* (Brescia) 59 (2004): 1012–38. Translated by
Wicks in *Doing Theology*, 187–223. Mahwah, N.J.: Paulist Press, 2009.

———. "Pieter Smulders and *Dei Verbum*: 5, A Critical Reception of the
Schema *De revelatione* of the Mixed Commission (1963)." *Gregorianum* 86
(2005): 92–134.

———. "Review of *Das Konzil und die Seminare: Die Ausbilding der Priester
in der Dynamik des Zweiten Vatikanums* by Alois Greiler." *Theological
Studies* 67 (2006): 205–6.

———. Reviews of *Il concilio inedito: Fonti del Vaticano II*, edited by Massimo
Faggioli and Giovanni Turbanti; *A Brief History of Vatican II*, by Giuseppe
Alberigo; and *La fatica della libertà: L'elaborazione della dichiarazione
Dignitatis humanae sulla libertà del Vaticano II*, by Silvia Scatena. In
"New Light on Vatican Council II," *Catholic Historical Review* 92 (2006):
609–28.

———. "*De revelatione* under Revision (March–April 1964): Contributions
of C. Moeller and Other Belgian Theologians." In *The Belgian Contribution to the Second Vatican Council*, edited by Doris Donnelly et al.,
461–94. Leuven: Peeters, 2008.

———. "John Paul II and Lutherans: Actions and Reactions." In *The
Legacy of John Paul II*, edited by Gerald O'Collins and Michael A. Hayes,
139–202. London: Burns and Oates, 2008.

———. Reviews of *Carnets conciliaires de Mgr Gérard Philips, secétaire adjoint
de la Commission doctrinale*, edited by Karim Schelkens; *Lettres conciliaires (1962–1965)*, by Dom Helder Camara, edited by José De Broucker;
Il vescovo e il concilio. Modello episcopale e aggiornamento al Vaticano II,
by Massimo Faggioli; and *Un concilio per il mondo moderno. La redazione
della costituzione pastorale Gaudium et spes del Vaticano II*, by Giovanni
Turbanti. In "More Light on Vatican Council II," *Catholic Historical
Review* 94 (2008): 75–101.

———. "Six Texts by Prof. Joseph Ratzinger as *Peritus* Before and During
Vatican Council II." *Gregorianum* 89 (2008): 233–311.

———. Reviews of *Carnets du Concile*, by Henri de Lubac; *Vatican II: A Socio-
logical Analysis of Religious Change*, by Melisa J. Wilde; and *Vatican II:
Herméneutique et reception*, by Gilles Routhier. In "Further Light on
Vatican Council II," *Catholic Historical Review* 95 (2009): 546–69.

———. "Theologians at Vatican Council II." In his *Doing Theology*, 187–223.
Mahwah, N.J.: Paulist Press, 2009.

———. "Vatican II on Revelation—From Behind the Scenes." *Theological
Studies* 71 (2010): 637–50.

————. "Cardinal Willebrands's Contributions to Catholic Ecumenical Theology." *Pro ecclesia* 20 (2011): 6–27.

————. "Dalla *Dei Verbum* al sinodo sulla Parola di Dio." In *Commento alla Verbum Domini*, edited by Carmen Aparicio Valls and Salvador Pie-Ninot, 33–39. Rome: Gregorian and Biblical Press, 2011.

————. "Cardinal Bea's Unity Secretariat: Engine of Renewal and Reform at Vatican II." *Ecumenical Trends* 41 (December 2012): 1–5, 15.

————. "Lutheran–Catholic Dialogue: On Foundations Laid in 1962–1964." *Concordia Journal* 39 (2013): 296–309.

————. "Lutheran–Roman Catholic International Dialogue: Selected Remarks." In *Celebrating a Century of Ecumenism: Exploring the Achievements of International Dialogues*, edited by John A. Radano, 55–76. Grand Rapids, Mich.: Eerdmans, 2012.

————. "On the Fiftieth Anniversary of the Opening of Vatican II." *Lutheran Forum* 46 (Fall 2012): 41–44.

————. "Review of *Catholic Theology of Revelation on the Eve of Vatican II: A Redaction History of the Schema* De fontibus revelationis *(1960–1962)*, by Karim Schelkens." *Zeitschrift für Kirchengeschichte* 123 (2012): 408–9.

———— "Review of *Vatican II: Canadian Experiences*, edited by Michael Attridge et al." *American Catholic Studies* 123 (2012): 77–79.

————. Reviews of *Dialogo e rinnovamento*, edited by Mauro Velati; *Konzilstagebuch S. Tromp*, vol. 2, edited by Alexandra von Teuffenbach; *The Council Notes of E. Schillebeeckx 1962–63*, edited by Karim Schelkens; and *Il concilio Vaticano II: Una storia mai scritta*, by Roberto de Mattei. In "Still More Light on Vatican Council II," *Catholic Historical Review* 98 (2012): 476–502.

————. "Vatican II Taking Hold of Its (and Pope John's) Council Goals, September 1962–May 1963." *Josephinum Journal of Theology* 19 (2012): 172–86.

————. "Vatican II Living On in the Bilateral Ecumenical Dialogues." *Ecumenical Trends* 42 (2013): 122–25.

————. "Vatican II's Turn in 1963: Toward Renewing Catholic Ecclesiology and Validating Catholic Ecumenical Engagement." *Josephinum Journal of Theology* 19 (2012 [published 2014]): 194–206.

————. "Scripture Reading Urged *vehementer* (DV 25): Background and Development." *Theological Studies* 74 (2013): 555–80. Reprinted in *50 Years On: Probing the Riches of Vatican II*, edited by David G. Schultenover, 365–90. Collegeville, Minn.: Liturgical Press, 2015.

————. "Tridentine Motivations of Pope John XXIII Before and During Vatican Council II." *Theological Studies* 75 (2014): 847–62.

————. Reviews of *Julius Cardinal Döpfner: Konzilstagebücher, Briefe und Notizen zum Zweiten Vatikanischen Konzil*, edited by Guido Treffler; *Zur Lehre des Zweiten Vatikanischen Konzils, Formulierung Vermittlung*

Deutung, in Joseph Ratzinger, *Gesammelte Schriften*, Vols. 7/1–2; *Das Zweite Vatikanische Konzil (1962–1965)*, *Stand und Perspektiven der kirchenhistorischen Forschung im deutschsprachigen Raum*, edited by Franz Xaver Bischof; *Erneuerung in Christus, Das Zweite Vatikanische Konzil (1962–1965) im Spiegel Münchener Kirchenarchive*, edited by Andreas R. Batlogg, SJ, Clemens Brodkorb, and Peter Pfister; and *Personenlexikon zum Zweiten Vatikanischen Konzil*, edited by Michael Quisinsky and Peter Walter. In "Light from Germany on Vatican Council II," *Catholic Historical Review* 99 (2013): 727–48.

———. "Vatican II in 1964: Major Doctrinal Advances, but also Fissures on Addressing the Modern World." *Josephinum Journal of Theology* 20 (2013 [published 2015]): 4–19.

———. "Augustin Cardinal Bea, SJ: Biblical and Ecumenical Conscience of Vatican II." In *The Legacy of Vatican II*, edited by Massimo Faggioli and Andrea Vicini, SJ, 185–202. Mahwah, N.J.: Paulist Press, 2015.

———. Reviews of *Bibliographie du Concile Vatican II*, by Philippe J. Roy; *Les membres du Coetus internationalis Patrum au Concile Vatican II*, by Philippe Roy-Lysencourt; and *Separati ma Fratelli: Gli oservatori non cattolici al Vaticano II (1962–1965)*, by Mauro Velati. In "Yet More Light on Vatican Council II," *Catholic Historical Review* 102 (2016): 97–117.

———. "Vatican II in 1965: Bringing in an Ample Harvest of Renewed Doctrine and Directives of Service." *Josephinum Journal of Theology* 22 (2015 [published 2016]): 4–22.

———. "The Fullness of Revelation in Christ in *Dei Verbum*." In *Josephinum Journal of Theology* 23 (2016 [published 2017]): 176–204.

Willebrands, Johannes G. M. *Les agendas conciliaires de Mgr. J. Willebrands*. Translated and annotated by Leo Declerck. Leuven: Peeters, 2009.

———. *"You Will Be Called Repairer of the Breach." The Diary of J. G. M. Willebrands, 1958–1961*. Edited by Theo Salemink. Leuven: Peeters, 2009.

Wiltgen, Ralph. *The Rhine Flows into the Tiber*. New York: Hawthorn Books, 1967; reprinted, Rockford, Ill.: TAN Books, 1985.

Witte, Jan. Successive versions of Ch. XI, *De oecumenismo* (1961–1962) of the Schema *De ecclesia* of the Vatican II Preparatory Theological Commission. Papers of Jan Witte, Archive of the Pontifical Gregorian University, Rome.

Wittstadt, Klaus. *Julius Kardinal Döpfner (1913–1976)*. Munich: Don Bosco, 2001.

World Council of Churches Central Committee. "The Church, the Churches, and the World Council of Churches." Toronto Statement, 1950. In *The Ecumenical Movement: An Anthology of Key Texts and Voices*, edited by Michael Kinnamon and Brian Cope, 463–68. Geneva: WCC Publications, 1997.

Index

Investigating Vatican II: Its Theologians, Ecumenical Turn, and Biblical Commitment was designed in Garamond, with Scala Sans and Garda Titling display type, and composed by Kachergis Book Design of Pittsboro, North Carolina. It was printed on 60-pound Natural Smooth Web and bound by Sheridan Books of Chelsea, Michigan.